LEGAL WRITING IN PLAIN ENGLISH

Chicago Guides
to *Writing*, Editing,
and Publishing

LEGAL WRITING IN PLAIN ENGLISH

A Text with Exercises

SECOND EDITION

BRYAN A. GARNER

THE UNIVERSITY OF CHICAGO PRESS
Chicago and London

The University of Chicago Press, Chicago 60637
The University of Chicago Press, Ltd., London
© 2001, 2013 by Bryan A. Garner
All rights reserved. Published 2013.
Printed in the United States of America

28 27 26 25 24 23 22 21   12 13

ISBN-13: 978-0-226-28393-7 (paper)
ISBN-13: 978-0-226-03139-2 (e-book)

Library of Congress Cataloging-in-Publication Data
Garner, Bryan A., author.
   Legal writing in plain English : a text with exercises / Bryan A. Garner. — Second edition.
      pages cm. — (Chicago guides to writing, editing, and publishing)
   Includes index.
   ISBN 978-0-226-28393-7 (paperback : alkaline paper) — ISBN 978-0-226-03139-2 (e-book)
   1. Legal composition. I. Title. II. Series: Chicago guides to writing, editing, and publishing.
KF250.G373 2013
 808.06′634—dc23

                                                                        2012045006

♾ This paper meets the requirements of ANSI/NISO Z39.48-1992 (Permanence of Paper).

OTHER BOOKS WRITTEN OR EDITED BY BRYAN A. GARNER

Garner's Modern American Usage
Garner's Dictionary of Legal Usage
Black's Law Dictionary (all editions since 1996)
Garner on Language and Writing (foreword by Justice Ruth Bader Ginsburg)
Reading Law: The Interpretation of Legal Texts (with Justice Antonin Scalia)
Making Your Case: The Art of Persuading Judges (with Justice Antonin Scalia)
The Redbook: A Manual on Legal Style
The Elements of Legal Style
The Chicago Manual of Style, chap. 5, "Grammar and Usage" (15th & 16th eds.)
The Winning Brief
The Winning Oral Argument
Ethical Communications for Lawyers
Securities Disclosure in Plain English
Guidelines for Drafting and Editing Court Rules
A New Miscellany-at-Law by Sir Robert Megarry
The Oxford Dictionary of American Usage and Style
The Rules of Golf in Plain English (with Jeffrey Kuhn)
The HBR Guide to Better Business Writing
A Handbook of Basic Legal Terms
A Handbook of Business Law Terms
A Handbook of Criminal Law Terms
A Handbook of Family Law Terms
Texas, Our Texas: Remembrances of the University

For my beloved daughter
ALEXANDRA BESS GARNER

CONTENTS

PREFACE

This book takes a practical approach to legal writing. It derives from my experience over the past several decades in working with law students and—in far greater numbers—practicing lawyers and judges. So the book is intended not just for law students and paralegals but also for practitioners—even experienced ones. In devising the exercises for each section, I envisioned either a writing class or an informal group of legal writers who meet periodically to work through the book.

Particularly in its approach to exercises, the book differs markedly from other legal-writing texts. Each of the 50 sections contains a basic, an intermediate, and an advanced exercise. (Model answers for the basic exercises are in the back of the book.) Some of these exercises are open-ended, requiring you to supply examples of particular writing problems. This simply means that you'll have to pay some attention to style in your legal reading. Other exercises require you to research the literature on effective writing. Why? Because as professional writers, lawyers should know this literature. After all, workaday questions about writing are generally *much* easier to answer than the legal questions that arise in practicing law. If you worry about points of grammar and usage, see § 48. Better yet, make friends with the nearest librarian. Librarians are there to help you, and they're generally eager to do it.

The book's organization reflects the different types of writing that lawyers do. Some techniques apply to virtually all legal writing (§§ 1–20). Others apply mostly—though not quite exclusively—to analytical and persuasive writing (§§ 21–30). Still others apply mostly to transactional drafting (§§ 31–40), though these techniques also address problems that occasionally arise in the other types of legal writing. Then there are two other groupings of techniques: those that lead to readable typography (§§ 41–45) and those that lead to ongoing improvement (§§ 46–50).

Much of the advice in this book depends on—and even promotes—sound legal analysis. That might not be what people expect from a book on legal writing. Yet many sections are essentially about thinking straight. This is crucial, since it's impossible to separate good writing from clear thinking.

Here you'll find discussed and illustrated the primary techniques for improving your writing style. Some sections will serve only as reminders of what you've heard before but perhaps forgotten. Other techniques will probably be new to you. What matters most, in the end, is how you apply sound practices in your writing. You'll have to use good judgment. No blackletter rule can substitute for that.

Finally, a word about "plain English." The phrase certainly shouldn't connote drab and dreary language. Actually, plain English is typically quite interesting to read. It's robust and direct—the opposite of gaudy, pretentious language. You achieve plain English when you use the simplest, most straightforward way of expressing an idea. You can still choose interesting words. But you'll avoid fancy ones that have everyday replacements meaning precisely the same thing.

I hope that you'll enjoy and profit from the book. The examples are drawn from all practice areas, and the exercises are practical and realistic. If you can handle them capably, you're quite a legal writer. If not, keep working. This book is meant to offer both help and hope.

ↀ ↀ ↀ

The more books I write, the more abettors I have. Among the indispensable contributors to this book were the participants in continuing-legal-education seminars—as well as law students—who have contributed to my knowledge of legal writing and legal language over more than 20 years. Although the group numbers in the hundreds, it is a select group among the some 155,000 lawyers and students who have been exposed to many of the principles discussed in these pages. On the subject of effective writing, my curiosity is boundless. So to the lawyers and students whose comments gave insight and energy to this investigation, a genuine thank-you.

Some debts are so specific that I must name names. Two English professors at the University of Texas—John R. Trimble and Betty Sue Flowers—have occasionally team-taught with me for a decade, and I've learned volumes from them. Trimble influenced my thinking especially in §§ 15, 20, 25, 29, and 50, and Flowers provided the intellectual framework for § 2.

I greatly benefited from the suggestions of several readers who acted as consultants for the second edition: Joel Atlas of Cornell Law School; Elizabeth S. Duquette of University of Chicago Law School; Elana Einhorn of University of Texas School of Law; Robert Harrison of Yale Law School; Susannah Tobin of Harvard Law School; and Kathleen Vinson of Suffolk University Law School.

I'm indebted to Michael L. Atchley, Thomas D. Boyle, Beverly Ray Burlingame, Charles Dewey Cole Jr., Tina G. Davis, Jerome R. Doak, Ronald Dworkin, Lawrence Friedman, Michael A. Logan, Richard A. Posner, and Steven C. Seeger for the good models I've cited. They are splendid writers, and I am delighted to be able to showcase their work.

Several brilliant legal-writing instructors reviewed the manuscript of the first edition and made excellent suggestions. My profound gratitude goes to Kathleen Coles, A. Darby Dickerson, Kay Kavanagh, Joseph Kimble, Karen Larsen, Kathleen O'Neill, and Kathryn Tullos.

I had the help of many able editors. Linda J. Halvorson of the University of Chicago Press originally invited me to write the book and made many helpful suggestions, as did Mary Laur on this second edition. Many others contributed in myriad ways: my heartfelt thanks to Ryden McComas Anderson, David Bemelmans, Beverly Ray Burlingame, Karolyne H. C. Garner, Heather C. Haines, Cynde L. Horne, Tiger Jackson, Karen Magnuson, Becky R. McDaniel, Jeff Newman, Elizabeth C. Powell, Wanda Raiford, David W. Schultz, Joseph F. Spaniol Jr., and David J. Zheng.

I wrote the first edition in July and August of 1999 in Oxford, England, at the Bodleian Law Library. Many thanks to my generous friend Professor Tony Honoré, both for his electric wit (on any subject) and for his many kindnesses (including the extended use of his library carrel).

My wife, Karolyne, and my two daughters, Caroline and Alexandra, were as supportive as ever. I believe they know how grateful I am.

Bryan A. Garner
DALLAS, TEXAS

INTRODUCTION

"Notwithstanding anything to the contrary contained in any other document (or any part thereof) . . . ." No. Strike that.

There's an age-old cycle of poor legal writing. You can help break it.

The first part of the cycle is familiar enough. Start with the premise that writing well isn't easy. Most people don't do it well—even many college graduates who think they do. Most doctors, accountants, and businesspeople—even professors—aren't accomplished writers. Why should it be any different for lawyers?

The second part of the cycle is insidious: when you plunge groups of mediocre writers into a complex field with its own mind-boggling jargon, rife with bloated expressions that displace everyday words, the results are predictable enough. But it's even worse: Make law students pore over reams of tedious, hyperformal, creaky prose. Acculturate them to pomposity. Then what do you suppose you'll get? You'll end up with average legal writers: wordy, stuffy, artificial, often ungrammatical, and largely unreadable.

In the last part of the cycle, each generation of lawyers trains the next to follow its ingrained habits. Meanwhile, generation after generation, lawyers get ridiculed for their pompous writing.

It doesn't have to be this way—for you or anybody else. Even if you're entering the legal profession as a fairly weak writer, you can help break the cycle. You don't have to blindly adopt the worn-out, ineffective writing habits of the past.

Although it won't be easy, once you become a skillful writer—especially a skillful writer on legal subjects—your rewards will be great. But before we talk about rewards, let's ponder some obstacles you must overcome.

First, though anyone can learn to write effectively, it takes hard work. Good style is something you must strive to attain. In that way it's like a sport: there are relatively few really good players, and they don't attain that level of competence haphazardly. They work at it. So remember: writing is like any other skill—you can improve, but you'll have to dedicate yourself to it. The easier path is to settle for being a so-so writer.

If you want to become a first-rate writer, you'll have to make a commitment.

Second, since you're in law, you're already swimming in a sea of bad writing. We learn our trade by struggling through oceans of linguistic dreck — jargon-filled, pretentious, flatulent legal prose that seems designed to drown any flair for language. When on the job, we read poor prose almost exclusively. It's wordy, heavy, and antique-sounding. A part of you may well come to believe that you must sound that way to be truly lawyerlike.

You'll have to inoculate yourself against legalese.

Third, the world is complex, and so is the law. You might think that good legal writing is necessarily complex. You might even be tempted to make your writing more complex than necessary just to impress. You'll feel the impulse to shun simplicity.

But you'll have to be willing to embrace simplicity — while always resisting oversimplification. Of all the hurdles we've considered, this will be the most difficult. It will require intelligence and maturity.

This brings us to the fourth and final point. You'll have to be psychologically mature. It's a prerequisite. After all, law school is a life-changing experience. When you're through with it, you're a different person — perhaps better, perhaps not, but undeniably different. Ultimately, you'll have to answer a question that your parents started helping you answer before you understood a single word: What kind of person are you? And every time you write, you'll be answering some related questions: What kind of person are you as a writer? What do you sound like?

If you want to write well, you'll have to resist sounding like a machine. Or a foreign philosopher in translation. You'll have to learn to sound like yourself. It's even possible that you'll find yourself by learning to write well.

Yet the rewards are more tangible than that. They're by-products of good writing. Because legal employers prize writing ability more highly than almost any other skill, you'll gain several immediate advantages:

- You'll be more likely to get and keep whatever job you want.
- You'll be more likely to be promoted quickly.
- You'll have greater opportunities for career mobility, with a broader range of possibilities.

If you can write — really write — people will assume certain other things about you. The most important is that you're a clear thinker.

But you'll surely encounter some workplace obstacles along the way. You'll undoubtedly find that time pressures make writing and revising difficult. Maybe an employer will tell you that you're being *too* clear in your writing — that you should learn to obfuscate. Maybe the advice will be to leave a court paper vague so that the specific arguments can be fashioned orally before the judge — a seat-of-the-pants approach. Maybe an employer will disapprove of your departing from some mind-numbing convention that ill-informed legal writers cling to, such as doubling up words and numerals. Good writers hear all this bad advice and much more. So how are you to deal with it?

The answer is twofold. First, do what you must in the short run. Don't butt heads with someone who refuses to engage in an intelligent discussion about writing. If that person happens to be your supervisor, simply learn what you can from the situation. (The lessons may have more to do with the human psyche than with good writing.) Second, don't lose your critical sense; instead, cultivate it. Think independently about why you consider some writing good and other writing bad.

In the end, you might learn to write in a bold, clear, powerful way. It will be a struggle for you — as it is for anyone. You'll be combating both the natural human tendency to write poorly and the unnatural pressure from colleagues to write poorly. But you'll have struck a blow for yourself and for the law. You'll be championing clarity and cogency — even truth. The law could certainly stand to have those qualities in greater abundance.

But let's not get ahead of ourselves. The journey toward clear thinking is only beginning.

PART ONE

Principles for All Legal Writing

There are many types of legal writing—demand letters, opinion letters, research memos, motions, briefs, judicial opinions, contracts, statutes, and ordinances, to name just a few. Although each type presents a unique challenge, they all have some things in common. That is, certain principles of good writing apply to the whole gamut. These 20 principles make up Part One, which is divided into three subparts:

- *Framing Your Thoughts*
- *Phrasing Your Sentences*
- *Choosing Your Words*

Whatever the document, you'll be doing those three things. The 20 tips that follow should help you do them better.

1

Framing Your Thoughts

§1. Have something to say — and think it through.

What's your biggest challenge as a writer? It's figuring out, from the mass of possibilities, exactly what your points are — and then stating them coherently, with adequate reasoning and support.

Although this advice might seem obvious, legal writers constantly ignore it. The result is a mushy, aimless style. Even with your point well in mind, if you take too long to reach it, you might as well have no point at all. Only readers with a high incentive to understand you will labor to grasp your meaning.

That's where law school comes in. Every law student must read and digest scads of diffuse writing. You read through old cases that take forever to convey fairly straightforward points. You read law-review articles that take 50 pages to say what might be said more powerfully in 5. And as you read, your incentive for gleaning the main message remains high because your future in law depends on it. You have no choice but to wade through all that opaque prose.

Take, for example, a sentence from a judicial opinion. See if you can follow the court's point:

> And in the outset we may as well be frank enough to confess, and, indeed, in view of the seriousness of the consequences which upon fuller reflection we find would inevitably result to municipalities in the matter of street improvements from the conclusion reached and announced in the former opinion, we are pleased to declare that the arguments upon rehearing have convinced us that the decision upon the ultimate question involved here formerly rendered by this court, even if not faulty in its reasoning from the premises announced or wholly erroneous in conclusions as to some of the questions incidentally arising and necessarily legitimate subjects of discussion in the decision of the main proposition, is, at any rate, one which may, under the peculiar circumstances of this case, the more justly and at the same time, upon reasons of equal cogency, be superseded by a conclusion whose effect cannot be to disturb the integrity of the long and well-established system for the improvement of streets in the incorporated cities and towns of California not governed by freeholders' charters.[1]

---

1. *Chase v. Kalber*, 153 P. 397, 398 (Cal. Ct. App. 1915).

What's the court saying? In a highly embellished style, it's simply saying, "We made a mistake last time." That's all.

If you add sentence after sentence in this style—all filled with syntactic curlicues—you end up with an even more impenetrable morass of words. The only readers who will bother to penetrate it are either law students or lawyers who are paid to do so.

However willing you might be to pierce through another writer's obscurity, you must insist that your own writing never put your readers to that trouble. On the one hand, then, you'll need a penetrating mind as a reader to cut through overgrown verbal foliage. On the other hand, you'll need a focused mind as a writer to leave aside everything that doesn't help you swiftly communicate your ideas.

That's the start to becoming an effective legal writer.

Exercises

Begin each of the following exercises by looking up the case cited. Then write a case brief for each one—that is, a short case synopsis that follows a standard form: (1) case name and citation (in proper form); (2) brief facts; (3) question for decision; (4) holding; and (5) reasoning. Your finished product should fit on a five-by-seven-inch index card (front and back). The exercises are increasingly challenging for either or both of two reasons: first, the increasing complexity of the legal principles involved; and second, the increasing difficulty of the language used in the opinions. When you're finished, have a friend assess how easy it is to understand what you've written. Here's an example of a case brief:

> **Case:** *Henderson v. Ford Motor Co.,* 519 S.W.2d 87 (Tex. 1974).
>
> **Facts:** While driving in city traffic, Henderson found that, despite repeated attempts, she couldn't brake. To avoid injuring anyone, she ran into a pole. An investigator later found that part of a rubber gasket from the air filter had gotten into the carburetor. Henderson sued Ford on various theories, including defective design. Her expert witness didn't criticize the design of the gasket, carburetor, or air filter, but did say that the positioning of the parts might have been better. No one testified that the air-filter housing was unreasonably dangerous from the time of installation. Yet the jury determined that the air-filter housing was defective and that this defect had caused Henderson's damage.
>
> **Question:** The expert witness didn't testify that the design was unreasonably dangerous—only that it could be improved on. Is this testimony sufficient to support a jury finding that a product's design is unreasonably dangerous?
>
> **Holding:** Mere evidence that a design could be made better—without evidence that the design itself was unreasonably dangerous—is insufficient to impose liability on a manufacturer.
>
> **Reasoning:** A plaintiff in a design-defect case must provide some evi-

dence that the design of the product made it unreasonably dangerous. Specifically, the evidence must show that a prudent manufacturer who was knowledgeable about the risks would not have placed the particular product in the stream of commerce. Mere speculation that a product might be improved on does not constitute evidence of a design defect. A manufacturer is not required to design the best product that is scientifically possible.

Basic

Write a case brief for *People v. Nelson*, 132 Cal. Rptr. 3d 856 (Ct. App. 2011). If you belong to a writing group or class, circulate a copy of your case brief to each colleague.

Intermediate

Write a case brief for *Wilburn v. Commonwealth*, 312 S.W.3d 321 (Ky. 2010). If you belong to a writing group or class, circulate a copy of your case brief to each colleague.

Advanced

Write a case brief for *District of Columbia v. Heller*, 554 U.S. 570 (2008). If you belong to a writing group or class, circulate a copy of your case brief to each colleague.

§ 2.   For maximal efficiency, plan your writing projects. Try nonlinear outlining.

Writers work in various ways, often experimenting with many methods before settling into certain habits. But most writers need a way to set down their yet-unformed ideas in some way other than a top-to-bottom order.

Once you've thought of some points to make — even if they're not fully formed — you've already begun the writing process. But you're not yet ready to begin writing sentences and paragraphs. You're ready to start outlining, which itself can be a multistep process. Here I'll discuss producing an outline that probably won't resemble the outlines you've tried for other writing projects. More on this in a moment. First, let's break down the writing process into its component parts.

It's useful to think of writing as a four-step process:

1. Think of things you want to say — as many as possible as quickly as possible.

2. Figure out a sensible order for those thoughts; that is, prepare an outline.

3. With the outline as your guide, swiftly write out a draft.

4. After setting the draft aside for some time (whether minutes or days), come back to it and edit.

These four steps derive from a system developed by Betty Sue Flowers, a former University of Texas English professor. She has named each of the steps: (1) *Madman*, the creative spirit who generates ideas; (2) *Architect*, the planner who ensures that the structure is sound and appealing; (3) *Carpenter*, the builder who makes the corners square and the counters level; and (4) *Judge*, who checks to see whether anything has gone wrong.[2] Each character represents a separate intellectual function that writers must work through.

The Madman, essentially, is your imagination. This character, though sometimes brilliant, is almost always sloppy. When you're in the Madman phase, you're going for copious thoughts — as many as possible. Ideally, though, you won't be writing out sentences and paragraphs. Rather, you'll be jotting down ideas. And if you get into the swing of it, your jottings will come fast and furious.

You'll need to protect the Madman against the Judge, who hates the Madman's sloppiness. If you don't restrain the Judge in these early stages of the writing process, the Madman could be at considerable risk. Writers commonly have little battles in their heads if the hypercritical Judge is allowed to start censoring ideas even as the Madman is trying to develop them. The result is writer's block. The one thing all slow writers seem to have in common is that they will not go on to sentence two until sentence one is perfect. By the time they get to the end of the paragraph, the Judge still isn't satisfied, so they cross it out and start again. Fast writers *never* bring in the Judge that early in the writing process; this enables them to use the process to discover what they have to say. The perfectionistic, Judge-dominated writers view their initial efforts as producing a final product, which is why it takes them so much longer to get it done. So learn to keep the Judge out of the Madman's way.

The other steps are equally important.

Once you've let the Madman come up with ideas — in no particular order — the Architect must arrange them. But it's virtually impossible for the Architect to work well until the Madman has had free rein for a while. Although initially the Architect's work might be nonlinear, you'll ultimately need a linear outline — a plan that shows the steps on the way from the beginning, through the middle, to the end. Typically, in legal writing, you'll arrange your points from the most to the least important — and then clinch the argument or analysis with a strong closer.

The Architect's work product should be in complete sentences — not

---

2. *See* Betty S. Flowers, *Madman, Architect, Carpenter, Judge: Roles and the Writing Process*, 44 Proceedings of the Conference of College Teachers of English 7–10 (1979).

mere phrases. Why? You should be working with full propositions, not just scraps of ideas. A good outline can be as simple as three propositions arranged in their most logical and powerful order.

Next is the Carpenter's turn in the lead. This is where you begin writing in earnest. Following the Architect's specifications, the Carpenter builds the draft, joining sentence to sentence and paragraph to paragraph. Of course, the Architect's blueprint makes the Carpenter's job much easier. Ideally, the Carpenter writes quickly, treating the outline as a series of points that need elaboration.

For many people, the carpentry is the most unpleasant part of writing. They find it hard to sit down and produce a draft. But this problem stems largely from skipping the Madman and Architect stages—as if any writer could do three things at once: think of ideas, sequence them, and verbalize them. That's not the way it works, even for superb writers. In any event, the Carpenter's job becomes relatively easy if the Madman and Architect have done competent work beforehand.

Again, the Judge must stay out of the Carpenter's way. If you're constantly stopping yourself to edit the Carpenter's work, you're slowing yourself down. And you're getting into a different frame of mind—that of editor, as opposed to writer. Still, though, the Carpenter exercises considerable discretion in following the Architect's plans and makes architectural refinements here and there when producing paragraphs and sections.

When you have a draft, no matter how rough, the Judge can finally take over. For many writers, this is where the fun begins. You have the makings of a solid piece of writing, but now you can fix the ragged edges. The Judge does everything from smoothing over rough transitions to cutting unnecessary words to correcting grammar, spelling, and typos. An alternative name for the Judge is "Janitor" because a big part of what the Judge does is tidy up little messes.

Each character has an important role to play, and to the extent that you slight any of them, your writing will suffer. If you decide, for example, to "rough out" a draft by simply sitting down and writing it out, you'll be starting the whole process at the Carpenter phase. You'll be asking the Carpenter to do not just the carpentry but also the Madman's and the Architect's work. That's a tall order. People who write this way tend to produce bad work. And they tend to procrastinate.

If you decide that you can begin an outline with a Roman numeral, you'll still be asking a lot: the Architect will have to dream up ideas and sequence them simultaneously. And worse: whatever your I–II–III order happens to be at this early stage will probably become fossilized in later drafts. Most writers' minds aren't supple enough to allow part IV to become part I(D) in a later draft, even if it logically belongs there.

That's why it's critical to let the Madman spin out ideas in the early phases of planning a piece. Ideally, the ideas will come to you so fast and fluidly that it's hard to get them all down as your mind races.

One way to do this — to get yourself into the Madman frame of mind — is to use a nonlinear outline. Among lawyers, the most popular type of nonlinear outline is the whirlybird. It starts out looking like this:

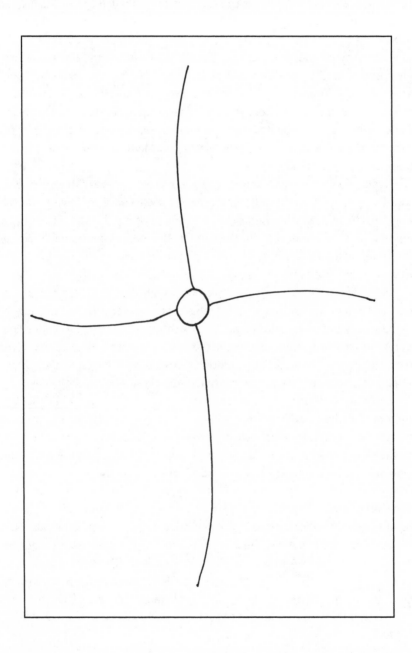

A shorthand name for the project goes in the center. Then you begin adding ideas — the more the better. For every major idea you have, use a branch off
the center circle. For supporting ideas, try branching off from a major branch.
Everything you might want to mention goes into the whirlybird — which has
no top and no bottom. You're striving for copious thoughts without having
to worry about where they go, how they fit together, or what they'll look like
when put in the right order. Here's an example:

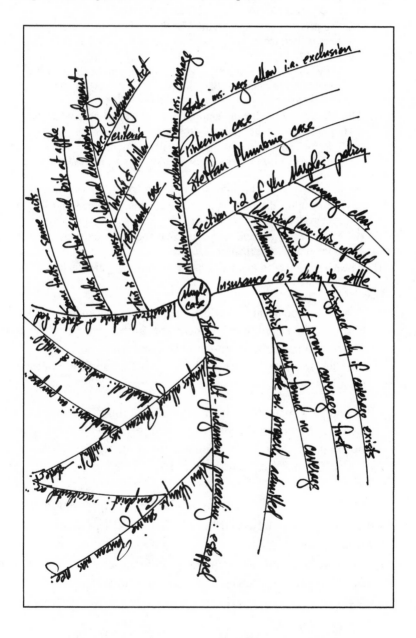

Once you've finished a whirlybird—whether it takes ten minutes or ten hours—you'll probably find it easy to work the elements into a good linear outline. You'll know all the materials. It will just be a matter of having the Architect organize them sensibly. The next step might look like this:

I. **An insurer's duty to settle is triggered only upon "compelling evidence" of actual coverage.**
  (A) The trial court properly found that there was no compelling evidence of actual coverage in the Marples' policy.
  (B) The Marples only now argue—for the first time on appeal—that "compelling evidence" exists. By their delay, they have waived the point.
  (C) In the absence of compelling evidence—and given the Marples' own contrary evidence—State Mutual had more than a good-faith basis for asserting that they had no duty to settle.

II. **The Marples are judicially estopped to contradict here what they earlier claimed and proved in state court.**
  (A) The policy does not cover intentional actions, and the state-court evidence of Panzan's willfulness is fatal to their claim against State Mutual.
  (B) In state court, the intentional nature of Panzan's act was crucial to obtaining the default judgment, and the Marples presented abundant evidence of intent.
  (C) The Marples' contradictory attempt in the trial court to prove lack of intention belies their negligence claim.

III. **The Marples' lawsuit constitutes an improper use of a declaratory-judgment action.**

Once you have this type of linear outline—something that many writers can create only if they do a nonlinear outline first—writing your first draft becomes much less intimidating. More on this in a moment.

Lawyers who have tried using the whirlybird before drafting a linear outline commonly cite several advantages:

- It encourages creativity. It helps you think of things you might otherwise miss. Brainstorming becomes easier because the creative mind tends to jump around. You eliminate the straitjacketing effect of As, Bs, and Cs, which can cause you to force ideas into premature categories.
- At the same time, the whirlybird can help in free-form categorizing.
- It makes getting started fairly easy. It's stress free. You can avoid writer's block.
- As some of the same ideas emerge in different contexts, you can see more clearly the interconnections between your ideas.
- It's a great way to discover your key points—and to distill your thoughts.

- Once you know all the options, you can more confidently select what your lead will be.
- The whirlybird is an excellent reminder of ideas that might otherwise get dropped.

Once the Architect has finished organizing the Madman's ideas, the Carpenter's job — the one that writers most often put off — becomes easier. It's just a matter of elaborating. Further, the Judge will be able to focus on matters of form and style, and that's what the character is best suited for. The Judge shouldn't have to think on several levels at once.

If you were to give me a pile of writing samples, I'd critique them according to this paradigm:

- The writer whose prose is "correct" but dry and dull needs work on the Madman.
- The writer who uses no headings (see § 4) — and for whom it would be difficult to devise headings once a draft is done — needs work on the Architect.
- The writer who has problems with transitions (see § 25) needs work on the Carpenter.
- The writer who allows typos in the final draft needs work on the Judge.

Each character in the Flowers paradigm must have its time at the helm. What you don't want to do is let one character dominate so much that the others get squeezed out. Your writing will suffer.

Perhaps the most crucial phases — because they're the most unpredictable and mysterious — are the first two: Madman and Architect. They will determine the degree of originality and insight in your writing. If you don't consciously involve them, the Carpenter will waste a lot of time. A carpenter must follow *plans*.

So as you can see, writing well is much more than getting the grammar and spelling right. Those are matters for the Judge, who in the end should tidy things up. Don't underestimate this tidying: it requires loads of know-how and serious stamina. Meanwhile, though, your Judge won't contribute many interesting or original thoughts.

Although you might fear that you'll never have time to go through all four phases, try it: it's one of the surest and quickest ways to good writing. In a one-hour span, you might spend 10 minutes as Madman, 5 minutes as Architect, 25 minutes as Carpenter, and 10 minutes as Judge — with short breaks in between. That's a productive way to spend an hour. But it won't happen without conscious planning — and ensuring that you allocate meaningful time to each stage. You have to plan how you're going to turn mushy thoughts into polished prose.

Exercises

Basic

While planning and researching a writing project, fill out a whirlybird. (You're ready to begin once you know enough about the problem to have an idea or two.) Use unruled paper. Take your time. Fill as many major and minor branches as you can, and feel free to add more. Then, when the paper starts getting full — and only then — create a linear outline consisting of three full-sentence propositions. Once you've written those, rethink their order and make any necessary adjustments. Remember that you're working on the basic unit of organization; once you have that, you'll organize further according to issues and answers.

Intermediate

Do the same with a trial or appellate brief. Fashion your full-sentence propositions into point headings.

Advanced

Do the same with a journal article or continuing-legal-education paper. For this one, your whirlybird may require a large sheet of butcher paper.

§ 3.   Order your material in a logical sequence. Present facts chronologically. Keep related material together.

Though ordering your material logically might not seem difficult, it will often be one of your biggest challenges, especially because of some odd conventions in law. One example among many is the stupefying use of alphabetized organization in certain contracts. That is, some formbooks actually have provisions in alphabetical order according to headings: assignments, default, delivery, indemnity, notices, payment, remedies, and so on. A far better strategy — if clarity is the goal — is to follow the logic and chronology of the deal. What are the most important provisions? In what order are the parties to do things?

Even when narrating events, legal writers often falter when it comes to chronology. Disruptions in the story line can result from opening the narrative with a statement of the earlier steps in litigation. Here, for example, is a judge's opener that recites events in reverse chronological order — a surprisingly common phenomenon:

> This is an appeal from an order of the Circuit Court of Jackson County entered February 10, 2011, affirming the June 20, 2010 order of the Mississippi Workers' Compensation Commission directing the Jackson County

School District to pay immediately the assessed amount of $52,218 to the South Mississippi Workers' Compensation Fund.

For most readers, that doesn't easily compute.

Even if the order isn't a strictly reversed chronology but merely starts in the middle of a story, the reader's difficulties can be insurmountable. Consider a before-and-after example. It comes from an amicus brief submitted to a state supreme court, seeking to overturn a lower court's ruling on an aspect of the state's oil-and-gas law. Here is the original two-paragraph opener, in which the two meanings of *hold* in the first paragraph present a stumbling block:

I. Introduction

The Court of Appeals held that capability of the lease to produce in paying quantities does not hold an oil and gas lease after the primary term and that actual marketing is necessary to perpetuate the lease in the secondary term. The Court of Appeals' holding is contrary to the fundamental principle of Arkansas oil and gas law that marketing is not essential to hold a lease where there is a well capable of producing in paying quantities.

The Court of Appeals' decision will create title uncertainty in thousands of oil and gas leases in this state. As this Court is well aware, thousands of wells across Arkansas have been shut-in or substantially curtailed from time to time. Under the Court of Appeals' decision, it will be argued that many of these currently productive and profitable Arkansas oil and gas leases terminated years ago if there was a timeframe when gas was not taken from the lease in paying quantities for the period specified in the cessation of production clause — often as short a time as sixty days. The issues of this case already affect a dozen or more cases now being litigated in Arkansas. The Court of Appeals' decision will encourage waste of a valuable natural resource and harm lessors and lessees by requiring continuous marketing of gas even at fire-sale prices.

Could you track the argument there? Does it hold any dramatic value?

Now consider a revision that emphasizes the underlying story. The editor has achieved clarity partly by highlighting the historical perspective, partly by tucking in some transitional words, and partly by specifying that the whole case hinges on the meaning of the word *produced* (admittedly in an obscurely named clause: the habendum clause). Note, too, the heightened drama of the case (on which huge sums of money were riding):

I. Introduction

Since first considering the issue more than 30 years ago, the Arkansas Supreme Court has consistently held that the word *produced* — as used in the habendum clause of an oil-and-gas lease — means "capable of producing in paying quantities." The Court of Appeals in this case overrode that settled principle by holding that (1) capability to produce in paying quantities does not maintain an oil-and-gas lease after the primary term — rather, gas sales and deliveries are necessary to perpetuate a lease in the secondary term; and (2) the cessation-of-production clause is a special limitation to the habendum clause. The court further held, incorrectly, that equities may be ignored in determining whether a lease terminates.

These holdings, besides being legally incorrect, are apt to prove cata-
strophic, since they will create title uncertainty in oil-and-gas leases across
this state. As this Court well knows, thousands of Arkansas wells have been
shut in or substantially curtailed from time to time. Under the new ruling,
litigants can now argue that many currently productive and profitable Arkansas oil-and-gas leases actually terminated years ago — if, for example,
gas was not taken from a lease in paying quantities for the period specified
in the cessation-of-production clause — often as short as 60 days. Indeed,
the issues in this case already affect a dozen or more Arkansas cases in various stages of litigation. The Court of Appeals' decision, besides encouraging waste of a vital natural resource, and besides spawning needless litigation, will harm lessors and lessees alike by requiring continuous marketing
of gas, even at fire-sale prices.

What qualities distinguish the two versions? What is the sequence of each?
Which one is more logically organized, assuming that these are the first words
a reader encounters? Did either version seem impenetrable when you first
started reading it? What does that say about the writing?

Exercises

Basic

Improve the sequence of ideas in the following sentence. Start like this:
"In March 2010, Gilbert Spaulding applied to the Workforce Commission for extended unemployment benefits." Then use one or two extra
sentences.

- The lower court did not err by affirming the Workforce Commission's denial of Spaulding's request for extended unemployment benefits, since those
  benefits were not available during the period for which he sought eligibility.

Improve the sequence and phrasing of ideas in these sentences, perhaps
by breaking them into separate sentences:

- The state supreme court reversed the intermediate appellate court's affir-
  mance of a summary judgment granted to Pilsen Corporation, the plaintiff,
  which had only requested a partial summary judgment on the discrete issue
  of fraud.
- The issue is whether Davis Energy has granted its neighbors an easement
  to use a private road that enters a Davis fuel-storage yard, when for three
  years Davis has had a guard at the road's entrance but has posted no other
  notice about private property or permission to enter, and for seven years
  the owners of adjacent property have used the road to reach their own
  property.
- The Plaintiff Los Angeles Dodgers, a corporation with offices and its principal office in Los Angeles, California, is the owner of a professional baseball team that, since 1958, has played baseball in Los Angeles, California,
  and before 1958 played baseball in Brooklyn, New York, under the name
  "the Brooklyn Dodgers," but in that year moved the site of its home games
  from Brooklyn to Los Angeles.

Intermediate

Rewrite the following passages to reassemble the elements in chronological order. Again, you might need to break one or more sentences into separate sentences.

- This action arose out of a request by Pan-American to cancel its surety bond posted with the Land Reclamation Commission to ensure reclamation on a portion of the Prelancia Fuels mine site. The Commission filed a petition for declaratory judgment and application for a temporary restraining order and preliminary injunction on February 16, 2006, to determine whether Pan-American could lawfully cancel its surety bond. Pan-American made its request after legislation had been passed that, according to Pan-American, would increase its liability under the bonds. The trial judge disagreed with Pan-American. At the request of the Commission, after a brief evidentiary hearing, a temporary restraining order and preliminary injunction were granted on February 16, 2006, preventing Pan-American from canceling the bond at issue until final judgment on the declaratory-judgment action.

- In *Sinclair*, the court awarded the niece of Sinclair a constructive trust. Sinclair's niece was suing Purdy's estate for one-half interest in property that she claimed her uncle owned and had promised to bequeath to her in exchange for caring for him until his death. The court observed that the property was purchased in his sister's name. This was done for business purposes and because he and his sister shared a close relationship. There was also an agreement between the siblings that the sister would be allowed to keep only half the property. The court ruled that withholding the property from the niece would be a breach of promise; hence, a constructive trust was awarded in favor of the niece.

- Kathcart filed the instant patent application on April 11, 2012, more than one year after he filed counterpart applications in Greece and Spain on November 21, 2010. Kathcart initially filed an application in the U.S. on November 22, 2009, claiming most of the same compounds as in the instant application. When he filed abroad, however, in 2010, he expanded his claims to include certain ester derivatives of the originally claimed compounds. It is the claims to these esters, which Kathcart has made the subject of a subsequent continuation-in-part application, the application now before the court, that are the issue here. Both foreign patents issued before the instant application in the U.S., the Greek patent on October 2, 2011, and the Spanish patent on January 21, 2012.

Advanced

Find a published case in which the presentation of the facts is marred by disruptions in chronology. Write a short explanation specifying why the narrative was difficult for you to read. Rewrite the factual statement as best you can, omitting irrelevant facts and putting in brackets any facts you might want to add (but weren't given in the case itself). If you belong to a writing group or class, circulate a copy of your before-and-after versions to each colleague.

§ 4.   Divide the document into sections, and sections into subparts as needed. Use informative headings.

Once you've determined the necessary order of your document in the out-lining stage, divide it into discrete, recognizable parts. This may well pre-sent a serious challenge because the legal mind isn't very good at division. Its strength is multiplication — multiplying thoughts and multiplying words. Still, with a little effort, you can learn to divide a document into readable segments of text. You can do this even as you're writing.

While you're figuring out a structure, make its parts explicit. Doing so will help you as well as your readers. The more complex your project, the simpler and more overt its structure should be. When writing a memo or brief, try thinking of its contents as a series of points you wish to make. Each point will account for a chunk of the whole — a chunk on this, a chunk on that, yet an-other chunk on this other point. For each of these parts, ask yourself, "What would make a pithy section heading here?" Then put it in boldface so it really stands out. You may need to go even further by devising subheadings as well. Busy readers welcome having a stream of information divided up this way.

In fact, headings have many advantages:

- They help you organize your thoughts into categories.
- They give readers their bearings at a glance.
- They provide some visual variety to your pages.
- They make the text skimmable — an important quality for those in a hurry and those who want to return to a specific part of your argument.
- They instantly signal transitions.
- When collected into a table of contents, they provide a road map for the whole document, however long it might be (see § 45).

You'd think these things would be obvious. But to many writers they're not.

Let's take a short example — a paragraph from an amended agreement of sale. At first it might look all right:

4.5 Upon the additional property closing, the Purchaser will:
  (A) authorize the title company to release the additional property escrow funds to the Additional Property Seller;
  (B) execute and deliver such documents as may be reasonably re-quired by the Additional Property Seller or the title company;
  (C) deliver a certificate of good standing, a certificate of Pur-chaser's corporate existence, and copies of all documents requested by the Additional Property Seller to show the Pur-chaser's corporate existence;
  (D) execute and deliver the additional bill of sale, assuming the ob-ligations under the additional contracts from the date of the

additional property closing and the obligation relating to the physical and environmental condition of the additional property;

(E) at the additional property closing, Purchaser and the Additional Property Seller will execute and deliver an additional closing statement setting forth the amount held in the additional property escrow and all prorations, adjustments, and credits to that escrow, and, if necessary, a post-closing agreement for the additional property closing for any adjustments based on estimates that are to be readjusted after the additional property closing.

The problem is that paragraph 4.5 has been plopped into the midst of paragraphs 4.1, 4.2, 4.3, 4.4, 4.6, and so on — not one of which has a heading. Without significant effort, the reader won't be able to see what each paragraph is about.

"Well," the naysayer might object, "agreements of sale aren't supposed to be pleasure reading. After all, other lawyers are paid to read them!" But that's not really an argument you can make with a straight face. And we're not talking just about making the reader's task more pleasurable.

When we put a heading on the paragraph, look what happens:

4.5 Purchaser's Obligations upon Closing. Upon the additional property closing, the Purchaser will:

(A) authorize the title company to release the additional property escrow funds to the Additional Property Seller;

(B) execute and deliver such documents as may be reasonably required by the Additional Property Seller or the title company;

(C) deliver a certificate of good standing, a certificate of Purchaser's corporate existence, and copies of all documents requested by the Additional Property Seller to show the Purchaser's corporate existence;

(D) execute and deliver the additional bill of sale, assuming the obligations under the additional contracts from the date of the additional property closing and the obligation relating to the physical and environmental condition of the additional property;

(E) *at the additional property closing, Purchaser and the Additional Property Seller will execute and deliver an additional closing statement setting forth the amount held in the additional property escrow and all prorations, adjustments, and credits to that escrow, and, if necessary, a post-closing agreement for the additional property closing for any adjustments based on estimates that are to be readjusted after the additional property closing.*

Subparagraph (E) suddenly sticks out: it doesn't fit within the category of the heading, and it doesn't fit with the other subparagraphs. (On parallelism, see § 8.) We'll need to move it somewhere else. Depending on the larger context, we'll either make it as a subparagraph in another section or make it a paragraph of its own. But all this might have been difficult to see if we hadn't gone to the trouble to think about headings for every decimal-level paragraph.

State and federal judges routinely emphasize the importance of point headings in briefs. They say that headings and subheadings help them keep their bearings, let them actually see the organization, and afford them mental rest stops. Headings also allow them to focus on the points they're most interested in. The key characteristics of sound point headings for persuasive writing are that they (1) are complete sentences; (2) contain (typically) 10 to 35 words; (3) are capitalized normally (*never* in all caps) but set in single-spaced boldface type; and (4) contain not just a conclusion but ordinarily a reason as well. In the following example, from the United States Solicitor General's Office, the point headings as they appear in the table of contents convey the gist of the argument at a glance:

A device as simple as headings can help you think more clearly.

Exercises

Basic

Go to the website of the US Solicitor General's Office: http://www
.justice.gov/osg. Find two briefs with particularly effective headings. If
you're a member of a writing group or class, circulate a copy of the table
of contents and be prepared to discuss why you think the headings are so
effective.

Intermediate

Find a state statute or regulation having at least three sections with headings that don't adequately describe the sections' contents. Devise better headings. If you're a member of a writing group or class, be prepared to explain why your edits would improve the regulation.

Advanced

Find a transactional document with long stretches of uninterrupted text. Break up the long paragraphs into smaller paragraphs and add headings where appropriate. For a model of this approach, see Garner, *Securities Disclosure in Plain English* §§ 41–43 (1999). If, as a result of this exercise, you find that the organization is poor, note the organizational deficiencies. If you're a member of a writing group or class, circulate a copy of the relevant pages and be prepared to explain where your headings would go and to discuss any organizational problems you uncovered.

2

Phrasing Your Sentences

§5.   Omit needless words.

Three good things happen when you combat verbosity: your readers read faster, you crystallize your thoughts better, and your streamlined writing becomes punchier. Both you and your readers benefit.

The following sentence, at 35 words, isn't grossly overlong, but still it's verbose. It comes from the Code of Federal Regulations:

> It is not necessary that an investment adviser's compensation be paid directly by the person receiving investment advisory services, but only that the investment adviser receive compensation from some source for his or her services.

Nearly two-thirds of the sentence can be cut with no loss in meaning—but with enhanced speed, clarity, and impact:

> Although the investment adviser must be paid, the source of the payment does not matter.

Imagine how this type of rewriting helps over a longer span—sentence after sentence and paragraph after paragraph.

Take a longer sentence, at 79 words, from a law-review article:

> Since, under the Equal Employment Opportunity Commission Guidelines pertaining to sexual harassment, an employer is liable for hostile-environment sexual harassment only if it knew or should have known of the harassment and failed to take prompt and effective steps to end the harassment, it is possible for employers to be exonerated from liability for hostile-environment sexual harassment when sexual harassment has occurred by individuals within an organization, but the organization took prompt action to prevent further harassment.[3]

That sentence meanders. Its basic point tends to get lost in the welter of words. Cut to its essence, the thought itself seems more coherent:

---

3. Elizabeth R. Koller Whittenbury, *Individual Liability for Sexual Harassment under Federal Law*, 14 Lab. Law. 357, 370 (1998).

EEOC Guidelines allow courts to exonerate an employer from liability for hostile-environment sexual harassment if the employer acts promptly to prevent further harassment.

At 24 words, the rewrite is less than a third the length of the original. But that figure only hints at the heightened vigor and lucidity.

The English language has vast potential for verbosity. Almost any writer can turn a 15-word sentence into a 20-word sentence that says the same thing. Many writers could make it a 30-word sentence. And a truly skilled verbiage-slinger could lard it out to 40 words without changing the meaning. In fact, almost all writers subconsciously lengthen their sentences this way.

But reversing this process is a rare art, especially when you're working with your own prose. You're likely to produce verbose first drafts—each sentence being probably a quarter longer than it should be. If you know this, and even expect it, you'll be much less wedded to your first draft. You'll have developed the critical sense needed to combat verbosity.

Meanwhile, of course, as you're tightening your prose, you must keep it natural and idiomatic—never allowing yourself to delete words whose omission will occasion miscues for readers. Don't delete articles (*a, an, the*) where they would customarily appear (*School is not liable for teacher's unforeseeable criminal acts*—insert *a* before *school* and before *teacher's*). And don't delete *that* if doing so will cause misreadings (*He denied the assertion made any difference*—insert *that* after *denied*).

Exercises

Basic

Delete at least four consecutive words in the following sentences and replace those words with just one word. You may rephrase ideas and rearrange sentences, but don't change the meaning.

- The general consensus of opinion on the court was that Business Corporation Law does not address the ability of a New York corporation to indemnify individuals who are not its employees.
- Even assuming that the fog caused the accident in which Cetera was involved, Pardone had no duty to prevent that injury because it was idiosyncratic, and Pardone could not have been expected to foresee such injury.
- At no time prior to the time of the initial public offering did the underwriters or any officers, directors, employees, or others have knowledge of any facts that would suggest that "Palm Harbor" could not be completed in a timely fashion and in accordance with specifications.
- Beale has wholly failed to allege facts that, if true, would establish that competition among the nation's law schools would be reduced or that the public has been in any way injured, and this failure to allege facts that would estab-

lish an injury to competition warrants the dismissal of her restraint-of-trade claim.

- The court examined a number of cases and stated that there appeared to be only a limited number of instances in which there would exist a duty to disclose the illegal conduct of persons who, through political campaigns, seek to be elected to a public office.

Intermediate

Revise the following sentences to make them as lean as you can without changing the meaning:

- The County sent an inspector who made observations as to the condition of the sidewalk and concluded that it was uneven.
- Although a review of the caselaw reflects that there are no decisions in the Eleventh Circuit concerning this issue, the great weight of federal authority favors the exclusion of third parties from a Rule 35 independent medical examination.
- There is caselaw for the proposition that use restrictions are not always strictly enforced when a lease is assigned by a tenant in bankruptcy and the property in question is not part of a shopping center.
- The court appeared to premise much of its opinion upon the argument that consumers stand at a significant disadvantage in product-liability actions based on ordinary negligence principles. Consequently, strict product liability was intended to relieve the plaintiff of the burden of having to prove actual negligence.
- With respect to matters not covered by the provisions of the Uniform Rules for the New York Court of Claims (the Uniform Rules), the Court of Claims adheres to the rules set forth in the Civil Practice Law and Rules (the CPLR). Ct. Cl. R. § 206.1(c). Because the Uniform Rules do not discuss disclosure of expert witnesses, it follows that the Court of Claims' rules on the subject are governed by the CPLR.
- There are cases that are factually similar to the present case, but that are controlled by older statutes — i.e., the pre-1965 legislative scheme. There are no cases that have been explicitly decided under § 1511 since the 1965 amendment, so it is unclear what effect the amendment has on cases that are factually similar to the present case.
- Arbitration as a means of settling disputes was at first viewed by the courts with much disfavor, but today is being used increasingly as a substitute for litigation for the adjudication of disputes arising out of contracts.
- The court rejected the defendant's argument that the headlines were not the product of sufficient skill or effort, finding that because many of the headlines consisted of eight or so words that imparted information, copying of the headlines might at least in some instances constitute copyright infringement.
- To say that one who has contracted to serve for a number of years at a low salary or at distasteful work and seeks to better his or her condition by a contract with another party should be penalized in every case by inability to enforce this second contract seems harsh, and under these or other extenuating circumstances, the courts have often deemed damages to be sufficient

recompense to the injured employer without also invalidating the second contract.

Advanced

Rewrite the following 193-word paragraph in fewer than 130 words without changing the meaning:

> In addition to the two cases cited just above, both (as mentioned) dealing with the California State Bar Rules of Conduct, Rule 3-310 of the California State Bar Rules of Professional Conduct describes circumstances in which an attorney is embroiled in the representation of adverse interests. Rule 3-310 is concerned primarily with situations in which the attorney's duty of loyalty and duty of confidentiality to clients are called into question. Therefore, to date, there are no Rule 3-310 cases disqualifying a district attorney as a result of a prosecution of an individual whom the district attorney used or is used as a witness in another prosecution. Most cases that involve district-attorney conflicts under Rule 3-310 consist of a former attorney–client relationship between an accused and a district attorney. In such cases, the rule serves to protect an accused from a prosecution in which a district attorney unfairly benefits from information gained during the course of his or her representation of the accused. Other Rule 3-310 cases involve overzealous prosecutions in cases where a district attorney is for one reason or another personally or emotionally interested in the prosecution of the accused.

or

Find a wordy sentence of at least 20 words that you can reliably cut in half without changing the meaning. Edit it. If you're a member of a writing group or class, circulate a copy of the before-and-after versions to each colleague.

§ 6.   Keep your average sentence length to about 20 words.

As much as any other quality, your average sentence length will determine the readability of your writing. That's why readability formulas rely so heavily on sentence length.[4]

But you don't just want a short average. You also want variety. You should have some 35-word sentences and some 3-word sentences. Just monitor your average, and work hard to keep it to about 20 words.

Unfortunately, in law many things converge to create overlong sentences. One is the lawyer's habit of overparticularization — the wretched practice

---

4. *See, e.g.,* Rudolf Flesch, *How to Write Plain English: A Book for Lawyers and Consumers* 20–27 (1979); Robert Gunning, *The Technique of Clear Writing* 32–34 (1952).

of trying to say too many things at once, with too much detail and too little sense of relevance (see § 23). Another is the fear of qualifying a proposition in a separate sentence, as if an entire idea and all its qualifications must be squeezed into a single obese sentence. A third is the nonsense baggage that so many writers lug around, such as the false notion that it's poor grammar to begin a sentence with *And* or *But*. A fourth is the ill-founded fear of being simple (and, by implication, seeming simpleminded)—or perhaps seeming to lack sophistication.

Many legal writers suffer from these turns of mind. And the ones who do must adjust their thinking if they want to pursue a clear, readable style.

Is a 20-word goal realistic? Many good writers meet it, even when discussing difficult subjects. Consider how Professor W. W. Buckland—with an average sentence length of 13 words—summed up part of the philosopher John Austin's thought:

> Austin's propositions come to this.[5] There is in every community (but he does not really look beyond our community) a person or body that can enact what it will and is under no superior in this matter.[32] That person or body he calls the Sovereign.[8] The general rules that the Sovereign lays down are the law.[11] This, at first sight, looks like circular reasoning.[8] Law is law since it is made by the Sovereign.[10] The Sovereign is Sovereign because he makes the law.[9] But this is not circular reasoning; it is not reasoning at all.[12] It is definition.[3] Sovereign and law have much the same relation as center and circumference.[12] Neither term means anything without the other.[7] In general what Austin says is true for us today, though some hold that it might be better to substitute "enforced" for "commanded."[23] Austin is diffuse and repetitive and there is here and there, or seems to be, a certain, not very important, confusion of thought. [23] But with the limitation that it is not universally true, there is not much to quarrel with in Austin's doctrine.[20][5]

The style is bold, confident, and quick. More legal writers ought to emulate it.

Is this type of style achievable in law practice? You bet. Here's a splendid example from a response to a motion to continue, by Thomas D. Boyle of Dallas:

> Gunther demanded an early trial date and breakneck discovery.[9] What Gunther wanted, Gunther got.[5] But now that Findlay seeks a hearing on its summary-judgment motion, Gunther wants to slam on the brakes, complaining that it needs more time to gather expert opinions.[28] Gunther ostensibly demanded the accelerated trial date to force a prompt resolution of its claims.[15] Yet now that Gunther may have that resolution, it does not want it.[13] Must Findlay's motion, already delayed once, be delayed again to accommodate Gunther's tactical timetable? . . .[14]
>
> Gunther's motion to continue is tactical only.[7] It is no more than an attempt to gain more time to answer Findlay's summary-judgment motion,

---

5. W. W. Buckland, *Some Reflections on Jurisprudence* 48 (1945).

which has already been reset once.[23] Even so, by the time Findlay's motion is heard on August 13, Gunther will already have had *eight weeks* to prepare its response.[23] If Gunther wants to defeat Findlay's motion, it need only identify a disputed fact for each point in the motion.[20] But Gunther spends much of its motion for continuance arguing the merits.[12] Rather than wasting time and money with dilatory tactics, Gunther should simply address the points in Findlay's motion head on.[20] If Gunther shows the existence of a genuine factual issue, then so be it.[14]

Although these sentences vary in length, the average is just 15 words. The variety, coupled with the short average, improves readability and generates both speed and interest. Keeping your sentences reasonably brief can also help you divide your ideas, simplify the punctuation, and enhance the clarity of syntax.

Exercises

Basic

Break each of the following long sentences into at least three separate sentences:

- Appellee Allied Indemnity of New York respectfully suggests that oral argument would be of little benefit because the dispositive issue has been recently authoritatively decided by the Texas Supreme Court in *National Union Fire Insurance Co. v. CBI Industries, Inc.,* 907 S.W.2d 517 (Tex. 1995), and by this Court in *Constitution State Insurance Co. v. Iso-Tex, Inc.,* 61 F.3d 405 (5th Cir. 1995), because the facts and legal arguments are adequately presented in the briefs and record, and because the decisional process would not be significantly aided by oral argument. [91 words]
- Although no Kansas cases were found that explicitly hold that Kansas requires a corporation to have a valid business purpose in order to engage in certain specified corporate transactions, either for mergers or consolidations, or for a sale of assets followed by a dissolution and liquidation, in a 2013 Supreme Court of Kansas case involving a cash-out merger where the dissenters claimed the defendant's board of directors breached its fiduciary duties to the dissenters, the court cited as one of the trial court's pertinent conclusions of law that it is not necessary for a corporation to show a valid corporate purpose for eliminating stockholders. [105 words]
- The court of appeals noted that the Environmental Protection Agency (EPA) had already issued the applicant a National Pollution Elimination System permit for the actual discharge of wastewater, which would occur from the outfall pipe, and that the issuance and conditions of such permits were generally exempt under the Clean Water Act from compliance with the Environmental Impact Statement (EIS) requirement, and accordingly the court concluded that the Corps had properly excluded the environmental implications of the discharges from the outfall pipe from its analysis and instead considered only the construction and maintenance of the pipeline itself in determining that the issuance of the permit did not constitute a major federal action. [112 words]

Intermediate

Rewrite the following passages to make the average sentence length under 20 words:

- At best, the lack of precise rules as to the treatment of routine corporate transactions forces investors and others who seek to understand accounting statements in all of their complex fullness to wade through pages of qualifying footnotes, the effect of which is often to express serious doubts about the meaningfulness and accuracy of the figures to which the accountants are attesting. Equally bad, while the footnotes, carefully read and digested, may enable the sophisticated analyst to arrive at a reasonably accurate understanding of the underlying economic reality, the comparison of figures published by one firm with those of any other is bound to result in seriously misleading distortions. Indeed, the figures for any given company may not be comparable from one year to the next, for although auditing standards require that the principles used by a firm must be "consistently applied" from year to year, the "presumption" of consistency may be overcome where the enterprise justifies the use of an alternative acceptable accounting principle on the basis that it is preferable. [Average sentence length: 57 words]

- It follows that in order for Wisconsin to compel school attendance beyond the eighth grade against a claim that such attendance interferes with the practice of a legitimate religious belief, it must appear either that the State does not deny the free exercise of religious belief by its requirement, or that there is a state interest of sufficient magnitude to override the interest claiming protection under the Free Exercise Clause. Long before there was general acknowledgment of the need for universal formal education, the Religion Clauses had specifically and firmly fixed the right to free exercise of religious beliefs, and buttressing this fundamental right was an equally firm, even if less explicit, prohibition against the establishment of any religion by government. The values underlying these two provisions relating to religion have been zealously protected, sometimes even at the expense of other interests of admittedly high social importance. The invalidation of financial aid to parochial schools by government grants for a salary subsidy for teachers is but one example of the extent to which courts have gone in this regard, notwithstanding that such aid programs were legislatively determined to be in the public interest and the service of sound educational policy by states and by Congress. [Average sentence length: 51 words]

- Some time subsequent thereto defendant, Brian Dailey, picked up a lightly built wood-and-canvas lawn chair that was then and there located in the back yard of the above described premises, moved it sideways a few feet and seated himself therein, at which time he discovered that the plaintiff, Ruth Garratt, was about to sit down at the place where the lawn chair had formerly been, at which time he hurriedly got up from the chair and attempted to move it toward Ruth Garratt to aid her in sitting down in the chair, whereupon, due to the defendant's small size and lack of dexterity, he was unable to get the lawn chair under the plaintiff in time to prevent her from falling to the ground. [Average sentence length: 126 words]

- Since it is undisputed that the sugar was stolen, and that it was purchased by Johnson, the question at issue for jury determination is the state of Johnson's mind when he purchased it. While the jury is unauthorized to convict unless it finds that Johnson himself had guilty knowledge, such knowledge may be proved by circumstances here to warrant the conclusion that Johnson, when he purchased the sugar, knew it to have been stolen and did not in fact honestly believe that the sellers were sugar dealers or were properly authorized by the Ralston Mill to sell sugar for it. In arriving at this conclusion, the jury might have considered the time and arrangements for the purchases, statements of Johnson to Gordon showing that he knew that he was taking a risk, the absence of any invoice or regular billing procedure, the contradictory statements of Johnson after his arrest, and the unlikelihood of the sellers' having come into possession of such large quantities of sugar to be sold below wholesale price in a legal manner. [Average sentence length: 58 words]

Advanced

Find a published piece of legal writing in which the average sentence length exceeds 40 words. Rewrite it to make the average under 20.

§ 7. Keep the subject, the verb, and the object together — toward the beginning of the sentence.

As you edit to ensure that your sentences are of manageable length, you should think about phrasing. Are the right words appearing in the right places? A sentence has two vital elements: a subject and a predicate (typically consisting of a verb and an object or complement). It seems simple:

> The partnership may buy a bankrupt partner's interest.

But legal sentences get complicated, and legal writers often complicate them unduly by separating the vital words:

> If any partner becomes a bankrupt partner, *the partnership*, at its sole option, exercisable by notice from the managing general partner (including any newly designated managing general partner) to the bankrupt partner (or its duly appointed representative) at any time prior to the 180th day after receipt of notice of the occurrence of the event causing the partner to become a bankrupt partner, *may buy*, and upon the exercise of this option the bankrupt partner or its representative shall sell, *the bankrupt partner's partnership interest*.

Even if you needed some of the details in that second version, you'd be better off keeping the related words together, at the outset — and breaking the one sentence into two:

> The partnership may buy any bankrupt partner's interest. To exercise its option to buy, the managing general partner must provide notice to the bankrupt partner no later than 180 days after receiving notice of the event that caused the bankruptcy.

Why should you put the subject and verb at or near the beginning? Because readers embarking on a sentence look for the action. So if a sentence has abundant qualifiers or conditions, state those after the subject and verb. Itemize them separately if you think a list might help the reader. You'd certainly want to restructure a sentence like this one:

> In the event that the Indemnitor shall undertake, conduct, or control the defense or settlement of any Claim and it is later determined by a court that such Claim was not a Claim for which the Indemnitor is required to indemnify the Indemnitee under this Article VI, the Indemnitee shall, with reasonable promptness, reimburse the Indemnitor for all its costs and expenses with respect to such settlement or defense, including reasonable attorney's fees and disbursements.

Putting the subject and predicate up front, as well as listing the two conditions separately (see § 34), makes the sentence easier to understand:

> The Indemnitee must promptly reimburse the Indemnitor for all its costs and expenses of settlement and defense, including reasonable attorney's fees and disbursements, if:
>
> (a) the Indemnitor undertakes, conducts, or controls the defense or settlement of any claim; and
>
> (b) a court later determines that the claim was not one for which the Indemnitor must indemnify the Indemnitee under this Article VI.

Remember: keep related words together. So important is this principle that—as you will observe in the examples just given—it can overcome the chronological-order principle (§ 3).

Exercises

Basic

Edit the following sentences to cure the separation of related words:

- Ms. Lenderfield, during the course of her struggle to provide for her children as a single parent, accrued considerable debt to her family and others.
- Chesapeake's assertion that it is not a proper defendant in this case and, therefore, that relief cannot be granted is incorrect.
- The court, in finding that Officer McGee was acting more as a school employee than as a police officer in searching Robinson, ruled that an official's primary role is not law enforcement.

Intermediate

Edit the following sentences to cure the separation of related words:

- Plaintiff's testimony that he had never had a back injury and had never been treated by a doctor for a back ailment before this workplace accident is suspect.

- The Trustee, at any time, by an instrument in writing executed by the Trustee, with the concurrence of the City Council evidenced by a resolution, may accept the resignation of or remove any cotrustee or separate trustee appointed under this section.
- In *Barber v. SMH (US), Inc.,* the Michigan Court of Appeals held that the plaintiff's reliance on a statement made by the defendant that "as long as he was profitable and doing the job for the defendant, he would be defendant's exclusive representative" as establishing an oral contract for just-cause employment was misplaced.
- Taxes imposed by any governmental authority, such as sales, use, excise, gross-receipts, or other taxes relating to the equipment, except for the personal-property tax, for which Biltex, Inc. is assessed and liable by applicable law, must be reimbursed by Calburn, Inc.

Advanced

Find a published legal example of either subject–verb separation or verb-object separation. (The worse the separation, the better your example.) Retype the sentence, with the citation, and then type your own corrected version below it. If you're a member of a writing group or class, circulate a copy of your page to each colleague, and be prepared to discuss your work.

§ 8.   Use parallel phrasing for parallel ideas.

Just as you should generally put related words together in ways that match the reader's natural expectations, you should also state related ideas in similar grammatical form. Parallelism harmonizes your language with your thoughts. At its simplest, it's a device for balancing lists:

Adverbs

> The jury weighed the evidence carefully, skillfully, and wisely.

Adjectives

> The arguments were long, disorganized, and unpersuasive.

Nouns

> The facilities are available to directors, officers,
> and corporate counsel.

Verbs

> The perpetrator drove to Minnesota, changed cars,
> and dropped the box on the side of the road outside St. Cloud.

The simplest, most common errors include a noun–noun–verb sequence, as here: "She was a law professor, environmental activist, and wrote mystery novels." For the sake of parallelism, the final element should be *writer of mystery novels*. In legal writing, though, an almost equally common error is to intersperse parenthetical numerals in a sentence without regard for whether the enumerated items match grammatically — as here:

> To prove a claim of false advertising under the Lanham Act, Omega must show that Binnergy (1) made a false or misleading statement, (2) that actually deceived or was likely to deceive a substantial segment of the advertisement's audience, (3) on a subject material to the decision to purchase goods or services, (4) about goods or services offered in interstate commerce, (5) that resulted in actual or probable injury to Omega.

In that passage, #1 is a predicate, #2 is a subordinate clause beginning with *that,* #3 and #4 are prepositional phrases, and #5 is another *that*-clause. Let's instead try leading off all the items with verbs, using only one *that* to introduce the list:

> To prove a claim of false advertising under the Lanham Act, Omega must show that Binnergy made a statement that (1) was false or misleading, (2) actually deceived or was likely to deceive a substantial segment of the advertisement's audience, (3) related to a subject material to the decision to purchase goods or services, (4) related to goods or services offered in interstate commerce, and (5) resulted in actual or probable injury to Omega.

Many grammatical constructions require parallelism. Among the most frequent are "correlative conjunctions," which must frame matching parts. The four most common pairs are these:

> Both . . . and
> Either . . . or
> Neither . . . nor
> Not only . . . but also

For example, if a verb follows *not only*, then a verb must likewise follow *but also*. Here, though, the writer got it wrong:

> Domestic violence is a force that *not only* causes suffering to the victim of an attack, *but also* detrimental effects on any children in the home.

The sentence needs matching parts for the *not only . . . but also* construction. Hence:

> Domestic violence causes suffering not only to the victim of an attack but also to any children in the home.

Be sure that whenever you list items or use correlative conjunctions, you phrase the corresponding ideas so that they correspond grammatically. Doing so shows an orderly mind at work.

Exercises

Basic

Revise the following sentences to cure the unparallel phrasing:

- The court relied heavily on the district court's statement that the would-be intervenors retained the right to appear through counsel, to participate in the fairness hearing, to conduct discovery, and standing to appeal the court's approval or disapproval of the class-action settlement.
- Tenant will probably not be able to have the lease declared void and unenforceable for vagueness because it contains all the essential elements of a lease: a description of the premises, the amount of rent to be paid, the term of the lease, and identifies the parties.
- The *Younger* doctrine also applies to a state civil proceeding that is (1) ongoing, (2) implicates important state interests, and (3) affords an adequate opportunity to raise federal claims.

Intermediate

Rewrite the following paragraph from a loan agreement so that you highlight the parallel phrases. The parenthetical letters — except for "(A)" — have been deleted. Simply reinsert the missing parenthetical letters "(B)" and "(C)" for the phrases that are parallel to the phrase introduced by "(A)." Study the passage first. Once you've decided where the letters should go, set off the listed items separately (see § 34). You might want to edit the sentence, of course. But be careful not to change the meaning.

> **2.1 *No Default or Violation of the Law.*** The execution and delivery of this Loan Agreement, or the bond indenture, and any other transaction documents by the Authority, will not result in a breach of the terms of, or constitute a default under, (A) any indenture, mortgage, deed of trust, lease, or other instrument to which the Authority is a party or by which it or any of its property is bound or its bylaws or any of the constitutional or statutory rules or regulations applicable to the Authority or its property.

Advanced

Revise the following sentences to cure the unparallel phrasing:

- The essential elements of a fraud claim under New York law are that:
  (a) the defendant made a misrepresentation
  (b) of a material fact
  (c) that was intended to induce reliance by the plaintiff
  (d) which was in fact relied upon by the plaintiff
  (e) to the plaintiff's detriment.
- Where there are already allegations of defects in design, manufacturing, and warnings, a claim that the manufacturer should have recalled its 2009 products is redundant, prejudicial, and directed to the wrong institutional forum.
- Under Georgia law, the elements necessary for the application of equitable estoppel are (1) a false representation or concealment of facts, (2) it must

be within the knowledge of the party making the one or concealing the other, (3) the person affected thereby must be ignorant of the truth, (4) the person seeking to influence the conduct of the other must act intentionally for that purpose, and (5) persons complaining must have been induced to act by reason of such conduct of the other.

§ 9.   Prefer the active voice over the passive.

Think of it this way: if you're active, you do things; if you're passive, things are done to you. It's the same with subjects of sentences. In an active-voice construction, the subject does something (*The court dismissed the appeal*). In a passive-voice construction, something is done to the subject (*The appeal was dismissed by the court*).

The active voice typically has four advantages over the passive:

- It usually requires fewer words.
- It better reflects a chronologically ordered sequence (ACTIVE: actor → action → recipient of action), as opposed to the reverse (PASSIVE: recipient of action → action → actor).
- It makes the reading easier because its syntax meets the English speaker's default expectation that the subject of a sentence will perform the action of the verb.
- It makes the writing more vigorous and lively (*John wrote to the company* as opposed to *The company was written to by John*).

Although these advantages generally hold true, they are not absolutes. You'll occasionally find exceptions — situations in which you'll want the passive (such as when the actor can't be identified or is relatively unimportant). If you can reliably spot passive-voice constructions and quickly assess the merits of an active-voice alternative, you'll be able to make sound judgments.

Reliably spotting the passive will prove a challenge. Fewer than half of lawyers can do it consistently. But it's not so hard if you keep this fail-safe test in mind: if you see a *be*-verb (such as *is, are, was*, or *were*) followed by a past-tense verb, you have a passive-voice construction. Look for phrases like these:

is	dismissed
are	docketed
was	vacated
were	reversed
been	filed
being	affirmed
be	sanctioned
am	rewarded

And there is also the *got* passive, usually confined to informal contexts: *The statute got repealed.*

So all the following sentences are passive:

- In 2011, only ten executives *were covered* by Article 12.
- Prospective investors *are urged* to consult their own tax advisers.
- The 2012 Plan *is intended* to facilitate key employees in earning a greater degree of ownership interest in the Company.

You can improve these sentences by changing them to the active voice:

- In 2011, Article 12 covered only ten executives.
- We urge prospective investors to consult their own tax advisers.
- With our 2012 Plan, we intend to help key employees obtain a greater ownership interest in the Company.

With a little effort, you'll find yourself marking passages in this way:

> *In the absence of proper venue, this Court should dismiss the petition.*
>
> B. ~~Venue is improper in this district, and the petition should (be dismissed).~~
>
> *ERISA venue provision (29 U.S.C. § 1132(e)(2)) governs the*
> The Plaintiff's choice of forum, ~~in this instance (is governed) by the ERISA venue provision, 29 U.S.C. § 1132(e)(2).~~ Section 1132(e)(2) does not allow *the Plaintiff to maintain* this action ~~to (be maintained)~~ in the Eastern District of New York. Further, *Court should dismiss the* this action ~~should (be dismissed)~~ under 28 U.S.C. § 1406(a) because the Plaintiff is engaged in blatant forum-shopping. In such circumstances, ~~it is~~ *Court need not transfer the case.* ~~not required that~~ the ~~case be transferred,~~ since the Defendants do not have significant contacts with the Eastern District of New York:
>
> - At the time ~~when~~ *of* the Plaintiff's claim for benefits ~~was denied,~~ *unsuccessful)* the ~~offices of the~~ Plan Administrator ~~were located~~ *kept offices* in Bethlehem, Pennsylvania.
> - As of September 10, 1999, ~~the offices of~~ the Plan Administrator ~~(were moved)~~ to Omaha, Nebraska. *does not*
> - ~~No office of~~ the Plan Administrator ~~(is maintained)~~ *an office* in the Eastern District of New York.
> - The ~~benefits under the~~ Plan ~~(are insured) by~~ *'s insurer* Cosmopolitan Casualty and Life, in New York. *operates*

Plaintiff also lacks any connection to the Eastern District of New York. When she filed her claim for benefits, she resided in Manhattan, which ~~(is located)~~ in the Southern District of New York. Plaintiff currently resides in Westchester County, ~~which is~~ likewise in the Southern District.

Once you learn to edit that way, you'll have mastered the passive voice. And in gaining this skill, you'll find that there are many subtleties.

One subtlety is that in some passive-voice constructions the *be*-verb is understood in context. That is, although a grammarian would say it's implied, you won't be able to point to it in the sentence. For example:

> Last week, I heard it argued by a client that national insurance should cover all legal fees.

Grammatically speaking, that sentence contains the implied verb *being* after the word *it*, so part of the sentence (not *I heard* but *it argued*) is in the passive voice. To make it active, you'd write this:

> Last week, I heard a client argue that national insurance should cover all legal fees.

With the so-called "truncated passive," the actor is omitted altogether — so that the sentence becomes vague and perhaps mysterious:

> Last week, I heard it argued that national insurance should cover all legal fees.

The truncated is especially common among litigators who tell courts that their motions should *be granted* and that their opponents' motions should *be denied*. Although it's clear who is to do the granting or denying (the court), the lawyers who write this way miss an opportunity to flatter the very court they are trying to persuade. That is, by explicitly placing *this Court* as the subject of the sentence, they proclaim that only *this Court* has the power to do as they request.

In sum, the active voice generally saves words, says directly who does what, and makes for better, more interesting prose.

Exercises

Basic

Edit the following sentences to eliminate the passive voice:

- Testimony was heard from the plaintiff and from three witnesses on behalf of the defendant.
- This is a purely legal question to be determined by the court.
- McCormick's motion for partial summary judgment on the duty to defend should be denied.
- Plaintiff's opposition violates Rule 313 of the California Rules of Court and may be disregarded by the court.

Intermediate

Count the passive-voice constructions in the following paragraphs. Decide which ones you would change to active voice. Change them.

- The intention of the donor is established at the moment the funds are dedicated to a charitable cause. This dedication imposes a charitable trust for the donor's objective as effectively as if the assets had been accepted subject to an express limitation providing that the donation was to be held in trust by a trustee solely for the purpose for which it was given. It is imperative that the objectives of individuals who give to charity be strictly adhered to.
- There are situations in which a motion for rehearing should be granted. Before the enactment of CPLR § 5517, it was held that when such a motion was granted, any appeals from the prior order would be dismissed. The CPLR was amended to "alter caselaw holding that an appeal from an order had to be dismissed upon entry in the court below of a subsequent order." [Citation.] Thus today, § 5517(a) states that after a notice of appeal from an order has been served, the original appeal will not be affected if a motion for rehearing is entertained. The appeal will be neither mooted nor canceled by the grant or denial of a motion for rehearing.
- Jurisdiction was conferred on the district court by 28 U.S.C. § 1331. The complaint was dismissed with prejudice on March 31, 2009, and judgment was entered in favor of the Cauthorns. A timely notice of appeal was filed by Perkins on April 7, 2009. Jurisdiction is conferred on this court by 28 U.S.C. § 1291.
- During the taxable years at issue, the replacement fuel assemblies had not begun to be used by the company for their specifically assigned function, namely, to generate electrical power through nuclear fission. Nor were the assemblies placed in a state of readiness for their intended use during the years in which they were acquired. That did not occur until the spring of 2010, when, after more than a year of careful planning, the reactor was shut down, various maintenance tasks were performed, spent fuel assemblies were removed, the reactor was reconfigured using the new fuel assemblies in conjunction with partially spent assemblies that were not replaced, and low power testing was performed to ensure that the reconfigured reactor core performed safely in accordance with specifications. Only after those procedures had been successfully completed did the replacement fuel assemblies generate salable electric power and, hence, income to taxpayers. Only at that point could the replacement fuel assemblies be considered to have been placed in service.

Advanced

Find a published passage — two or three paragraphs — in which more than 50% of the verbs are in the passive voice. Retype it, providing the citation. Then, beneath the original, show your rewritten version.

or

In the literature on effective writing, find three authoritative discussions of situations in which the passive voice can be preferable to the active. Consolidate what those authorities say. In how many situations is the passive voice better?

§ 10. Avoid multiple negatives.

When you can recast a negative statement as a positive one without changing the meaning, do it. You'll save readers from needless mental work.

A single negative often isn't very taxing:

> No more than one officer may be in the polling place at a given time.

Still, the positive form is more concise and direct — and equally emphatic:

> Only one officer may be in the polling place at a given time.

But when a sentence has more than one needless negative, the meaning can get muddled:

> A member who has no fewer than 25 years of credited service but has not yet attained the age of 60 years and is not eligible for retirement may not voluntarily retire early without first filing a written application with the board.

Change *no fewer than* to *at least*; *has not yet attained* to *is under*; and *may not . . . without* to a different construction entirely, using *must*. Then make a few other edits, and the sentence becomes much more cogent:

> Even if you're a member who is not otherwise eligible for retirement, you may voluntarily retire if you are under the age of 60 and have at least 25 years of credited service. To do so, you must file a written application with the board.

This revisory technique won't always work, of course. If you're stating a prohibition, you'll need to use a negative ("Don't litter"). One airline avoids this type of directness in a lavatory sign: "Please discard anything other than tissue in the trash dispenser." What this really means is "Please don't discard anything except tissue in the toilet." You wonder how many people bother to puzzle out the roundabout message of the original — which seems prompted by a desire to avoid using the word *toilet*. Still, avoiding the negative in that instance is awkward at best.

As Groucho Marx once said, "I can't say that I don't disagree with you."

Exercises

Basic

Recast the following sentences in a more positive, straightforward way:

- Notice will not be effective unless it is delivered in person or by certified mail, return receipt requested.
- In the absence of any proof to the contrary, the court should presume that the administrator's functions have not ceased.
- No termination will be approved unless the administrator reviews the application and finds that it is not lacking any requisite materials.

- It was not unreasonable to find that the jurors did likely believe Payton's mitigation evidence beyond their reach. The jury was not left without any judicial direction.

Intermediate

Recast the following sentences in positive form:

- Notwithstanding the due-diligence requirement, the granting of a motion to vacate a judgment of conviction will not be precluded where there is nothing in the record to indicate that the defendant's failure to acquire the evidence before or during trial was unreasonable.
- There is no issue of material fact that Renfro cannot establish that Aniseed, Inc. owed her a duty to prevent the injury she claims to have suffered.
- Bendola cannot be permitted to stand on nothing more than unsubstantiated and self-laudatory statements as a basis for denying summary judgment.
- No reason for refusing confirmation of the master's report not covered by the exceptions in the rule is disclosed by the record or urged by the defendants.
- A plan shall not be treated as not satisfying the requirements of this section solely because the spouse of the participant is not entitled to receive a survivor annuity (whether or not an election has been made), unless both the participant and the spouse have been married throughout the one-year period ending on the date of the participant's death.

Advanced

Find a sentence in published writing that is burdened with at least two negatives that you can easily recast in the positive with no change in meaning. If you're a member of a writing group or class, provide each colleague with a copy of the original (with a citation) and your revised version.

§11. End sentences emphatically.

Unskilled writers often compose sentences that, at the very end, fizzle. But skillful writers know that a sentence's final word or phrase, whatever it may be, should have a special kick. So if you want to avoid sounding like a bureaucratic bore, perk up your endings. Consider:

- Melinda Jackson died three weeks later in Columbus, Ohio.
- Melinda Jackson died in Columbus, Ohio, three weeks later.
- Three weeks later, while visiting Columbus, Melinda Jackson died.

The first emphasizes the place of death—probably a poor strategy. The second emphasizes the time of death—again, probably ill-advised. The third emphasizes the death itself. That's almost certainly what the writer intended.

With virtually any sentence, you have a choice about what you want to stress. Make it a conscious choice.

Again and again, you'll find that the most emphatic position in a sentence isn't the beginning but the end. Just as it's unwise to end a sentence with a date (unless the date is all-important), it's usually unwise to end one with a rule number or a citation:

> Fenster International Racecourse, Inc. respectfully asks this Court to enter a summary judgment and, further, to find that there is no just reason to delay enforcement or appeal pursuant to Illinois Supreme Court Rule 304A.

A little reordering can make a big difference:

> Fenster International Racecourse, Inc. respectfully asks this Court to enter a summary judgment. Under Illinois Supreme Court Rule 304A, there is no just reason to delay enforcement or appeal.

When you make this type of adjustment in sentence after sentence, you brighten the style.

Exercises

Basic

Rewrite the following passages to make the sentence endings more emphatic:

- This Court dismissed the whistleblower claims against the Governor on August 27 in response to the Governor's Plea to the Jurisdiction.
- The right to stop the work is the single most important factor in determining whether a party is in charge of the work within the meaning of the Act.
- The Commission is not in a position to provide additional affidavits and other evidence to support its contention that Bulworth and Islington are an integrated enterprise at this time.
- The court may authorize a preappearance interview between the interpreter and the party or witness if it finds good cause.
- Silver Sidings contends that it had no control over the hazardous substance released to create the emergency, and that the Department of Natural Resources therefore has no jurisdiction over Silver Sidings under the Spill Bill (see § 260.510, RSMo 1994). In fact, Silver Sidings owned the property where the release occurred, owned the underground storage tanks from which the hazardous substance was released, permitted the hazardous substances to be stored in its tanks on its property, and had every right as a landowner to control how its land and tanks were used — all relevant factors under the Spill Bill. Thus, Silver Sidings is "a person having control over a hazardous substance involved in a hazardous-substance emergency" within the meaning of the Spill Bill.

Intermediate

Find a journalist's article in which the last word is especially arresting. Be prepared to explain why.

or

In published legal writing, find a paragraph in which the sentence endings are unemphatic. Rewrite the paragraph to spruce it up.

Advanced

In the literature on effective writing, find support for the idea that sentences should end emphatically. If you belong to a writing group or class, prepare a page with at least three quotations to this effect. Provide full citations to your sources.

3

Choosing Your Words

§ 12. Learn to detest simplifiable jargon.

Polish in writing requires not only grammatical consistency and simplicity but also the avoidance of unnecessary jargon. Every profession has its own jargon. In a medical record, you shouldn't be surprised to read that the doctor "observed a fungal infection of unknown etiology on the upper lower left extremity." For some doctors, the word *etiology* (meaning "cause")—as well as dozens of other phrases such as *the patient is being given positive-pressure ventilatory support* (meaning "the patient is on a ventilator")—reinforces one's identity as a doctor.

Similarly, in police reports you'll frequently encounter passages like this one:

> When Officer Galvin entered the lot, he observed the two males exiting the lot. He then initiated a verbal exchange with a female white subject, who stated that she had observed two male whites looking into vehicles. When she pointed out the subjects as the two male whites who had exited the lot previously, Officer Galvin promptly engaged in foot pursuit of them.

All this gets recorded with a straight face. For the police officer, linguistic oddities such as *engaging in foot pursuit of* (meaning "running after")—as well as absurdly formal word choices like *observed* ("saw"), *exiting* ("leaving"), *initiated a verbal exchange* ("spoke"), *stated* ("said"), *male whites* ("white men")—are part of what makes one feel like a genuine police officer. But make no mistake: they do not contribute to precision—nor even to the "clinical" nature of the description.

Similar types of unnecessary jargon afflict most lawyer talk.

To the educated person who isn't a doctor, a police officer, or a lawyer, those who use jargon sound more than a little silly.

Consider something as commonplace as a law firm's jarringly antiquated e-mail disclaimer, full of verbosity and legalese:

> The foregoing message may, in whole or in part (including but not limited to any and all attachments hereto), contain confidential and/or privileged

information. If you are not the addressee denominated in the foregoing recipient box designated for the purpose of such denomination, or you are
not a person or persons authorized to receive this message for said recipient, then you must not use, copy, disclose, or take any action on said message or on any information hereinabove and/or hereinbelow. If said message has been received by you in error, please advise the sender forthwith
by reply e-mail and delete said message. Unintended transmission of said
message shall not constitute a knowing waiver of attorney-client privilege
or of any other privilege to which the unintentional sender may be entitled
at law or in equity.

That ludicrous disclaimer reflects negatively on the sender. Instead, it could
be much more direct:

This message, together with any attachments, may contain privileged or
confidential information. Unless you're the intended recipient, you cannot
use it. If you've received this e-mail by mistake, please reply to let us know
and then permanently delete it. We don't waive any privilege with mis-
delivered e-mail.

What a different impression the revised version conveys.

When first studying law, you labor to acquire legalese (it's something you
must understand). But if you ultimately hope to write well, you must labor to
give it up in your own speech and writing—that is, if you want to speak and
write effectively. Legalisms should become part of your reading vocabulary,
not part of your writing vocabulary.

But what, exactly, is a legalism? The term refers not to unsimplifiable
terms of art (like *habeas corpus*) but to legal jargon that has an everyday English
equivalent. Among the extreme examples are these:

Legalism	Plain English
anent	about
case sub judice	this case
dehors the record	outside the record
inter sese	among themselves
motion for vacatur	motion to vacate
sub suo periculo	at one's own peril

These examples are extreme because few legal writers use them today. They
don't present much of a threat to your writing style because you'll be sensible
enough to avoid them.

The real danger comes with commonplace legalisms that inhabit every
paragraph of murky legal writing:

Legalism	Plain English
as to	about, of, by, for, in
bring an action against	sue
herein	in this [agreement, etc.]
inasmuch as	since, because
instant case	here, this case
in the event that	if
not less than	at least
prior to	before
pursuant to	under, by, in accordance with
said (adj.)	the, this, that
same (pron.)	it, them
subsequent to	after
such	that, this, those, the
thereafter	later
therein	in it, in them, inside

While these and other legalisms might seem precise, they don't lend precision to the discussion. They're no more precise than the ordinary words.

In the following example, the drafter's fondness for *said*, *same*, and *such* has produced an unnecessarily opaque tongue-twister:

> The Undersigned hereby extends said lien on said property until said indebtedness and Loan Agreement/Note as so modified and extended has been fully paid, and agrees that such modification shall in no manner affect or impair said Loan Agreement/Note or the lien securing same and that said lien shall not in any manner be waived, the purpose of this instrument being simply to extend or modify the time or manner of payment of said Loan Agreement/Note and indebtedness and to carry forward the lien securing same, which is hereby acknowledged by the Undersigned to be valid and subsisting.

With a little effort — and by giving "the Undersigned" a name — it's possible to boil that legal gibberish down to this:

> Williams extends the lien until the Note, as modified, has been fully paid. The modification does not affect any other terms of the Note or the lien, both of which otherwise remain in force.

Lawyers recoil from this type of edit until they've acquired some experience. But with experience and insight comes the knowledge of just how unnecessary legal claptrap is.

Acquire that knowledge ravenously, and you might short-circuit years of befuddlement.

Exercises

Basic

Translate the following passages into plain English:

- A prehearing conference was held on July 15, 2010, and the result of said conference was that Rawson was given an extension of time until August 6 to respond to Vicker's motion. Rawson subsequently failed to file any response thereto.
- In the event that any employee is requested to testify in any judicial or administrative proceeding, said party will give the company prompt notice of such request in order that the company may seek an appropriate protective order.
- The court asks whether the plaintiff is guilty of unreasonable delay in asserting its rights. Such determination is committed to the trial court's sound discretion. The emphasis is on the reasonableness of the delay, not the length of such delay.
- Subsequent to the Bank's dishonor and return of the forged check, the U.S. Attorney served the aforementioned subpoena upon the Bank and directed the Bank to deliver to his office forthwith, upon receipt, at any time and from time to time, any and all bank checks, cashier's checks, and similar items stolen in the robbery that transpired on July 2, 2010.

Intermediate

Translate the following passages into plain English:

- All modifications, interlineations, additions, supplements, and/or changes to this Contractual Amendment are subject to and conditioned upon a fully executed, signed, and dated acceptance, approval, and confirmation at Pantheon's corporate headquarters.
- An interpreter is needed if, after examining a witness, the court arrives at the conclusion that the witness is without the ability to understand and speak English at a sufficient level of proficiency to comprehend the proceedings in such a way as to assist counsel in the conduct of the case.
- This letter shall confirm our understanding and agreement that if your loan application on the above-described property is approved, you shall occupy the same as your primary residence within thirty (30) days of the closing date. You are aware that if you shall fail to do so, such failure shall constitute a default under the Note and Security Instrument executed in connection with your loan, and upon occurrence of such default the full and entire amount of the principal and interest payable pursuant to said Note shall become immediately due and payable at the option of the holder thereof.
- Pursuant to the provisions of §§ 3670, 3671, and 3672 of the Internal Revenue Code of the United States, notice is hereby given that there have been assessed under the Internal Revenue Code of the United States, against the following-named taxpayer, taxes (including interest and penalties) which after demand for payment thereof remain unpaid, and that by virtue of the above-mentioned statutes the amount (or amounts) of said taxes, together with penalties, interest, and costs that may accrue in addi-

tion thereto, is (or are) a lien (or liens) in favor of the United States upon all property and rights to property belonging to said taxpayer.

Advanced

Find a published piece of legal writing that is thick with legalese. Prepare a short memo—no more than three pages—in which you (1) show at least two paragraphs from the original, (2) show how you would edit the passage, and (3) explain briefly why you made your edits. If possible, cite authority (such as a usage guide—see § 48) in support of your edits.

or

Review three of the following books and write a summary of what they say about using plain language:

- Mark Adler, *Clarity for Lawyers: The Use of Plain English in Legal Writing* (2d ed. 2007).
- Rudolf Flesch, *How to Write Plain English: A Book for Lawyers and Consumers* (1979).
- Joseph Kimble, *Lifting the Fog of Legalese: Essays on Plain Language* (2006).
- David Mellinkoff, *The Language of the Law* (1963).
- Peter M. Tiersma, *Legal Language* (2000).

§ 13.   Use strong, precise verbs. Minimize *is*, *are*, *was*, and *were*.

Despite many notable exceptions—as in "I think, therefore I am," "To be or not to be," or "It depends on what the meaning of *is* is"—*be*-verbs often lack force. When they appear frequently, the writing can become inert. Legal writers often overindulge, as in these passages:

- If there *is* information to which the company has reasonable access, the designated witness *is* required to review it so that the witness *is* prepared on all matters of question.
- Affecting vitally the problem of the burden of proof *is* the doctrine of presumptions. A presumption occurs in legal terminology when the fact-trier, whether a court or a jury, *is* required from the proof of one fact to assume some other fact not directly testified to. A well-known example *is* the presumption that a person *is* dead after seven years if he or she has been shown to have been absent for seven years without being heard from.

We can recast each of those passages with better, more picturesque verbs:

- If the company has reasonable access to information, the designated witness must review it to prepare for all matters of questioning.

- The doctrine of presumptions vitally affects the burden-of-proof issue. A presumption occurs in legal terminology when the fact-trier, whether a court or a jury, must deduce from one fact yet another that no one has testified about directly. For example, the law presumes that a person has died if that person has been absent for seven years without being heard from.

As you might gather, relying on *is* and its siblings can easily turn into a habit. And wherever you find the various forms of the verb *to be* congregating, you're likely to find wordy, sluggish writing. Although the English language actually has eight *be*-verbs—not only *is*, *are*, *was*, and *were* but also *been*, *being*, *be*, and *am*—this section targets the big four. They're the ones that you'll need to focus on most. So mentally—or even physically—highlight every *is*, *are*, *was*, and *were*, and see whether you can improve the sentence by removing it.

Many writers, by the way, erroneously believe that a *be*-verb always signals passive voice. In fact, it's only half of the passive-voice construction (see § 9). But even if *be*-verbs don't always make sentences passive, they can certainly weaken your prose on their own. So they merit your critical attention.

Exercises

Basic

Rewrite the following sentences to eliminate the *be*-verbs:

- Jones is in agreement with Smith.
- The professional fees in this project are entirely dependent upon the planning techniques that the client is in favor of implementing.
- The judge is of the opinion that it is within sound judicial discretion to determine whether, once the claim is asserted, the crime-fraud exception is applicable.
- Where there is no express agreement, it is ordinarily taken that the authority was to last for what was a reasonable time in light of all the circumstances.

Intermediate

Rewrite the following passages to eliminate the *be*-verbs:

- There was no light-duty work that was available at the company. The company's actions were hardly discriminatory when there was no showing that the company was practicing any type of discriminatory preference.
- Several members were in attendance, and those present were in agreement that the board's action was violative of the bylaws.
- This evidence is indicative that the company was desirous of creating a monopoly with the operating system.
- Since there is a limited number of persons with the requisite skills, it is increasingly difficult for the company to hire personnel who are qualified.

Advanced

In a piece of published legal writing, find two meaty paragraphs — consecutive ones — in which *be*-verbs predominate. Type the paragraphs, preserve an unedited version, and then revise them to reduce the number of *be*-verbs by at least 75%. If you're part of a writing group or class, circulate a copy of the before-and-after versions to each colleague.

§ 14. Simplify wordy phrases. Watch out for *of*.

In working to shorten sentences, phrase by phrase, you'll need to become a stickler for editing out the usual suspects — the recurrent phrases that bloat legal writing. Each one typically displaces a single everyday word:

Bloated Phrase	Normal Expression
an adequate number of	enough
a number of	many, several
a sufficient number of	enough
at the present time	now
at the time when	when
at this point in time	now
during such time as	while
during the course of	during
for the reason that	because
in the event that	if
in the near future	soon
is able to	can
notwithstanding the fact that	although
on a daily basis	daily
on the ground that	because
prior to	before
subsequent to	after
the majority of	most
until such time as	until

You'll need to remember this list — and the reliable one-word translations.

More than that, though, you can strengthen your writing by cultivating a skepticism toward the one word in the English language that most commonly signals verbosity: *of*. Although this may sound simplistic, it actually works: focus on each *of* to see whether it's propping up a wordy construction. You might be surprised at how often it does that. When editing on a computer, try searching for "[space]of[space]" to see how many *of*s you can safely eliminate.

Reducing the *of*s by 50% or so can greatly improve briskness and readability. With a little experience, you'll find that you carry out three or four predictable edits.

First, you'll sometimes delete a prepositional phrase as verbiage:

> Under New York corporate law, an action may be brought against one or more officers or directors ~~of a corporation~~ to compel them to account for their official actions if those actions resulted in the corporation's losing assets.

Although the edit may seem minor, deleting *of a corporation* helps streamline the sentence. This edit — by which you brand the *of*-phrase needless — is especially common in phrases such as *the provisions of* and *the terms and conditions of*. Instead of writing that an agency's actions are "subject to the provisions of the 2010 legislation," simply write that they are "subject to the 2010 legislation." Phrases like *the provisions of* typically add nothing.

Second, you'll sometimes change an *of*-phrase to a possessive form. For example:

> Profit-sharing was a means by which the employees were given a lump-sum reward for the success, ~~of the company.~~ *company's*

That's an easy edit. It also puts a punch word at the end of the sentence (see § 11).

Third, you'll sometimes replace a prepositional phrase with an adjective or adverb. For example:

> The sale proceeds came predominantly from the Historical Society's collection of European paintings and decorative arts, the maintenance of which contributed little to the study of ~~the~~ *California* history, ~~of California.~~

Although we might want to keep one *of* in the final phrase, we'll need to delete the other one and use *California* as an adjective.

Finally, you'll often just find a better wording. For example:

> The company advised Coleman ~~of the lack of a~~ *that he had no* factual or legal basis for the lawsuit.

This edit is especially common with *-ion* words, as here:

> Under New York law, any corporate act that is merely convenient ~~for~~ *to effectuate* ~~the effectuation of~~ the corporation's purpose is now viewed as a power that is subject to § 202.

Changing *effectuation* to *effectuate* immediately eliminates a preposition and improves the style.

Selectively deleting *of*s is surprisingly effective: even the most accomplished writer can benefit from it.

Exercises

Basic

Revise these sentences to minimize prepositions:

- Jenkins knew of the existence of the access port of the computer.
- This Court did not err in issuing its order of dismissal of the claims of Plaintiff.
- Courts have identified a number of factors as relevant to a determination of whether the defendant's use of another's registered trademark is likely to cause a state of confusion, mistake, or deception.
- One way in which a private party can act preemptively to protect the enforceability of the rest of the provisions of a contract, in the face of one void provision, is to insert a severability clause.
- Any waiver of any of the provisions of this Agreement by any party shall be binding only if set forth in an instrument signed on behalf of that party.

Intermediate

Revise the following passages to minimize prepositions:

- Henry II had genius of a high order, which never manifested itself more clearly than in his appreciation of the inevitability of the divergence of the paths of crime and of tort, and in his conception of crimes as offenses against the whole community.
- The recognition of the propriety of a court's overruling its own decisions places those decisions on the plane of merely persuasive authority and causes our theory of judicial precedent to be substantially like the theory held on the continent of Europe.
- Penfold had no knowledge of the amount of money paid — and could not have had knowledge of this — in advance of Penfold's review of its financial position in 2010. Thus, Penfold's profit-sharing is neither deserving of nor subject to the protections of Title III.
- In the case of *R.E. Spriggs Co. v. Adolph Coors Co.*, 94 Cal. App. 3d 419 (Ct. App. 1979), the Court of Appeal of California addressed the estoppel effect of a cease-and-desist order. The court was of the view that the trial court erred in failing to apply the doctrine of collateral estoppel, since the factual issue in dispute had been litigated and decided in an earlier case involving the enforcement of an FTC cease-and-desist order.

- One or both of the aspects of the function of the court must suffer. Either consideration of the merits of the actual controversy must yield to the need of detailed formulation of a precedent that will not embarrass future decision, or careful formulation must give way to the demand for study of the merits of the case at hand.

Advanced

Find a published passage in which you can improve the style by cutting the *of*s by at least half. Type the original, and then handwrite your edits so that they're easy to follow. If you're part of a writing group or class, circulate a copy to each of your colleagues.

§ 15. Turn *-ion* words into verbs when you can.

It's not just passive voice (§ 9) and *be*-verbs (§ 13) that can sap the strength from your sentences. So can abstract nouns made from verbs. Avoid using words ending in *-ion* when you can. Write that someone has violated the law, not that someone *was in violation of* the law; that something illustrates something else, not that it *provides an illustration of* it; that a lawyer has decided to represent the defendant, not that the lawyer has *made the decision* to *undertake the representation of* the defendant; that one party will indemnify the other, not that the party will *furnish an indemnification to* the other.

In each of those alternatives, there's the long abstract way of saying it, and there's the short concrete way. The long way uses weak verbs and abstract nouns ending in *-ion*. The short way uses a straightforward verb. Legal writing is full of flabby phrases containing *-ion* words:

Wordy	Better Wording
are in mitigation of	mitigate
conduct an examination of	examine
make accommodation for	accommodate
make adjustments to	adjust
make provision for	provide for
provide a description of	describe
submit an application	apply
take into consideration	consider

Of course, when you need to refer to mediation or negotiation as a procedure, then you must say *mediation* or *negotiation*. But if a first draft refers to *the mediation of the claims by the parties*, you might well consider having the second draft refer to *the parties' mediating the claims*.

Why concentrate on editing *-ion* words? Three reasons:

- You'll often avoid inert *be*-verbs by replacing them with action verbs (see § 11).
- You'll generally eliminate prepositions in the process, especially *of* (see § 14).
- You'll humanize the text by saying who does what.

The underlying rationale in all this is concreteness. By uncovering buried verbs, you make your writing much less abstract — it becomes far easier for readers to visualize what you're talking about.

If you still have doubts, compare that preceding sentence with this one: "After the transformation of nominalizations, the text will have fewer abstractions; readers' capability for visualization of the discussion is enhanced."

Be alert to words ending in *-ion*. When you can, eliminate them.

Exercises

Basic

Improve the following passages by changing all but one or two of the *-ion* words. Do any *-ion* words need to stay?

- An interested party may make an application for a modification or revocation of an antidumping order (or termination of a suspension agreement) in conjunction with an annual administrative review. A revocation application will normally receive no consideration by the board unless there have been no sales at less than fair value for a period of at least three consecutive years.
- In analyzing the ADA claim, the court noted that the decedent's termination and the reduction in AIDS benefits by the company occurred before the ADA became effective. Plaintiff nonetheless made the allegation that maintaining the limitation on AIDS benefits beyond the effective date of the ADA — in effect discrimination between plan members with AIDS and members without AIDS — constituted a violation of the general rule of Title I.
- The determination that reasonable grounds exist for the revocation of parole should first be made by someone directly involved in the case. Yet we need make no assumptions in arriving at the conclusion that this preliminary evaluation, and any recommendations resulting therefrom, should be in the hands of someone not directly involved.

Intermediate

Edit the following sentences to reduce the number of words ending in *-ion*:

- In the event of termination of this Agreement by Sponsor before expiration of the project period, Sponsor must pay all costs that the University has accrued as of the date of termination.

- The federal district courts have discretion over supervision of the discovery process, the imposition of sanctions for discovery violations, and evidentiary rulings.
- Although compliance with the terms of the Act should provide Hince some protection from state or local actions, the actual degree of protection remains uncertain because of the absence of any prior judicial interpretation of the Act.
- Any violation of the terms of probation established by the Board will result in revocation of VanTech's authority to conduct itself as a public-utility operation.
- In addition, the imposition of punitive damages here would be a violation of the constitutional provision containing the prohibition of ex post facto laws.

Advanced

Find a paragraph in published legal writing with at least three *-ion* words that need editing. Retype the paragraph, with its citation, and then type your own revised passage below it. If you're a member of a writing group or class, circulate a copy of your page to each colleague, and be prepared to discuss your work.

or

Research the literature on effective writing for additional support for eliminating *-ion* words. What are the various terms that writing authorities use for these words?

§ 16. Avoid doublets and triplets.

Legal writing is legendarily redundant, with time-honored phrases such as these:

> alienate, transfer, and convey (*transfer* suffices)
> due and payable (*due* suffices)
> give, devise, and bequeath (*give* suffices)
> indemnify and hold harmless (*indemnify* suffices)
> last will and testament (*will* suffices)

The list could easily be lengthened. Perhaps you've heard that these strung-along synonyms once served a useful purpose in providing Latin, French, and Anglo-Saxon translations when legal language was not fully settled. This explanation is largely a historical inaccuracy.[6] But even if it were accurate, it would have little relevance to the modern lawyer.

---

6. *See Garner's Dictionary of Legal Usage* 294–297 (3d ed. 2011).

The problem isn't just that doublets and triplets, old though they may be, aren't legally required. They can actually lead to sloppy thinking. Because courts must give meaning to every word—reading nothing as mere surplusage[7]—lawyers shouldn't lard their drafts with unnecessary words. The idea isn't to say something in as many ways as you can but to say it once as well as you can.

To avoid needless repetition, apply this rule: if one word swallows the meaning of other words, use that word alone. To put it more technically, if one term names a genus of which the other terms are merely species—and if the genus word supplies the appropriate level of generality—then use the genus word only. Hence use *encumbrances* alone, not *liens and encumbrances*—which wrongly suggests that a lien is not an encumbrance. And if the two words are simply synonyms (*convey and transport*), simply choose the one that fits best in your context.

What about *indemnify and hold harmless*? Is there a nuanced distinction? Historically, and in most states today, no. But in some states, yes: courts have fabricated a historical distinction between *indemnify* and *hold harmless* on the assumption that every word must be given effect. For the full story—a rather sad one—see *Garner's Dictionary of Legal Usage* (3d ed. 2011) under *indemnify*.

Exercises

Basic

Edit the following sentences to eliminate the redundancies without changing the meaning:

- Licensee will perform the work in compliance with all applicable laws, rules, statutes, ordinances, and codes.
- A party may not challenge a witness's truthfulness and veracity by the introduction or injection of extrinsic evidence relating to matters not already in the record.
- If the bailee fails, refrains, or refuses to perform any obligation under this agreement, the bailor may, at its option, perform the obligation of the bailee and charge to, bill, or otherwise recover from the bailee the cost of this performance.
- Seller must cooperate with and assist Buyer in this process, without bearing the costs or expenses associated therewith.

---

7. *See* Antonin Scalia & Bryan A. Garner, *Reading Law: The Interpretation of Legal Texts* 174–79 (2012) (discussing the presumption against surplusage). *See also, e.g., Lowe v. SEC,* 472 U.S. 181, 208 (1985) ("[W]e must give effect to every word that Congress used in the statute"); *Reiter v. Sonotone Corp.,* 442 U.S. 330, 339 (1979) ("[I]n construing a statute we are obliged to give effect, if possible, to every word"); *Burdon Cent. Sugar-Ref. Co. v. Payne,* 167 U.S. 127, 142 (1897) ("[T]he contract must be so construed as to give meaning to all its provisions, and . . . that interpretation would be incorrect which would obliterate one portion of the contract in order to enforce another part").

Intermediate

Find two examples of doublets or triplets in your apartment lease, mortgage, car-loan agreement, or other personal contract. Suggest a revision that eliminates the redundancy without (in your opinion) changing the meaning. If you're part of a writing group or class, circulate a copy of the before-and-after versions to each colleague.

Advanced

In the literature on legal language, find at least three discussions of the origin and modern use of doublets and triplets. Write a short essay (300–500 words) reporting your findings.

§ 17. Refer to people and companies by name. Never use corresponding terms ending in *-ee* and *-or*.

Imagine a world in which all novelists used the terms "Protagonist" and "Antagonist" as the names of their principal characters. Assume that playwrights and screenwriters did the same. The stories would grow tedious, wouldn't they?

Legal writers have traditionally spoiled their stories by calling real people "Plaintiff" and "Defendant," "Appellant" and "Appellee," or "Lessor" and "Lessee." It's a noxious habit that violates the principles of good writing.

You can do better: call people McInerny or Walker or Zook. Or refer to the bank or the company or the university. (If you want to—if you're feeling particularly nervous—you can capitalize them: the Bank, the Company, or the University. But see § 18.) Then make sure your story line works. Do what you can, however, to avoid legal labels as party names.

Most people, you see, don't think of themselves as intervenors, mortgagors, obligors, prosecutrixes, and the like. Even lawyers end up having to backtrack and continually translate. You're better off supplying the translations in advance.

By the way, you'll sometimes hear litigators say that it's a good idea to humanize your client (*Johnson*) while dehumanizing your adversary (*Defendant*). This advice is almost always unsound: it not only makes your writing halfway dull but also suggests that you lower yourself to transparently cheap tricks. Besides, if your adversary has really done bad things, the reader will readily associate those bad acts with a name (*Pfeiffer*) but won't with a legalistic label (*Defendant*).

Yet the preference for real names does have two limited exceptions: (1) when you're briefly discussing a case other than the one you're currently involved in, *the plaintiff* and *the defendant* (both lowercase) may work fine; and (2) when multiple parties are aligned in such a way that a single name is inaccurate, as in a class action, you may need *Plaintiffs* or *Defendants* (capitalized). Otherwise, use real names for parties — even your opponents.

As for *-or/-ee* correlatives, they typify poor legal drafting: *indemnitor/indemnitee, licensor/licensee, mortagagor/mortgagee, obligor/obligee,* etc. They have three major drawbacks. First, using such pairs means that you are differentiating the parties with nothing but a two-character suffix: you're inviting typographical errors, misreadings, and confusion. Second, you're making your document look as if you copied it from a formbook — and it is understandable that people will think you did just that. Third, you will review your own work less attentively if you use these boring labels — and you are therefore more likely to make substantive mistakes.

You are *much* better off personalizing your documents by using particular names, whether you're preparing pleadings, briefs, or transactional documents.

Exercises

Basic

Rewrite the following paragraph from a summary-judgment brief. Substitute names for procedural labels. Assume that the movant (your client) is Pine National and that the plaintiff is Peter Foster. You'll undoubtedly see the need for other edits, so improve the style as best you can.

> Movant has conclusively established that Plaintiff did not initiate this lawsuit against Movant until after the expiration of the applicable limitations period. Plaintiff does not dispute this. Instead, Plaintiff seeks to avoid application of the limitations bar by (1) asserting that this is a case of misnomer, in which case limitations would be tolled, and (2) asserting that, under *Enserch Corp. v. Parker,* 794 S.W.2d 2, 4–5 (Tex. 1990), factual issues exist as to whether Movant was prejudiced by the late filing. Yet the evidence before the Court establishes as a matter of law that this is a case of misidentification (which does not toll limitations), not one of misnomer. Further, Plaintiff has not responded with any proof of a basis for tolling limitations under the equitable exception to the statute of limitations described in *Enserch.* The exception is inapplicable under the facts before this Court, and, therefore, prejudice or the lack thereof to Movant is not a relevant inquiry. Plaintiff's claims against Movant are barred by limitations as a matter of law.

Intermediate

Find a legal document in which defined legal labels, such as *mortagagor* and *mortgagee,* have caused the drafter to avoid pronouns, as a result of which the style becomes embarrassingly repetitious. Rewrite a paragraph or two of the example. If you're part of a writing group or class, provide each colleague with a copy of the example and the revision.

Advanced

Find some authority that supports (or contradicts) the idea that you should refer to parties by name. Look at the relevant literature on brief writing and contract drafting. If you're part of a writing group or class, be prepared to discuss the authority you've found.

§18. Don't habitually use parenthetical shorthand names. Use them only when you really need them.

Ever read a newspaper article that begins this way?

> A powerful Russian industrialist named Mikhail Khodorkovsky (hereinafter "the Industrialist" or "Khodorkovsky"), whose empire (hereinafter "the Khodorkovsky Empire") is under investigation in the money-laundering inquiry (hereinafter "the Inquiry") at the Bank of New York (hereinafter "the Bank"), said yesterday that a large part of the billions of dollars (hereinafter "Russian Capital") moved through the Bank was controlled by Russian officials (hereinafter "the Officials") who used the Khodorkovsky Empire to protect their fortunes by shipping the Russian Capital abroad before Russian markets collapsed last year (hereinafter "the Russian Collapse").

Although that's absurd—and no professional journalist would ever do it— many lawyers are smitten with the idea:

> Gobel Mattingly ("Mattingly"), shareholder on behalf of Allied Ready Mix Company, Incorporated ("Allied") and Jefferson Equipment Company, Incorporated ("Jefferson"), has appealed from a nunc pro tunc order (the "Nunc Pro Tunc Order") of the Jefferson Circuit Court (the "Court Below") in this stockholder derivative action ("the Action").

Even without *hereinafter*s, that's nonsense. There's only one Mattingly, one Allied, and one Jefferson involved. And if you tell the story competently, any reader will know what order, what action, and what trial court you're talking about. As it is, the parentheticals impede comprehension.

So if you avoid the rote, mechanical use of parenthetical shorthand names, when might you actually need them? Only when there's a genuine need, which typically arises in just two instances. First, if you're going to refer to the General Agreement on Tariffs and Trade as *GATT*—something you may well do because the acronym is well established (see § 19)—then you might want to do this:

> Signed originally in 1948, the General Agreement on Tariffs and Trade ("GATT") promotes international trade by lowering import duties.

That way, the reader who encounters *GATT* won't be momentarily confused. Second, if you're writing about a case with two or more entities having confusingly similar names, a shorthand reference will dispel the confusion:

> Seattle Credit Corporation ("Seattle Credit") has sued Seattle Credit Engineering Corporation ("SC Engineering") for trademark infringement.

Although these situations sometimes occur, they aren't the norm.

Exercises

Basic

Rewrite the following paragraph to eliminate the shorthand names:

> The statement of the procedural history of this matter, as stated in the Appellant's brief, is essentially correct. The claimant, Keith W. Hillman (hereinafter "Hillman"), filed his claim for benefits from the Criminal Injuries Compensation Fund, Va. Code §§ 19.2-368.1 et seq., on July 27, 2010. His claim was denied by the Director of the Division of Crime Victims' Compensation (hereinafter "the Director") on August 27, 2010, because his conduct contributed to the infliction of his injury and because he had failed to cooperate with law enforcement. On December 20, 2010, Hillman requested a review of the denial of benefits. On April 8, 2011, Hillman was given an opportunity for an evidentiary hearing before a deputy commissioner pursuant to Administrative Bulletin No. 25, attached hereto as Addendum A (hereinafter "Add. A").

Intermediate

Find a judicial opinion in which the parties are methodically defined at the outset. If you're part of a writing group or class, circulate a copy of the first two pages. Be prepared to discuss whether you think the definitions serve any valid purpose.

Advanced

Find a legal document in which the introduction of shorthand names seems pedantic — or, worse still, absurd. Decide how you would deal with the issue if you were the writer. If you belong to a writing group or class, be prepared to discuss your findings and your proposed solutions.

§ 19. Shun newfangled acronyms.

Some acronyms are fine. People don't hesitate over *ATM cards*, *FAA regulations*, *GM cars*, *IBM computers*, or *USDA-inspected beef*. And lawyers are well familiar with acronyms such as ADA, DOJ, UCC, and USC.

But specialists often glory in concocting an alphabet soup that no one else finds digestible. They haven't learned how to write in plain English. Their acronyms are shortcuts, all right — but for themselves, not for their readers. This, for example, is a word-for-word passage (only the names have been changed) from a summary-judgment opposition filed by a major law firm:

> Plaintiff Valhalla Imports, Inc. ("VII") is correct in pointing out that Maine Casualty Corporation ("MCC") was represented at the voluntary settlement conference ("VSC") by Matthew Tabak, a claims representative. Tabak attended the VSC as MCC's claims representative handling Grosse's claim against the Randall County Water District ("RCWD"), which was listed as an additional insured under MCC's insurance policy. MCC simply was not involved in the worker's compensation ("WC") proceeding, had no responsibility for that proceeding, nor any duty in regard to the settlement of that proceeding, including the settlement of the serious and willful ("S&W") application. Rather, MCC's involvement in the facts giving rise to the action was limited to the following: MCC agreed to defend and indemnify (1) the RCWD under the insurance policy against Grosse's civil claims, and (2) VII against RCWD's cross-complaint. When Tabak contributed the aggregate limit of the MCC policy at the VSC, MCC did all it could do or was required to do to promote settlement.

Refuse to engage in that type of self-important obscurity. If you worry enough about your reader's convenience, you'll translate ideas into ordinary words that more readers — even more *legal* readers — can understand. Instead of the example just quoted, you might write it up as a good journalist would. Give the reader credit for having read the title that shows the full name of Valhalla. You might write something like this:

> Plaintiff Valhalla correctly points out that Maine Casualty was represented at the voluntary settlement conference by Matthew Tabak, a claims representative. Tabak attended the conference as the company's claims representative. He was handling Grosse's claim against the Randall County Water District, which was listed as an additional insured on the Maine Casualty policy. But the company was not involved in the worker's-compensation proceeding, had no responsibility for that proceeding, and had no duties in any of the settlement discussions in that proceeding. Rather, Maine Casualty's involvement was limited to the following: it agreed to defend and indemnify (1) the Water District under the insurance policy against Grosse's civil claims, and (2) Valhalla against the Water District's cross-complaint. When Tabak contributed the aggregate limit of the insurance policy at the voluntary settlement conference, Maine Casualty did all it was required to do to promote settlement.

When it comes to overused acronyms, environmental lawyers are among the grossest offenders. In environmental law, it's common to see discussions in which small-quantity handlers of universal wastes are defined as "SQHUW" (singular in form but plural in sense!), large-quantity handlers as "LQHUW" (again plural in sense), and conditionally exempt small-quantity generators as "CESQGs" (plural in form and in sense). Then, before you know it, you're reading that "the requirements for SQHUW and CESQGs are similar" and that "SQHUW and LQHUW are distinguished by the amount of on-site waste accumulated at any one time." Then, just as you're about to master these acronyms, you see references to "SQHUW handlers" and "LQHUW handlers." (The phrases are, of course, redundant.) Finally, when all these acronyms get intermingled with references to statutes such as RCRA, CERCLA, and FIFRA, you really do wonder what language you're reading.

Exercises

Basic

In a law journal, find a passage that contains too many acronyms. Pick out one paragraph, type it (with citation), copy it, and then revise it to minimize the acronyms while you avoid repeating cumbersome phrases. If you're part of a writing group or class, circulate a copy of your before-and-after versions to each colleague.

Intermediate

In a book or article, find 10 to 20 acronyms. On a single page, present the acronyms together with their meanings. If you're part of a writing group or class, circulate a copy to each colleague and be prepared to discuss (1) the extent to which you think the acronyms save time in communication among specialists, (2) the extent to which you think they impede understanding for ordinary readers, and (3) the relative desirability and feasibility of making the field more understandable to more people.

Advanced

In the literature on effective writing, find two sources that discuss the use of acronyms. Distill their guidance and write a one-page report on your findings. If you're part of a writing group or class, circulate a copy to each colleague.

§ 20. Make everything you write speakable.

Whenever you write, whether you know it or not, you're answering a question: What do you sound like? You might be stuffy (many legal writers are), whiny, defensive, aloof, or chummy. You probably don't want to be any of those things.

Generally, the best approach is to be relaxed and natural sounding. That tone bespeaks confidence. It shows that you're comfortable with your written voice. It's worth remembering, as the late Second Circuit judge Jerome Frank once put it, that the primary appeal of the language is to the ear.[8] Good writing is simply speech heightened and polished.

To the legal reader, few things are more pleasing than the sense that a writer is talking directly to you — one intelligent being to another. It's unusual enough to be genuinely refreshing. Consider the following example. It's the opener to a memorandum of law that Charles Dewey Cole Jr. of New York filed in federal court:

Grieg's Response in Support of Denying Wilson's Late Designation of Expert Witnesses

You wouldn't know it from reading Wilson's objections, but what is at stake is not Grieg's inability to depose Wilson's employees (or even Grieg's inability to depose them fully). What these objections are about — and this is all that they are about — is Wilson's unexcused failure to serve its expert-witness disclosure by the deadline: July 13, 2011. Because Wilson didn't serve a medical report by then, Grieg assumed that Wilson would forgo medical testimony, and Grieg in turn decided against having Walim Alibrandi examined by a physician.

The plaintiffs' attorney must have assumed that whatever injuries Mr. Alibrandi received in the collision (and they were slight indeed), the cost of a physical examination and of preparing a medical report simply wasn't justified — an understandable decision given a comparison of that cost with the anticipated recovery. What the plaintiffs' attorney did not anticipate was that the defendants weren't about to settle the case, and he found himself in the unenviable position of having let the discovery deadline run without having served a medical report. And he had no excuse.

Because the plaintiffs' lawyer had no justification for failing to serve any medical expert-witness disclosure, he dressed up his application before the magistrate judge to include all sorts of stuff about how the defendants had impeded discovery so that he couldn't take a whole bunch of unnecessary depositions. The magistrate judge recognized this for what it was and concluded that the plaintiffs' lawyer "had no excuse for his failure to have served his own medical expert disclosure." So she refused to reopen the period for discovery at the October settlement conference.

The relaxed tone, achieved partly through contractions, shows confidence. The point about contractions isn't to use them whenever possible, but rather whenever natural. Like pronouns, they make a document more readable: "*Write as You Talk* is the accepted rule of writing readably — and in English, the most conspicuous and handiest device of doing that is to use contractions."[9] A 1989 study confirmed this: it found that frequent contractions enhance readability.[10] This advice applies not just to briefs but also to contracts, rules, and other legal documents.

---

8. Jerome Frank, *The Speech of Judges: A Dissenting Opinion*, 6 Scribes J. Legal Writing 97, 99 (1996–1997), *reprinted from* 29 Va. L. Rev. 625 (1943).

9. Rudolf Flesch, *The Art of Readable Writing* 82 (1949).

10. *See, e.g.,* Wayne A. Danielson & Dominic L. Lasorsa, *A New Readability Formula Based on the Stylistic Age of Novels*, 33 J. Reading 194, 196 (1989).

A word of caution: you might not be allowed to use contractions much until you achieve a certain level of experience or seniority. The applicability of this admonition will depend on your work situation. If you're in a junior position, you may have to be patient. My coauthor of two books, Justice Antonin Scalia, disapproved of contractions, much to my surprise — so although in our first joint book we used them throughout (he made concessions to my style), in our second book we abstained.[11]

What are the other characteristics of a natural, spoken style?

One is the use of first-person and second-person pronouns — especially *we* and *you*—as opposed to third-party references such as *resident* or *mortgagor* or *vendee* (see § 17). Readers are much more engaged by a text that speaks to them directly. For example, the U.S. Air Force years ago began to remedy the problem of unnatural, hard-to-understand language in its directives. To translate a grievance procedure into plain English, the revisers used *you* instead of *employee*. One sentence originally read:

> If the employee feels that an interview with the immediate supervisor would be unsatisfactory, he or his representative may, in the first instance, present his grievance to the next supervisor in line.

That sentence is much clearer with the personal word *you*:

> If you feel that your supervisor will not handle your case fairly, you may go directly to your supervisor's supervisor.[12]

In sum, when you address readers directly, they more readily see how the text applies to them.

Another point is to begin sentences with *And*, *But*, and *So*—especially *But*. You do this in speech all the time. Good writers routinely do it in print — nearly 10% of the time.[13] But legal writers often lapse into stiffer sentence openers like *Similarly, However, Consequently*, and *Inasmuch as*. Try replacing these heavy connectors with faster, more conversational ones.

Here's a good test of naturalness: if you wouldn't say it, then don't write it. You'll give your writing much more credence if you come across as sincere, honest, and genuine. Your words will be plainer, your style more relaxed, and your prose more memorable. You should probably try reading your prose aloud to see whether you'd actually say it the way you've written it.

---

11. *See* Antonin Scalia & Bryan A. Garner, *Making Your Case: The Art of Persuading Judges* 114–19 (2008) (debating contractions); Antonin Scalia & Bryan A. Garner, *Reading Law: The Interpretation of Legal Texts* (2012) (containing no contractions).

12. *See* Arthur O. England, *Getting Your Message Across by Plain Talk*, 34 J. Applied Psychol. 182, 182 (1950).

13. Francis Christiansen, *Notes Toward a New Rhetoric*, 25 College English 9 (1963); *see also* Bryan A. Garner, *On Beginning Sentences with "But,"* 3 Scribes J. Legal Writing 87 (1992).

Exercises

Basic

Rewrite the following openers and closers from letters to make them speakable:

- Enclosed please find the following documents:
- Pursuant to your instructions, I met with Roger Smith today regarding the above-referenced cause.
- Please be advised that the discovery cutoff in the above-referenced cause is Monday, March 10, 2014.
- Pursuant to my conversation with Alex in your office on today's date, I contacted the trustee.
- This letter is for the purpose of retaining your services as a consultant regarding the above-referenced matter.
- Thank you in advance for your courtesy and cooperation in this regard. Please do not hesitate to contact me should you have any questions regarding this request.

Intermediate

In a law review, find a long sentence or a short to medium paragraph that strikes you as particularly unspeakable. Type it, provide a citation, and set out a bulleted list of reasons why you consider it difficult to read aloud. If you belong to a writing group or class, circulate a copy to each colleague.

Advanced

In a judicial opinion, find a two- or three-paragraph passage that strikes you as being particularly unspeakable. Type it, provide a citation, and set out a bulleted list of reasons why you consider it difficult to read aloud. Rewrite the passage. If you belong to a writing group or class, circulate a copy of your before-and-after versions to each colleague.

PART TWO

Principles Mainly for Analytical and Persuasive Writing

The phrase "analytical and persuasive writing" encompasses general expository prose: letters, memos, briefs, judicial opinions, and the like. The only excluded items, essentially, belong to the category known as "legal drafting" (see Part Three). In writing to analyze or persuade, strive for these major goals:

- *Get your point across quickly with a concrete summary up front.*
- *Focus the analysis or argument.*
- *Make it interesting.*
- *Supply smooth transitions.*
- *Quote smartly and deftly.*

Most legal writers don't attain these goals. The tips that follow will allow you to stand out as one who does attain them.

§ 21. Plan all three parts: the beginning, the middle, and the end.

All good expository writing has three parts: an introduction, a main body, and a conclusion. You'd think everyone knows this. Not so: the orthodox method of brief writing, and the way of many research memos, is to provide only one part — a middle.

How so? Well, formbook-style openers typically just restate the title. For example: *Plaintiff Pantheon Corporation, by and through its attorneys of record [full address], files this, Pantheon's Memorandum in Support of Its Motion for Summary Judgment.* Hence the title. That's why it's called "Pantheon's Memorandum in Support of Its Motion for Summary Judgment" just an inch above this wasteful sentence. In some briefs, the hence-the-title sentence starts with *Now come . . .*

The conclusion, meanwhile, is equally formulaic: *For all the foregoing reasons . . .* or (in antique language) *Wherefore, premises considered, . . .* These concluding refusals to summarize are every bit as common as stale openers.

If you're writing that way, you're neglecting the most critical parts of the brief: the beginning and the end.

A Proper Opener

The ideal introduction concisely states the precise points at issue — concretely — in a way that is fully comprehensible to any intelligent reader in a first reading. Stripped of all extraneous matter, the intro serves as an executive summary: it places the essential ideas before the reader.

Fortunately, you're almost always able to put a preliminary statement on the first page of a brief, even if the rules don't call for it. Just put it there — as far up front as you can. In at least two jurisdictions, New York and New Jersey, including a preliminary statement is the norm — though few lawyers put them to good use. And in most other jurisdictions, very few lawyers use intros. But a good one is always advisable.

How do you decide what goes into an introduction? Figure out first how many arguments you want to make, and then turn each one into an issue statement.

Let's say you have a single issue. You might begin this way:

Motion for Summary Judgment

Preliminary Statement

In ruling on this motion, the Court faces the following issue— all else being peripheral:

> Section 7300 of the Internal Revenue Code prohibits the unauthorized disclosure of a taxpayer's tax audit by an IRS agent. While drinking at a hotel bar, IRS Agent Harold Collins confronted Susan Jones, who was dining with her family in an adjoining restaurant, and shouted, "Ms. Jones, if I had your audit case, I'd have you in jail by now." Did Agent Collins make an unauthorized disclosure of Susan Jones's tax audit?

That type of opener uses the "deep issue" technique (see § 22)—in which the issue is framed in separate sentences totaling fewer than 75 words.[1]

Although the deep issue is hard to beat, you can also state the issue less formally in the preliminary statement. Here's an example from another summary-judgment motion:

> Under Alabama law, a personal representative can bring a wrongful-death action on behalf of a decedent only if the decedent could have maintained a claim at the time of death. (Ala. Code § 6–5–410(a).) The decedent's medical records establish that he was diagnosed with lung cancer in 2006. So the applicable two-year statute of limitations on the decedent's personal-injury claim elapsed no later than 2008 — nearly two years before his death. Because the two-year statute of limitations would have barred the decedent from pursuing a lawsuit at the time of his death in 2010, his personal representative is likewise barred from bringing suit.

In short, don't depend on a rule to tell you to put the issues up front. True, some court rules require them at the outset, as U.S. Supreme Court Rule 14 does. But many rules, especially in trial courts, don't say anything about them at all. And even on appeal, various state-court rules require mere "Points Relied On" or "Points of Error"—something rather different from true issues. Despite these requirements — which you must comply with — always add a preliminary statement that highlights the issues. Your judicial readers will be grateful.

---

1. *See* Garner, *The Winning Brief* §§ 8–12, at 53–97 (2d ed. 2004); *see also* Antonin Scalia & Bryan A. Garner, *Making Your Case: The Art of Persuading Judges* 85–87 (2008).

A Satisfactory Middle

The middle should—with a series of headings and perhaps subheadings (see § 4)—develop the reasoning by which the writer seeks to prove the affirmative or the negative of the issues stated in the introduction. How do you do that? First, select the main ideas that prove your conclusion. Then arrange them in a way that shows the relations they naturally bear to one another and to the essential idea or ideas. All the main headings and subheadings should drive the reader toward your conclusion.

Let's say you have three issues. You'll have three parts in the body, typically proceeding from the strongest to the least strong. (Forget the weak arguments.) Each part will be organized to do four things:

- Set forth the legal rule embedded in the issue statement.
- Show how the factual points fit into this rule.
- Deal with counterarguments.
- Drive the point home with an additional reason or set of reasons.

That's the basic way to organize the argument for each issue.

A tricky part is dealing with counterarguments (see § 30). You must weigh and address all serious ones, and the dialectical method of arguing is the best tool for this. A dialectic is something like a pendulum through time. At its simplest, its form is thesis–antithesis–conclusion. You'll need to counter the antithesis to your position.

A Strong Closer

The conclusion should briefly sum up the argument. If you're writing as an advocate, you'll need to show clearly what the decision maker should do and why. One good method is to answer the questions posed in the opener.

Just as your opener is crucial, so is your closer. It's your chance to sum up—preferably in a fresh, expansive way. Yet the classic *Wherefore, premises considered,* . . .—a form with regional variations throughout the country—is a formulaic cop-out that says nothing.

To close forcefully, recapitulate your main points concisely—and, if you can, freshly. Put them in a nutshell, without vague references to "the foregoing reasons" or "the aforementioned argument." You'll project an image of confidence and professionalism.

A Sea Change

All this may sound obvious. But judging from what lawyers actually do, it's little known. Go down to the courthouse sometime and look at the filings: you'll see that more than 85% of them have stock openers and closers. They're all middle. This absence of logical structure—more than anything else—explains why so many briefs are inadequate. Likewise, many if not most research memos assume that the reader is as familiar with the subject as the writer—as a result of which no good, comprehensible summary appears. Although you'll see a heading "Summary" or "Question Presented," the text is typically incomprehensible to anyone not already working on the matter. For a research memo, which should always have a long shelf life, that is quite bad.

Lawyers fear summarizing. They fear true openers and closers: they generally know that creating strong ones takes a lot of work. So they take the easy way out.

But remember what Samuel Johnson, the great English critic and dictionary writer, once said: "What is written without effort is in general read without pleasure."[2] Talk to judges, and they'll tell you that they generally read briefs without the remotest hint of pleasure. It shouldn't be that way.

Exercises

Basic

Find a brief or judicial opinion that has a particularly good opener and closer. (For a brief, you might look at books with model briefs. You might also look at continuing-legal-education materials on appellate practice.) If you belong to a writing group or class, circulate a copy to each colleague. Be prepared to explain why you think the introduction and conclusion are effective.

Intermediate

Find a research memo that has no proper opener or closer—that is, one that's all middle. Write both a summary that could be added at the start and a fresh conclusion. If you're part of a writing group or class, circulate a copy of your work to each colleague. Be prepared to discuss the problems in the original and how you tried to solve them.

Advanced

Find a motion (or memorandum in support) or a brief that launches straight into a statement of facts. Write a new preliminary statement that could be inserted at the beginning of the motion or brief. If you're part of a writing group or class, circulate a copy of your summary to each colleague. Be prepared to discuss the problems in the original and how you tried to solve them.

---

2. *Quoted in* Jon Winokur, *Writers on Writing* 111 (2d ed. 1987).

§ 22. Use the "deep issue" to spill the beans on the first page.

Virtually all analytical or persuasive writing should have a summary on page one — a true summary that encapsulates the upshot of the message. This upshot inevitably consists of three parts: the question, the answer, and the reasons. I don't know of any exceptions. It's true of good research memos, good briefs, and good judicial opinions. The summary is your opener.

American schools once taught what was called "précis writing"—and every American high-school student knew what a précis was: an accurate summary of a much longer piece. Teachers gave their students a three-page essay and asked them to state the gist of it in a single paragraph. Or the students would recast a three-page essay as a single paragraph. Schools did these drills frequently until the 1950s or so, when précis writing fell out of fashion.

If only it hadn't fallen into decline, students would enter law school much better equipped to do what good lawyers must do: work on a complicated case for months or even years but be able to distill its essence down to a page.

If you include an up-front summary, one major by-product will be that you'll think more clearly. Why? Because if you haven't isolated the most important idea, you haven't been thinking as clearly as you might. By highlighting the issues and conclusions on page one, you'll end up (1) testing the validity of those conclusions more thoroughly, (2) ensuring that you carry through with them when you get to the middle, and (3) eliminating slag that your research has produced but that doesn't help the analysis.

To summarize effectively, be sure that you include the issues, the answers, and the reasons for those answers. If you're writing a memo, page one ends up looking something like the example on page 74. If you're writing a brief, page one should start with a preliminary statement that looks akin to the one on page 75.

Have you noticed that the issue here contains more than one sentence? There's a reason for that: it's by far the best way to frame issues. You can do it in one sentence, of course, but that method typically ruins the chronology, forces you into overlong sentences, makes the issues unduly abstract, and results in altogether incomprehensible statements.

Instead, try the "deep-issue" method, which means that you'll:

- Put the issues first.
- Never — never — begin with *Whether* or any other interrogative word.
- Break each issue into separate sentences.
- Keep each issue to 75 or fewer words.

Memorandum

To: Partner
From: Associate
Date: June 6, 2010
Re: Jimmy Gilmartin—Landlord-Tenant Dispute; Eviction Suit

Questions Presented

1. **Vague Lease Provisions.** Our client, Jimmy Gilmartin, signed a lease containing several vague clauses, including one that requires him to "obey all rules of the building and to cooperate fully with the building management." Do vague provisions such as that one make the lease void and unenforceable?

    Short Answer: No. A lease is enforceable if it describes the premises, identifies the parties, states the duration of the lease and the rental amounts, and is signed by both parties. If those elements are present in the lease, other vague provisions will not render the lease unenforceable.

2. **Housing-Code Violations.** Gilmartin's apartment has several housing-code violations: a hole in the bedroom floor, mice infestation, and a continually malfunctioning toilet. What is the effect of these violations on the landlord's ability to collect back rent?

    Short Answer: If the defects existed when Gilmartin signed the lease, then the landlord won't be able to collect back rent. But rather than being free from all obligation, Gilmartin will be treated as a tenant at sufferance who must pay the fair rental value of the housing, given its condition.

3. **Eviction-Suit Defenses.** The landlord has sued for eviction, claiming that Gilmartin has violated various lease terms. What are Gilmartin's possible defenses or counterclaims?

    Short Answer: Gilmartin may seek abatement of any rent paid in excess of the fair rental value of the premises—a remedy in the nature of recoupment. In the alternative, he may seek damages for breach of the implied warranty of habitability—a remedy that is considered a positive counterclaim. The distinction can be important because only in the action for damages can the tenant recover money, as opposed to merely reducing the landlord's recovery.

State of Illinois
County of St. Clair

IN THE CIRCUIT COURT OF ST. CLAIR COUNTY
CRIMINAL DIVISION

People of the State of Illinois	§	
	§	
vs.	§	No. 12 CR 54965
	§	
Jorge Duren	§	

**Memorandum in Support of
Defendant's Motion to Quash Arrest and Suppress Evidence**

This motion presents the court with a single issue:

> Officer Bradley answered a complaint about possible gang-related
> drug activities outside an East St. Louis building. After arriving, he
> searched 12 people outside but found nothing. He then went inside,
> to the second floor, where he saw Jorge Duren. Without probable
> cause, he shouted that he would search Duren, who then dropped a
> bag containing contraband. Given that the threatened search would
> have been illegal, can the Court use the fruits of Officer Bradley's
> threat?

This issue swallows all the subissues relating to Duren's motion to quash
and suppress.

- Weave in enough facts, and arrange them chronologically, to show
  how the problem arises.
- Forget about whether the answer is yes or no.

If you're writing an analytical issue for a memo, the question will be open-
ended, as in these three:

- While investigating a complaint about loud music, Officer Smith knocked
  on Jimmy Jeffson's door. The music volume lowered suddenly, and Jeffson
  opened the door. Officer Jones then stepped into the apartment as Jeffson
  tried to close the door. If Officer Smith did not have a search warrant and
  no exigent circumstances existed, did his entry into the apartment violate
  Jeffson's Fourth Amendment privacy protections? [64 words]
- Under Georgia law, communications between psychiatrists and their pa-
  tients are absolutely privileged. Ms. Jenkins claims that Mr. Fulham's un-

welcome sexual advances caused her extreme emotional harm, triggering her need for psychiatric treatment. Given that Ms. Jenkins has placed her need for this treatment at issue, has she waived the psychiatrist-patient privilege? [52 words]

- Under Tennessee law, a judgment is not final until it is stamped "filed" by the court clerk. Fulmer was orally granted a divorce on November 10, 2009, and he "remarried" 30 days later. Yet the court clerk did not file-stamp the order from the November divorce until January 18, 2010. Is the remarriage valid? Has Fulmer committed bigamy? [59 words]

You don't know the answer when you read the question. The answer—the underlying legal rule—should immediately follow an analytical issue of this type.

If, on the other hand, you're writing a persuasive issue for a brief, the question should suggest the answer you want. The deep issue is cast as a syllogism, with the legal rule (major premise) first, then the factual premise (the minor premise preferably in chronological order), followed by a short, punchy question (the conclusion expressed interrogatively). Here are three good examples:

- In a testamentary bequest, an adjective used for identification purposes does not limit the gift. The will of Anton Dalby's paternal biological grandfather provides a bequest to "my grandson Anton." After the will was executed, Anton was adopted by his stepfather, and the biological father's parental rights were terminated. In the will, does the adjectival use of "grandson" make the gift contingent on the ongoing legal relationship, or does it merely help identify the legatee?

- Sixteen months before trial, Judge Fanchon established "litigation boundaries" for this case, holding that only evidence about oil wells within those geographical boundaries would be admissible. Nelson framed his discovery accordingly. But 27 days into the trial, Judge Fanchon suddenly removed the boundaries and allowed Celobar to introduce prejudicial evidence about land outside the litigation boundaries—land not in dispute. Given that Nelson couldn't rebut this evidence, was this evidentiary about-face reversible error?

- Under the Supreme Court's search-and-seizure law, a police officer is held to a more stringent standard than a private security guard. Officer McGee, a policeman working as a security officer, stopped a parent at Gordon Grammar School, flashed his badge, and identified himself as a Chicago policeman. When Officer McGee demanded to see Rothschild's jacket, Rothschild handed it over, exposing a gun in his vest. Was Officer McGee acting primarily as a private citizen?

Although you could rephrase those issues in single sentences, who would want to? You'd either torture the language or postpone the crux of the problem until later in the writing. The multisentence treatment in fewer than 75 words is the best method for achieving clarity, speed, and power. Once you master the technique, you'll be a certifiably clear thinker.

Exercises

Basic

In your own words, state the principal issue decided by a court in a published opinion. Use the deep-issue technique.

Intermediate

Find a judicial opinion that takes several paragraphs before getting to the point. Rewrite the opening paragraph with a more satisfactory opener. If you're part of a writing group or class, circulate a copy of both versions to each colleague.

Advanced

Take a published case that includes a dissenting opinion. Frame the deep issue decided by the majority. Then frame the most nearly corresponding issue that a dissenter would have wanted. If you're working in a group, be prepared to discuss the basic disagreement between the two sides. Below is an example of how you might frame divergent issues on the same point:

#1 Missouri's Spill Bill imposes liability on a "person having control over a hazardous substance" during a hazardous-substance emergency. Binary Coastal, as a landowner, controlled its land when it installed gasoline tanks and then leased the land to a service station. In February 2010, a hazardous-substance emergency occurred on the land. Was Binary Coastal a "person having control"?

#2 Missouri's Spill Bill imposes liability specifically on "a person having control over a hazardous substance" during a hazardous-substance emergency. In January 2010, Binary Coastal leased some land to a service station but had nothing to do with day-to-day operations or with the activities involving hazardous substances. In February, Binary Coastal's lessee experienced a release of hazardous substances. Did Binary Coastal have control of these substances at the time of release?

And here's an example from a published case[3]—one in which no judge dissented.

#1 Under principles of statutory construction, when statutes are in conflict, the specific controls over the general. In 1986, the Legislature narrowly tailored the retirement statutes so that a retiree over the age of 55 who decided on a lump-sum payment of benefits would forfeit certain other benefits. The Equal Employment Opportunity Commission now claims that this amendment is impermissible in light of the 1963 age-discrimination statute, which is broadly worded. Which statute controls?

---

3. *Nebraska Equal Opportunity Comm'n v. State Employees Retirement Sys.*, 471 N.W.2d 399 (Neb. 1991). For a discussion of this case, see Antonin Scalia & Bryan A. Garner, *Reading Law: The Interpretation of Legal Texts* 185–86 (2012).

#2 Since 1963, the statutory law of this state has prohibited age discrimination. Yet in 1986, the Legislature amended the retirement statutes in a way that forced retirees over the age of 55 to forfeit some of their benefits if they chose a lump-sum payment — but allowed those under 55 to make this choice with no such penalty. Did the Legislature intend this anomalous reversal of its long-held policy against age discrimination?

§ 23. Summarize. Don't overparticularize.

One requisite for clear exposition — and for getting thoughts across to readers — is knowing how to establish a context before embarking on details. Otherwise, your readers won't know what to make of the details. They'll get impatient, and they might well give up on you.

When you state the facts of a case, then, you need to be sure that you first give an introductory summary. That way, your readers will have a framework for understanding the case as the factual statement unfolds.

You'll have to work hard to distinguish what is necessary from what isn't. Although details can be important, you must omit the tedious ones. You're not trying to compile details; you're trying to select them knowledgeably. Here's a good test in winnowing important from unimportant facts: if it isn't necessary to understanding the issues or if it doesn't add human interest, then leave it out.

In legal writing, the overparticularized style most commonly manifests itself in litanies of dates, as in this statement of facts:

> On February 12, 2010, at or about 3:00 p.m., while showering, Plaintiff fell to the floor when her bathroom ceiling collapsed, striking her on the head. On February 12, 2010, at 4:06 p.m., paramedics took her, unconscious, to the hospital.
>
> On February 13, 2010, Plaintiff sued the apartment owner, alleging negligence and gross negligence in failing to maintain the premises. On March 6, 2010, Plaintiff visited Dr. Eugene Higginbotham, an orthopedic surgeon, who confirmed the diagnosis but concluded that surgery was not indicated, given Plaintiff's uncontrolled diabetes and her obesity. On the following dates, Plaintiff visited a physical therapist for her back condition: March 12, 2010, April 15, 2010, June 6, 2010, August 2, 2010, October 5, 2010, and November 16, 2010. The apartment owner settled the case for an undisclosed sum on December 10, 2010.
>
> On March 17, 2011, at or about 2:25 a.m., Plaintiff allegedly slipped and fell on a candy bar in a deserted hallway of Mega Electronics, Inc., where she worked as a night custodian. On March 17, 2011, at 2:40 a.m., Plaintiff reported the incident to the company nurse, who sent her home. On March 18 and 19, 2011, Plaintiff called in sick. On March 19, 2011, Plaintiff visited Dr. Felix Seaniz, who diagnosed her condition as a herniated disk caused by the recent fall at Mega Electronics. During the March 19, 2011 visit, when asked about previous back problems, Plaintiff failed to disclose

the fall in her shower on February 12, 2010. When asked why, she testified that she believed the February 12, 2010 fall unimportant because she had experienced no back pain since her last therapy session on November 16, 2010.

With the precise dates removed, and some relative times (such as *an hour later*) supplied, the passage becomes much cleaner. Readers can more easily focus on the story:

> In February 2010, while showering, Ms. Walker fell to the floor when her bathroom ceiling collapsed, striking her on the head. An hour later, paramedics took her, unconscious, to the hospital, where she was diagnosed with a herniated disk.
>
> The next day, Ms. Walker sued the apartment owner, alleging negligence and gross negligence in failing to maintain the premises. She then visited Dr. Eugene Higginbotham, an orthopedic surgeon, who confirmed the diagnosis but concluded that surgery was not indicated, given her uncontrolled diabetes and her obesity. During the next nine months, Ms. Walker visited a physical therapist six times for her back condition. In December 2010, a month after her last therapy session, the apartment owner settled the case for an undisclosed sum.
>
> Three months later, in March 2011, Ms. Walker allegedly slipped and fell on a candy bar in a deserted hallway of Mega Electronics, Inc., where she worked as a night custodian. Soon after the alleged fall, she reported the incident to the company nurse, who sent her home. For the next two days, she called in sick. She then visited Dr. Felix Seaniz, who diagnosed her condition as a herniated disk caused by the recent fall at Mega Electronics. During that visit, when asked about previous back problems, Ms. Walker failed to disclose the fall in her shower a year earlier. When asked why at trial, she testified that she believed the earlier fall unimportant because she had experienced no back pain since her last therapy session a few months earlier.

This rewrite reflects what happens when the writer considers the story from the reader's point of view — the only point of view that really matters.

Exercises

Basic

Rewrite the following passage to improve the story line by omitting needless details:

> On September 25, 2007, in a Texas federal district court, R&B Music sought injunctive relief against the McCoys to prevent them from any further use or disclosure of R&B's trade secrets. On September 26, 2007, the Texas court issued an order restraining the McCoys from using or disclosing certain R&B property and proprietary information. On September 26, 2007, the court set an evidentiary hearing for Tuesday, October 7, 2007, on R&B's preliminary-injunction motion.
>
> On October 6, 2007, the McCoys moved to dismiss for an alleged lack of venue and personal jurisdiction. Alternatively, they asked the court to transfer the case to an Illinois federal court under 28 U.S.C. § 1404 or § 1406.

On October 7, 2007, when the parties arrived for the injunction hearing, the Texas court indicated an intent to hear testimony and rule on the Mc-Coys' dismissal or transfer motion, to which R&B had been given no chance to respond. The testimony established that both of the McCoys had had significant contacts in Texas for the past eight years — including daily phone calls and faxes to and from R&B; their three visits to R&B's Texas headquarters; and their work in negotiating R&B contracts with Texas musicians.

On October 8, 2007, the Texas court transferred the case to this Court, noting that the transfer was for the reasons stated on the record. As the October 7, 2007, transcript reveals, the Texas court decided that while it has personal jurisdiction over John McCoy, it lacked personal jurisdiction over Kate McCoy. According to the court, the case should be transferred because "to accord relief to R&B down here while leaving the Illinois court to deal with Kate McCoy simply would not provide an effective situation" for any of the parties. The judge did not indicate which statutory section governed the transfer.

On October 8, 2007, in the same order, the Texas court further ruled that its September 26, 2007, order restricting both John and Kate McCoy from using or disclosing R&B's trade secrets would remain in effect until further orders of the Illinois court. On October 13, 2007, R&B filed the present supplemental motion for a preliminary injunction, asking this Court to extend and expand the injunctive relief already granted by the Texas court.

Intermediate

Rewrite the following passage to prune the overparticularized facts and to improve the story line. The passage comes from an appellant's brief — specifically from a section entitled "Nature of the Case and Material Proceedings in the Lower Courts," just after the preliminary statement.

On December 26, 2009, the Division of Child Support Enforcement ("DCSE") issued a Mandatory Withholding of Earnings Order directing the Social Security Administration to deduct $200.00 per month for current child support and $100.00 per month for payment on child-support arrears. On June 18, 2010, Skelton filed a Motion to Quash the Mandatory Withholding of Earnings Order with the Buchanan County Juvenile and Domestic Relations District Court. In the pleading, Skelton requested that the withholding order of the Division be reduced and that he be given credit against arrears for the amount of social-security benefits received by the children, and that the court recalculate the arrears. Hearings on the Motion to Quash in Buchanan County Juvenile and Domestic Relations District Court were held on September 11, 2010, and October 13, 2010. At the September 11, 2010 hearing, the court entered a temporary order requiring $28.50 per month toward current support and requiring $71.50 per month toward the arrears. The Motion to Quash was treated as a Motion for Reduction. The court took the issue of arrears under advisement and directed that the counsel for the parties prepare briefs on the issue concerning credit for a lump-sum social-security payment. The child support was set by using the appropriate code provisions, and neither party objected to the child-support award or the arrears payment.

On October 13, 2010, the Buchanan County Juvenile and Domestic Relations District Court denied the Motion to Quash and ruled that "credit

for social-security payments made to the children as to debt owed to the
Division is denied." The Court declined to exercise equitable relief for Mr.
Skelton (Appellee) as to any debt owed to custodial parent. Appeal was
noted in open court, so no bond was required for appeal."

This matter was subsequently appealed and tried de novo in the Circuit
Court of Buchanan County. At the circuit-court level, the court denied the
Division's request for an appeal bond and ruled that Skelton should receive
credit for the $7,086.10 lump-sum social-security benefits paid on behalf of
the children of Mr. Skelton. This reduced the child-support arrears from
$14,017.14 to $6,931.04. At the date of the circuit-court hearing, all the
children were over the age of 18.

The circuit court was reminded that on October 14, 2005, Skelton was
found guilty of contempt by the Buchanan County Juvenile and Domestic
Relations District Court and was advised "to immediately notify the court
of any change in employment, layoff, reduction in wages or hours worked."
The court further warned that "no further delinquency would be tolerated
and any change in circumstances must be followed up with a petition to
decrease, or else contempt sanctions will be imposed."

Advanced

Find a passage in which too much detail impedes the progress of the writer's thoughts. If you're part of a writing group or class, be prepared to
discuss why you think the detail is excessive and how you might prune it.

§ 24   Introduce each paragraph with a topic sentence.

Although it's possible to put a topic sentence last or in the middle, the best approach with persuasive writing is to open the paragraph with it. By stating the
controlling idea, a topic sentence will lend unity to a paragraph, which typically begins with a shift in focus from what has preceded. The topic sentence
will reorient readers to this new focus. And with well-introduced paragraphs,
the writing becomes much clearer: readers who are in a hurry will get your
point efficiently.

Good writers think of the paragraph — not the sentence — as the basic unit
of thought. The topic sentence ensures that each paragraph has its own cohe-
sive content. A good topic sentence centers the paragraph. It announces what
the paragraph is about, while the other sentences play supporting roles.

This principle sounds simple, yet legal writers often stumble over topic
sentences. The problem commonly occurs in discussing case law. Consider
the following paragraph, which begins with a case citation followed by an obscure judicial disposition:

In *Johnson v. Cass & Emerson*, 99 A. 633 (Vt. 1917), the Vermont Supreme
Court reversed the decision of a lower court that had held that the plaintiff

was "doing business" in a name other than its own without making the appropriate filing. *Id.* In that case the plaintiff, W. L. Johnson, used stationery in his dealings with the defendant which contained the words "Johnson's Employment Office, W. L. Johnson, Prop'r." *Id.* at 634. The court observed that the stationery "on its face showed Johnson as the owner of the business . . . [and that] no person could be reasonably misled by it." *Id.* at 634–35. The court further implied, however, that if the plaintiff had engaged in misleading acts in addition to the aforementioned stationery, such as the concurrent running of regular advertisements bearing only the name "Johnson's Employment Agency," it would have affirmed the decision of the court below. *Id.* at 635. Thus, in *Johnson,* the pivotal issue was whether the plaintiff was "doing business" under an unregistered assumed name during his relationship with the defendant, rather than if he had actually held himself out as someone else to the defendant.

That paragraph is quite difficult to follow partly because it lacks a good topic sentence and partly because of disruptions in chronology (see § 3). Both can be fixed with a little effort (citations, of course, would be footnoted — see § 28):

The Supreme Court of Vermont has held that the pivotal issue is whether a plaintiff "does business" under an unregistered assumed name while dealing with someone the plaintiff later tries to sue. In *Johnson v. Cass & Emerson,* W. L. Johnson, the plaintiff, transacted business with the defendant on stationery with the printed words "Johnson's Employment Office, W. L. Johnson, Prop'r." According to the court, the stationery showed that Johnson "was the owner of the business and was doing business under his own name," concluding that "no person could be reasonably misled by it." Apart from the stationery, there were no acts suggesting that "Johnson's Employment Agency" was a registered name. If there had been, the court implied, the result might have been different. But the court held that Johnson could sue in a Vermont court because he did not do business there under an unregistered name.

Notice how, in this revision, the case name doesn't come up until the second sentence. Delaying the citation typically enables you to write a stronger topic sentence.

Whether you're discussing cases or something else, look closely at your topic sentences when revising your prose. A reader should get most of the story from skimming the topic sentences.

Exercises

Basic

Write a new topic sentence for the following paragraph — one that you could insert at the beginning while leaving the following sentences intact:

Over the past 100 years, legal publishers developed an intricate set of printed materials that controlled the flow of legal information. Most of this apparatus was built around cases. Elaborate systems of reporting, digesting, tracing, and evaluating cases developed. Until very recently, mastering these systems was the essence of learning legal research. The lawyer graduating from law school in 1975 had to know much more than someone who graduated in 1875, because the use of traditional paper-based, case-centered tools had grown more complex. But it was still a system built on the old paradigm of the paper-information world. This old-style research is the only kind of research that some senior lawyers, judges, and law professors accept as legitimate. That will change in the course of the next generation, but it hasn't yet changed completely. Meanwhile, the new world of legal research is rooted in electronic information. In the past 30 years, the variety of electronic databases has grown, and the information that they store, as well as the search methods for using them, have improved enormously. Even the Internet carries a wide range of legal information. The modern researcher must know how to retrieve these modern tools.

Intermediate

In published legal writing, find a four-page passage with strong topic sentences. Underline them. If you're part of a writing group or class, bring copies of your work to the next meeting.

Advanced

In published legal writing, find a four-page passage with weak topic sentences. Edit the passage to strengthen them. If you're part of a writing group or class, circulate a copy of both the original and the edited version to your colleagues.

§ 25. Bridge between paragraphs.

Despite the topic sentence's importance in announcing the subject, its more important function is to provide a transition. That is, every paragraph opener should contain a transitional word or phrase to ease the reader's way from one paragraph to the next. Readers will then immediately see whether the new paragraph amplifies what has preceded, contrasts with it, or follows it in some other way.

Almost invariably, a good paragraph opener establishes a connection by using one or two of these devices:

- Pointing words — that is, words like *this, that, these, those,* and *the.*
- Echo links — that is, words or phrases in which a previously mentioned idea reverberates.
- Explicit connectives — that is, words whose chief purpose is to supply transitions (such as *also, further, therefore,* and *yet*).

Strong writers use all three techniques to establish continuity from paragraph to paragraph. Let's consider each one to see how they together work in context.

464   Jurisprudence without Foundations

tions—whether science, law, or religion—were the product of shifting human desires rather than the reflection of a reality external to those desires.

[This account] should help us see why "truth" is a problematic concept for a pragmatist. Its essential meaning, after all, is observer independence, which is just what the pragmatist is inclined to deny. It is no surprise, therefore, that the pragmatists' stabs at defining truth—truth is what is fated to be believed in the long run (Peirce), truth is what is good to believe (James), or truth is what survives in the competition among ideas (Holmes)—are riven by paradox. The pragmatist's real interest is not in truth at all but in belief justified by social need.

[This need] not make the pragmatist unfriendly to science—far from it—but it shifts the emphasis in the philosophy of science from the discovery of nature's laws by observation to the formulation of theories about nature (including man and society) on the basis of man's desire to predict and control his environment, both social and natural. The implication, later to become explicit in the writings of Thomas Kuhn, is that scientific theories are a function of human need and desire rather than of the way things are in nature, so that the succession of theories on a given topic need not produce a linear growth in scientific knowledge. Science in the pragmatic view is a social enterprise.

The [spirit of pragmatism] is not limited to the handful of philosophers who have called themselves pragmatists (and a tiny handful it is—Peirce himself, the founder, having renounced the term because he disagreed with William James's definition of it). Rival of pragmatism though it is thought to be, logical positivism, with its emphasis on verifiability and its consequent hostility to metaphysics, is pragmatic in demanding that theory make a difference in the world of fact, the empirical world. Popper's falsificationist philosophy of science is close to Peirce's view of science, for in both philosophies doubt is the engine of progress and truth an ever-receding goal rather than an attainment. Wittgenstein's emphasis on the "sociality" of knowledge marks him as pragmatist, while Habermas has acknowledged the influence of the pragmatists on his own theory of "conversational" rationality. Plainly we are dealing with an immensely diverse tradition rather than with a single, coherent school of thought.

[Latterly] [pragmatism] has come to be thought a left-wing ideology, a celebration of the plasticity of social institutions. The discussion in Chapter 12 of a recent article by Richard Rorty shows why, and Rorty is not even on the left of the neopragmatist movement. But the connec-

Pointing words—especially *this* and *that*—refer directly to something already mentioned. They point to an antecedent. If you first talk about land at 2911 Maple Avenue, and then you refer to *that property*, the word *that* points to the preceding reference. It establishes an unambiguous connection.

Pointing words often work in tandem with echo links. In fact, the word *property*—in the phrase *that property*—is an echo of *2911 Maple Avenue*. It's a different word in which the earlier reference reverberates. Imagine a friend

Is the Press Losing the First Amendment?   385

others. But there is no doubt where he stands. He is a partisan of free speech, and in this book there are victories and defeats for freedom, heroes and cowards of the press, friends and enemies of liberty.

[But]there is not much attempt at analysis of the philosophical grounds of free speech or freedom of the press, or much effort to find the limits of the freedoms and powers Hentoff wants to defend. In this respect he is typical of journalists who complain about the fate of the First Amendment in the courts, though he writes better and with more enthusiasm and knowledge than most. The press takes the Amendment as a kind of private charter, and attacks more or less automatically every refusal of the courts to find some further protection in that charter. The newspapers and networks denounced the decisions in the *Farber* and *Herbert* cases as fiercely—indeed even more fiercely—than those in the cases of *The Progressive* and *Snepp.*

[But] this strategy of automatic appeal to the First Amendment is, I think, a poor strategy, even if the press is concerned only to expand its legal powers as far as possible. For if the idea becomes popular that the Amendment is an all-purpose shield for journalists, warding off libel suits, depositions, and searches as well as censorship, then it must become a weaker shield, because it will seem obvious that so broad a power in the press must be balanced against other private and social interests in the community. What will then suffer is the historically central function of the First Amendment, which is simply to ensure that those who wish to speak on matters of political and social controversy are free to do so. Perhaps the surprising weakness of the First Amendment in protecting the defendants in *The Progressive* and *Snepp* cases, for example, is partly a consequence of the very effectiveness of the press in persuading the courts, in an earlier day, that the power of the First Amendment extends well beyond straight censorship cases.

In order to test this suspicion, we must consider an issue that Hentoff and other friends of the First Amendment neglect. What is the First Amendment for? Whom is it meant to protect? A variety of views is possible. The dominant theory among American constitutional lawyers assumes that the constitutional rights of free speech—including free press, which, in the constitutional language, means published speech in general rather than journalists in particular—are directed at protecting the audience. They protect, that is, not the speaker or writer himself but the audience he wishes to address. On this view, journalists and other writers are protected from censorship in order that the public at large may have access to the information it needs to vote and conduct its affairs intelligently.

In his famous essay *On Liberty*, John Stuart Mill offered a similar but more fundamental justification for the right of free speech. He said that if everyone is free to advance any theory of private or public morality, no matter how absurd or unpopular, truth is more likely to emerge from the

of yours saying that courts imprison too many people and thereby aggravate social problems, the ultimate result being greater levels of violence. You respond by saying, "That argument is fallacious for three reasons." The phrase *that argument* is a pointing word plus an echo link. You're off to a great start: now good luck in supplying the three reasons you've so deftly introduced.

Finally, there are explicit connectives. You won't be able to write well without them. Although some writers have a bias against explicit connectives—and they can indeed be overdone—professional writers find them indispensable. They typically clarify the relationship between two sentences. What follows is a handy list of some of the best ones. Photocopy it, tape it to a card, and prop it up by your computer or legal pad. Besides reminding you of the need for transitions, it will supply you with a generous range of options.

- **When adding a point:** and, also, in addition, besides, what is more, similarly, nor, along with, likewise, too, moreover, further
- **When giving an example:** for instance, for example, as one example, to cite but one example, for one thing, for another thing, likewise, another
- **When contrasting:** but, yet, instead, however, on the one hand, on the other hand, still, nevertheless, nonetheless, conversely, on the contrary, whereas, in contrast to, unfortunately
- **When comparing:** similarly, likewise, in the same way
- **When restating:** in other words, that is, this means, in simpler terms, in short, put differently, again
- **When introducing a cause:** because, since, when
- **When introducing a result:** so, as a result, thus, therefore, accordingly, then, hence
- **When conceding or qualifying:** granted, of course, to be sure, admittedly, though, even though, even if, only if, true, while, naturally, in some cases, occasionally, if, while it might be argued that, despite
- **When pressing a point:** in fact, as a matter of fact, indeed, of course, without exception, still, even so, anyway, the fact remains, assuredly
- **When explaining a sentence:** that is, then, earlier, previously, meanwhile, simultaneously, now, immediately, at once, until now, soon, no sooner, that being so, afterward, later, eventually, in the future, at last, finally, in the end
- **When summing up:** to summarize, to sum up, to conclude, in conclusion, in short, in brief, so, and so, consequently, therefore, all in all
- **When sequencing ideas:** First, . . . Second, . . . Third, . . . Finally, . . .

In creating bridges, Judge Richard Posner often uses explicit connectives. But in the passage on page 84, from *The Problems of Jurisprudence* (1990), he uses a pointing word and an echo link (*This account*), another pointing word plus an echo (*This need*), an echo (*spirit of pragmatism*), and an explicit connective (*Latterly*) followed by an echo (*pragmatism*).

A good writer generally combines all the methods for bridging. On page 85 is an example from *A Matter of Principle* (1985) by Ronald Dworkin, in which he uses an explicit connective (*But*), another (*But*), a pointing word coupled with an echo (*this suspicion*), and two explicit connectives (the comparatives *similar* and *more fundamental*).

Try this exercise: take something you've written, look at the paragraph breaks, and see whether you can spot bridging words. Circle them. If you find that you're bridging effectively in at least a third of the paragraphs, then you've already been (perhaps subconsciously) using this technique. Build on this strength—that is, start building bridges every time you make a new paragraph.

But if you find that you're seldom including a bridge, that probably means you have some discontinuities in the text. You're not writing with an unbroken train of thought—with a clean line. This technique should improve the structure of your writing even within paragraphs, where sentences must progress clause by clause. Yet the best test for effective bridging occurs in paragraph openers.

Exercises

Basic

The following sentences are consecutive paragraph openers from Lawrence Friedman's *Crime and Punishment in American History* (1993). Identify the bridging words, as well as the bridging method (pointing word, echo link, explicit connective), in each paragraph opener, beginning with the second. Remember that each of these paragraph openers is followed by several other sentences in the paragraph. You're not trying to link the sentences listed; rather, you're trying to spot words in each paragraph opener that relate explicitly to what must have come at the end of the preceding paragraph.

1. The automobile made its first appearance on the streets, for all practical purposes, in the first decade of this century.
2. By 1940, the United States had become an automobile society.
3. The numbers have continued to rise, as automobiles choke the roads and highways, and millions of people, living in the land of suburban sprawl, use the automobile as their lifeline—connecting them to work, shopping, and the outside world in general.
4. Thus, a person who parks overtime and gets a "ticket" will get an order to appear in court and face the music.
5. In many localities, traffic matters got handled by municipal courts, police courts, justices of the peace, and sometimes specialized departments of a municipal court.
6. The traffic court judge, as one would expect, did not have the prestige and dignity of a higher-grade judge.
7. The root of this evil was, perhaps, the fact that defendants did not—and do not—see themselves as criminals, but rather as unlucky people who got caught breaking a rule that everybody breaks once in a while.

8. This attitude came to the surface in a 1958 American Bar Association report on traffic matters in Oklahoma.

Intermediate

In published legal writing, find an exemplary passage (four pages or so) illustrating good bridges. At the outset of each paragraph, box the bridging
word or words. If you're part of a writing group or class, circulate a copy
to each colleague, provide the full citation on each copy, and be prepared
to discuss your findings.

Advanced

In published legal writing, find a passage (four pages or so) illustrating an
absence of bridges. Either add a bridge where needed or else explain in
the margin why the problem isn't fixable by an editor. If you're part of a
writing group or class, circulate a copy to each colleague, provide the full
citation on each copy, and be prepared to discuss your findings.

§ 26. Vary the length of your paragraphs, but generally keep them short.

Remember that the paragraph is the basic unit of thought. Have you ever done
a word count for your paragraphs? If not, you might find it revealing. Strive for
an average paragraph of no more than 150 words — preferably fewer — in three
to eight sentences. It's tempting to mandate a sentence count. The problem,
of course, is that an average of six sentences could still be horrendous if the
sentences were each 80 words long. So a word count is more reliable than a
sentence count.

As with sentence length (see § 6), you need variety in paragraph length:
some slender paragraphs and some fairly ample ones. But watch your average.
And remember that there's nothing wrong with an occasional one-sentence
paragraph. The superstition to the contrary is a remnant of half-remembered
grammar-school lessons.[4]

During the 20th century, paragraphs tended to get shorter. Although finding truly representative samples is a tricky matter, the following data — showing average numbers of words per paragraph in the works of noted 20th- and
21st-century legal writers — illustrate the trend:

---

4. For authorities debunking the false prohibition of one-sentence paragraphs, see John R.
Trimble, *Writing with Style* 92–93 (2d ed. 2000); Bryan A. Garner, *The Elements of Legal Style* 62
(2d ed. 2002); Theodore M. Bernstein, *The Careful Writer* 324 (1965).

Writer	Average Words per Paragraph
James Bradley Thayer[a] (1900)	655
Oliver Wendell Holmes[b] (1909)	270
James Barr Ames[c] (1913)	217
John Alderson Foote[d] (1914)	426
Charles Evans Hughes[e] (1928)	434
Harry D. Nims[f] (1929)	211
William F. Walsh[g] (1930)	286
Benjamin N. Cardozo[h] (1939)	322
William L. Prosser[i] (1941)	139
Samuel Williston[j] (1948)	189
Arthur L. Corbin[k] (1952)	116
Thomas E. Atkinson[l] (1953)	119
Karl N. Llewellyn[m] (1960)	151
Frederick Bernays Wiener[n] (1967)	127
Reed Dickerson[o] (1975)	95
Richard A. Posner[p] (1977)	153
Susan Estrich[q] (1987)	118
George T. Bogert[r] (1987)	85
Michael E. Tigar[s] (1993)	74
Karen Gross[t] (1997)	116
Charles Alan Wright[u] (1999)	84
Douglas G. Baird[v] (2001)	117
Elizabeth Warren & Jay Lawrence Westbrook[w] (2009)	97

[a] James Bradley Thayer, "Unilateral Mistake and Unjust Enrichment as a Ground for the Avoidance of Legal Transactions" (1900), in *Harvard Legal Essays* 466–89 (1934) (including three paragraphs containing 1,000+ words).
[b] Oliver Wendell Holmes, "Holdsworth's English Law" (1909), in *Collected Legal Papers* 285–90 (1920).
[c] James Barr Ames, "Two Theories of Consideration," in *Lectures on Legal History* 323–32 (1913).
[d] John Alderson Foote, *A Concise Treatise on Private International Jurisprudence* 126–42 (Coleman Phillipson ed., 4th ed. 1914) (including a one-sentence paragraph of only 22 words!).
[e] Charles Evans Hughes, *The Supreme Court of the United States* 57–67 (1928).
[f] Harry D. Nims, *The Law of Unfair Competition and Trade-Marks* §§ 259–60, at 688–95 (3d ed. 1929).
[g] William F. Walsh, *A Treatise on Equity* § 48, at 238–50 (1930).
[h] Benjamin N. Cardozo, *Law and Literature,* 52 Harv. L. Rev. 472 (1939) (entire essay).
[i] William L. Prosser, *Handbook of the Law of Torts* § 24, at 143–50 (1941).
[j] 2 Samuel Williston, *The Law Governing Sales of Goods* §§ 425–26, at 605–13 (rev. ed. 1948).
[k] Arthur L. Corbin, *Corbin on Contracts* § 532, at 487–90 (1952).
[l] Thomas E. Atkinson, *Handbook of the Law of Wills* § 96, at 499–505 (2d ed. 1953).
[m] Karl N. Llewellyn, *The Common Law Tradition: Deciding Appeals* 56–61 (1960).
[n] Frederick Bernays Wiener, *Briefing and Arguing Federal Appeals* § 62, at 197–200 (1967).
[o] Reed Dickerson, *The Interpretation and Application of Statutes* 1–5 (1975).
[p] Richard A. Posner, *Economic Analysis of the Law* § 4.5, at 74–79 (2d ed. 1977).
[q] Susan Estrich, *Real Rape* 58–63 (1987).
[r] George T. Bogert, *Trusts* § 113, at 408–11 (6th ed. 1987).
[s] Michael E. Tigar, *Federal Appeals* § 5.13 (2d ed. 1993).
[t] Karen Gross, *Failure and Forgiveness: Rebalancing the Bankruptcy System* 41–46 (1997).
[u] Charles Alan Wright, *Federal Practice and Procedure* § 1, at 1–5 (1999).
[v] Douglas G. Baird, *The Elements of Bankruptcy* 1–9 (2001).
[w] Elizabeth Warren & Jay Lawrence Westbrook, *The Law of Debtors and Creditors* 1–9 (6th ed. 2009).

Pity the poor readers of Thayer, Foote, and Hughes!

The sampling from Professor Wright's celebrated treatise *Federal Practice and Procedure*[5] illustrates the variety that adds interest and appeal. His longest paragraph contains 231 words. His shortest is a single sentence of 14 words.

Despite this powerful evidence, much contemporary legal writing contains massive paragraphs. An average of 250 words or more isn't uncommon, especially in law reviews. But a high average count occurs in court papers as well, and this raises a special problem. If you double-space, as court rules require, then a 250-word paragraph will occupy 85–90% of the page. You'll end up with about one paragraph per page. Double-spacing makes for an uninviting, blocklike density. The mere sight of it is enough to put off modern readers.

But if your average is under 150 words — or, better yet, under 100 — the reader can come up for air more frequently. You'll have an average of two or more paragraphs per page. Having some visual variety, the page will take on a more relaxed feel — whether you're double-spacing or single-spacing.

Exercises

Basic

In published legal writing, find a three- or four-page example of aptly varied paragraph lengths. Identify something specific that you like about the passage. If you belong to a writing group or class, circulate a copy to each colleague and be prepared to discuss your example.

Intermediate

Break down each of the following passages so that it contains three to five separate paragraphs. Find the best places for starting new paragraphs.

- When the courts of equity created the equity of redemption, they ignored the parties' explicit intention. They allowed the mortgagor to regain the property by performing the secured obligation after the legal title to the property had vested absolutely in the mortgagee. This vesting took place according to both the parties' express language in the mortgage deed and the effect that the law courts gave the language. After their original intervention, equity courts developed the doctrine prohibiting the clogging of the mortgagor's equity of redemption. Under this doctrine, even though the mortgage is in default, no agreement contained in the mortgage can cut off a recalcitrant mortgagor's equity of redemption without the resort to foreclosure by the mortgagee. Courts won't enforce a mortgagee's attempts to have the mortgagor waive the right to be foreclosed in the event of a default. The prohibition against clogging has been characterized by a variety of labels. The most common characterization associated with the doctrine

---

5. Charles Alan Wright et al., *Federal Practice and Procedure*, 55 vols. (1978–1999).

in the United States is "once a mortgage, always a mortgage." This is only another way of saying that a mortgage can't be made irredeemable. The clogging doctrine, as a corollary of the equity of redemption, prevented evasion by ingenious and determined mortgagees. These mortgagees had tried using many types of clauses that, while recognizing the existence of the equity of redemption, nullified or restricted its practical operation.

- Before an intelligent study of criminal law can be undertaken, it is necessary to focus on the single characteristic that differentiates it from civil law. This characteristic is punishment. Generally, in a civil suit, the basic questions are (1) how much, if at all, defendant has injured plaintiff, and (2) what remedy or remedies, if any, are appropriate to compensate plaintiff for his loss. In a criminal case, on the other hand, the questions are (1) to what extent, if at all, defendant has injured society, and (2) what sentence, if any, is necessary to punish defendant for his transgressions. Since the criminal law seeks to punish rather than to compensate, there should be something about each course of conduct defined as criminal that renders mere compensation to the victim inadequate. This follows from the truism that no human being should be made to suffer if such suffering cannot be justified by a concomitant gain to society. No rational assessment of the kinds of activity that should be punished can be undertaken without some analysis of the purposes of punishment. Those purposes most frequently mentioned are reformation, restraint, retribution, and deterrence.

- Declaratory remedies furnish an authoritative and reliable statement of the parties' rights. Other remedies may be added if necessary, but the declaratory remedy itself makes no award of damages, restitution, or injunction. The chief problem in obtaining declaratory relief lies in the rules of justiciability — rules that courts will not issue advisory opinions, decide moot cases or those that are not ripe, or deal in any dispute that does not count as a case or controversy. Although people might settle legal arguments between themselves by going to the law library or calling the librarian, they cannot call on the courts this way. These concerns grow out of procedural and process values. They involve what we think about the nature of courts and judicial work. Before declaratory-judgment statutes were enacted, plaintiffs obtained relief that was sometimes essentially declaratory by suing for injunctive relief, or to quiet title to land, or to rescind a contract. When the declaratory judgment performs an analogous function, the case is justiciable and such relief is appropriate. Yet it is not possible to describe adequately all the instances in which these concerns will prevent declaratory relief. This type of relief is often useful in contract disputes. A good example is the dispute over liability-insurance coverage. The insured tortfeasor, the insurer, and the injured victim all need to know whether insurance covers the claim. When the insurer insists that it does not cover the claim and the others insist that it does, declaratory judgment is a good resolution.

Advanced

In published legal writing, find an example of grossly overlong paragraphs. Suggest the natural points for additional paragraph breaks. If you belong to a writing group or class, circulate a copy with your paragraph markings to each colleague.

§ 27. Provide signposts along the way.

Headings (see § 4) are signposts, of course, but you'll also need textual signposts in all but the most elementary writing. If there are three issues you're going to discuss, state them explicitly on page one. If there are four advantages to your recommended course of action, say so when introducing the list. And be specific: don't say that there are "several" advantages. If there are four, say so. This greater level of specificity shows that you've thought through the problem.

Consider the following paragraph:

> Although stock-appreciation rights, including alternative settlements, can solve substantial problems encountered by corporate officers in realizing the value of their stock options, this solution also imposes costs on the corporation. Most obviously, alternative settlements result in a cash outflow from the corporation rather than the cash inflow that results from the exercise of an option. Alternative settlements also result in charges to corporate earnings — charges not required for ordinary stock options. All that is required for ordinary stock options is a disclosure of the options and balance-sheet charges against retained earnings when they are exercised.

That paragraph is difficult to wade through — unnecessarily so. Consider how helpful some simple signposts are (in boldface here only for pedagogical purposes):

> Although stock-appreciation rights, including alternative settlements, can solve substantial problems encountered by corporate officers in realizing the value of their stock options, this solution also imposes costs on the corporation **in two ways**. **First**, alternative settlements result in a cash outflow from the corporation rather than the cash inflow that results from the exercise of an option. **Second**, alternative settlements result in charges to corporate earnings — charges not required for ordinary stock options. All that is required for ordinary stock options is a disclosure of the options and balance-sheet charges against retained earnings when they are exercised.

Adding five words makes quite a difference. Three other words got deleted — so the net increase was only two.

Take another example. Most readers will find it unsettling to read, at the bottom of page one, "The examiner's reasoning was flawed"—followed by a long paragraph introduced by the words "In the first place . . . ." Of the two most obvious cures, the better one would be to write, "The examiner's reasoning was flawed for three reasons"—followed by a bulleted list (see § 43) succinctly introducing those reasons before you embark on a full explanation. The second-best cure would be to omit the bulleted list while mentioning that there are three reasons. But merely to refer vaguely to "several reasons" isn't really a cure at all. Phrases like that one often induce anxiety. How many reasons are there, after all?

Good signposts are especially important when the writing is double-spaced. In single-spaced text the paragraphs tend to be compact, but in double-spaced text the related sentences are more spread out. Page breaks come more frequently. And because much legal writing has to be double-spaced (as with briefs), signposts take on a special significance.

Exercises

Basic

Find a piece of published legal writing — such as a book chapter, a judicial opinion, or a law-review article — in which the writer uses signposts effectively. Photocopy a section that illustrates the signposts and highlight them. If you're part of a writing group or class, bring a highlighted copy to each colleague.

Intermediate

Find a piece of published legal writing — such as a book chapter, a judicial opinion, or a law-review article — in which the writer omits signposts where they're needed. Photocopy a section that illustrates the lack of signposts, and then edit the page by hand to supply them. If you're part of a writing group or class, circulate a copy to each colleague.

Advanced

One of your coworkers, in a hurry to leave for a two-week vacation, has come to you for help with a memo that needs to go out immediately. She leaves it with you. Although you don't know much about the subject — and don't know Ezra Bander, the recipient — do your best to rewrite the memo to clarify how many items your colleague is attaching.

> To: Ezra Bander
> From: [Your colleague's name]
> Subject: Group Annuity Policies
> Date: March 15, 2011
>
> Attached are two photocopies of the policy files for five of the six group annuity contracts the NY examiners selected for further review. To be as responsive as possible to the examiners' request, we have attached the applicable Administration section's complete file to each client relating to the contracts in question (other than FSR (GA-8192)). For FSR we have attached the Contract section's correspondence file since it is the most complete source of client information. Please note that for the GIC files (on page 1 of the list attached to your request), we consider certain pricing information to be proprietary and confidential. Therefore, we have added a Request for Confidential Treatment to the applicable portions of these files. We discovered that the jurisdiction for one of the contracts the ex-

aminers selected (GA-8180 Purgon) is actually Massachusetts. Please let us know if there is another contract you want to review. Due to the complexity of the SBCD Communications file, we created a timeline to facilitate the examiners' review (which was created solely to help the examiners follow the file). We are unable to send the original policy files since we have ongoing relationships with these clients. However, we have certified to NY (see attachment) that we have copied the files they requested. Also, attached to each of the five files are all related state filing materials, including any prefilings under Circular Letter 64-1, the submission packages to the Dept. of forms, any correspondence with the Dept., and approvals from the Dept. if received. The files have been reviewed by the business area and appropriate legal counsel.

If you have any questions, please call me.

§ 28. Unclutter the text by moving citations into footnotes.

Do you remember when you first started reading law? You were probably reading a judicial opinion, and surely among the most irksome things about the experience was encountering all the citations in the text. For beginning legal readers, the prose is quite jarring — as if you were driving down a highway filled with speed bumps.

These thought-interrupters were born of a technologically impoverished world. Originally, lawyers used scriveners who interspersed authorities in their writings. Then, in the 1880s, typewriters became popular, and it was all but impossible to put citations in footnotes. That's why citations have traditionally appeared in the text. They were there in 1800, they were there in 1900, and they were still there in 1975. It had become a hardened convention.

Meanwhile, of course, the number of cases being cited in legal writing skyrocketed during the years leading up to 1975. And by the turn of the 21st century, things had gotten even worse. With computer research and the proliferation of case law, it has become easier than ever to find several cases to support virtually every sentence.

So over time, the pages of judicial opinions, briefs, and memos have become increasingly cluttered. Some have become unreadable. Others can be read only by those mentally and emotionally intrepid enough to cut through the underbrush.

If citations plague readers, though, they plague writers every bit as much. When you put citations within and between sentences, it's hard to come up with shapely paragraphs. The connections between consecutive sentences get weaker. Even worse, legal writers often intend a single sentence, followed by a string citation with parentheticals, to stand for a paragraph. After all, it fills up a third or even half of the page. How would such a paragraph fare with a high-school composition teacher? It would flunk.

In short, it doesn't really matter whether readers can negotiate their way through eddies of citations — because, on the whole, writers can't.

Reference notes can cure these ills. That is, put citations — and generally only citations — in footnotes. And write in such a way that no reader would ever have to look at your footnotes to know what important authorities you're relying on. If you're quoting an opinion, you should — in the text — name the court you're quoting, the year in which it wrote, and (if necessary) the name of the case. Those things should be part of your story line. Just get the numbers (that is, the volume, reporter, and page references) out of the way.

If footnoting your citations seems like such a revolutionary idea, ask yourself why you've never seen a biography that reads like this:

> Holmes was ready for the final charge. His intellectual powers intact (Interview by Felix Frankfurter with Harold Laski, 23 Mar. 1938, at 45, unpublished manuscript on file with the author), he organized his work efficiently so that little time was wasted (3 Holmes Diary at 275, Langdell Law Library Manuscript No. 123-44-337; Holmes letter to Isabel Curtain, 24 June 1923, Langdell Law Library Manuscript No. 123-44-599). He volunteered less often to relieve others of their caseload (Holmes court memo, 24 July 1923, at 4, Library of Congress Rare Book Room Doc. No. 1923-AAC-Holmes-494), and he sometimes had to be reassured of his usefulness (Brandeis letter to Felix Frankfurter, 3 Mar. 1923, Brandeis Univ. Manuscript Collection Doc. No. 23-03-3-BF). His doctor gave him a clean bill of health (Mass. Archives Doc. No. 23-47899-32, at 1), told him his heart was "a good pump" (Holmes letter to Letitia Fontaine, 25 June 1923, at 2, Langdell Law Library Manuscript No. 123-44-651), and told him that very few men of Holmes's age were "as well off as he was" (*id.*) — to which Holmes drily replied that "most of them are dead" (Memo of Dr. Theobald Marmor, 26 June 1923, at 2, Morgan Library Collection, copy on file with the author). But he was pleased that the "main machinery" was "in good running order" (Holmes letter to Letitia Fontaine, 25 June 1923, at 1, Langdell Law Library Manuscript No. 123-44-651), and he frequently felt perky enough to get out of the carriage partway home from court and walk the remaining blocks with Brandeis (Brandeis letter to Clare Eustacia Bodnar, 22 July 1923, Brandeis Univ. Manuscript Collection Doc. No. 23-7-22-BCEBB).

No self-respecting historian would write that way. But brief writers commonly do something very much like it:

> Agency decisions are entitled to the greatest weight and to a presumption of validity, when the decision is viewed in the light most favorable to the agency. *Baltimore Lutheran High Sch. Ass'n v. Employment Security Admin.*, 302 Md. 649, 662–63, 490 A.2d 701, 708 (1985); *Board of Educ. of Montgomery County v. Paynter*, 303 Md. 22, 40, 491 A.2d 1186, 1195 (1985); *Nationwide Mut. Ins. Co. v. Insurance Comm'r*, 67 Md. App. 727, 737, 509 A.2d 719, 724, *cert. denied*, 307 Md. 433, 514 A.2d 1211 (1986); *Bulluck v.*

> *Pelham Wood Apartments*, 283 Md. 505, 513, 390 A.2d 1119, 1124 (1978).
> Thus, the reviewing court will not substitute its judgment for that of the
> agency when the issue is fairly debatable and the record contains substan-
> tial evidence to support the administrative decision. *Howard County v.
> Dorsey*, 45 Md. App. 692, 700, 416 A.2d 23, 27 (Md. Ct. Spec. App. 1980);
> *Mayor and Aldermen of City of Annapolis v. Annapolis Waterfront Co.*, 284
> Md. 383, 395–96, 396 A.2d 1080, 1087–88 (1979); *Cason v. Board of County
> Comm'rs for Prince George's County*, 261 Md. 699, 707, 276 A.2d 661, 665
> (1971); *Germenko v. County Board of Appeals of Baltimore County*, 257 Md.
> 706, 711, 264 A.2d 825, 828 (1970); *Bonnie View Country Club, Inc. v. Glass*,
> 242 Md. 46, 52, 217 A.2d 647, 651 (1966). The court may substitute its
> judgment only as to an error made on an issue of law. *State Election Board v.
> Billhimer*, 314 Md. 46, 59, 548 A.2d 819, 826 (1988), *cert. denied*, 490 U.S.
> 1007, 109 S.Ct. 1644, 104 L.Ed.2d 159 (1989); *Gray v. Anne Arundel County*,
> 73 Md. App. 301, 308, 533 A.2d 1325, 1329 (Md. Ct. Spec. App. 1987).

That's a fairly serious example of excessive citations, but it's actually mild
compared with what writers do when coupling parentheticals with the citations. Even if you have fewer citations, the reading becomes significantly worse
because it's harder to know what you need to read and what you can skip:

> To state a claim under Rule 10b-5, a complaint must allege that the de-
> fendant falsely represented or omitted to disclose a material fact in connec-
> tion with the purchase or sale of a security with the intent to deceive or
> defraud. *See Ernst & Ernst v. Hochfelder*, 425 U.S. 185, 96 S.Ct. 1375, 47
> L.Ed.2d 668 (1976). A party's specific promise to perform a particular act in
> the future, while secretly intending not to perform that act or knowing that
> the act could not be carried out, may violate § 10(b) and Rule 10b-5 if the
> promise is part of the consideration for the transfer of securities. *See, e.g.,
> Luce v. Edelstein*, 802 F.2d 49, 55 (2d Cir. 1986) (citing *McGrath v. Zenith
> Radio Corp.*, 651 F.2d 458 (7th Cir.), *cert. denied*, 454 U.S. 835, 102 S.Ct.
> 136, 70 L.Ed.2d 114 (1981)); *Wilsmann v. Upjohn Co.*, 775 F.2d 713, 719 (6th
> Cir. 1985) (concluding that plaintiff's securities-fraud claim against acquir-
> ing corporation was in connection with defendant's purchase of plaintiff's
> stock where plaintiff alleged that part of consideration for sale of stock was
> false promise by acquiring corporation concerning future payments for
> stock plaintiff received in acquired corporation but holding that evidence of
> fraud was insufficient to support jury's verdict), *cert. denied*, 476 U.S. 1171,
> 106 S.Ct. 2893, 90 L.Ed.2d 980 (1986). *But see Hunt v. Robinson*, 852 F.2d
> 786, 787 (4th Cir. 1988) (holding that defendant's failure to tender shares in
> new company in return for plaintiff's employment did not state securities-
> fraud claim because the defendant's alleged misrepresentation concerned
> its tender of shares as required by the terms of the employment contract,
> not the actual sale of stock). The failure to perform a promise, however,
> does not constitute fraud if the promise was made with the good-faith ex-
> pectation that it would be performed. *See Luce*, 802 F.2d at 56.

By the way, double-spacing aggravates this problem in a virulent way (see § 42).
    Even if you strip out the citations, something the careful reader will have
to do anyway (by mental contortion), you end up with unimpressive, wooden
prose:

> To state a claim under Rule 10b-5, a complaint must allege that the defendant falsely represented or omitted to disclose a material fact in connection with the purchase or sale of a security with the intent to deceive or defraud. A party's specific promise to perform a particular act in the future, while secretly intending not to perform that act or knowing that the act could not be carried out, may violate § 10(b) and Rule 10b-5 if the promise is part of the consideration for the transfer of securities. The failure to perform a promise, however, does not constitute fraud if the promise was made with the good-faith expectation that it would be performed.

Now it's possible to see what you're actually saying. You can more easily focus on style. So you edit the paragraph. Now it reads well:

> To state a claim under Rule 10b-5, a complaint must allege that the defendant — intending to deceive or defraud — falsely represented or failed to disclose a material fact about the purchase or sale of a security. A party's specific promise to do something in the future, while secretly intending not to do it or knowing that it can't be done, may violate Rule 10b-5 if the promise is part of the consideration for the transfer. But not performing the promise isn't fraud if the promisor expected in good faith to be able to perform.

The revised passage isn't a work of art. But it's much closer than the original — and probably as artful as most discussions of Rule 10b-5 ever could be.

Go back and look at the original 10b-5 passage. Look at how much more difficult it is to tease out the essential ideas. In your imagination try double-spacing it, so that you fill up the entire page. Now imagine page after page of this. You get the idea.

In sum, if you put citations into footnotes, while still naming in the text the important authorities you're relying on, your prose will improve. Here are ten advantages to using citational footnotes:

1. You're able to strip down an argument and focus on what you're saying.

2. You're able to write better, more fully developed paragraphs.

3. Meanwhile, your paragraphs will be significantly shorter than they would be with the citations in the text.

4. You're able to connect your sentences smoothly, with simple transitional words. When citations appear between sentences, writers tend to repeat several words that aren't necessary once the sentences are put together without citational interruptions.

5. You're able to use greater variety in sentence patterns, especially by sometimes using subordinate clauses.

6. You can't camouflage poor writing — or poor thinking — in a flurry of citations. And you won't be tempted to bury important parts of your analysis in parentheticals.

7. The long-decried string citation becomes relatively harmless. (I don't favor string citations, but I'm not adamantly opposed to them either — not if they're out of the way.)

8. You'll find it necessary to discuss important cases contextually, as opposed to merely relying on citations without ever discussing the cases you cite. You'll pay more respect to important precedent by actually discussing it instead of simply identifying it in a "citation sentence," which isn't really a sentence at all.

9. You give emphasis where it's due. That is, the court and the case and the holding are often what matters ("Three years ago in *Gandy*, this Court held . . ."), but the numbers in a citation never are ("925 S.W.2d 696, 698"—etc.). Numbers, when sprinkled through the main text, tend to distract.

10. Your pages end up looking significantly cleaner.

Many brief-writers and many judges have been persuaded by these points. They've begun using citational footnotes because they want to be better writers.

Seemingly the only argument against footnoting citations is the odd accusation that doing so diminishes the importance of precedent. No one ever leveled this accusation against Judge John Minor Wisdom or Judge Alvin Rubin, two highly respected Fifth Circuit judges who, from about 1983 to the end of their careers, footnoted all their citations. As Judge Wisdom put it in a 1993 article: "Citations belong in a footnote: even one full citation such as 494 U.S. 407, 110 S. Ct. 1212, 108 L. Ed. 2d 347 (1990), breaks the thought; two, three, or more in one massive paragraph are an abomination."[6]

Until the advent of personal computers in the 1980s, law offices had no choice. Citations had to go into the text. Only professional printers had a realistic option of footnoting citations. The computer has liberated us from this technological constraint.

Within a generation, the citational footnote may well be the norm in both judicial opinions and briefs. It will probably come to be viewed as one of the greatest improvements in legal writing.

Exercises

Basic

Look up (in hard copy, if possible) at least three cases listed below, all of which put citations in footnotes. Identify the stylistic differences you

---

6. John Minor Wisdom, *How I Write*, 4 Scribes J. Legal Writing 83, 86 (1993).

notice between these cases and other cases (in the same volume) having citations in the text.

- *Alizadeh v. Safeway Stores, Inc.*, 802 F.2d 111 (5th Cir. 1986).
- *Alamo Rent A Car, Inc. v. Schulman*, 897 P.2d 405 (Wash. Ct. App. 1995).
- *Warden v. Hoar Constr. Co.*, 507 S.E.2d 428 (Ga. 1998).
- *M.P.M. Enters., Inc. v. Gilbert*, 731 A.2d 790 (Del. 1999).
- *Aleck v. Delvo Plastics, Inc.*, 972 P.2d 988 (Alaska 1999).
- *State v. Martin*, 975 P.2d 1020 (Wash. 1999) (en banc).
- *In re Nolo Press/Folk Law, Inc.*, 991 S.W.2d 768 (Tex. 1999).
- *Williams v. Kimes*, 996 S.W.2d 43 (Mo. 1999) (en banc).
- *United States v. Parsee*, 178 F.3d 374 (5th Cir. 1999).
- *McGray Constr. Co. v. Director, Office of Workers' Comp. Programs*, 181 F.3d 1008 (9th Cir. 1999).
- *Minneapolis Public Hous. Auth. v. Lor*, 591 N.W.2d 700 (Minn. 1999).
- *Kohlbrand v. Ranieri*, 823 N.E.2d 76 (Ohio Ct. App. 2005).
- *McHenry v. State*, 820 N.E.2d 124 (Ind. 2005).
- *Admiral Ins. Co. v. Abshire*, 574 F.3d 267 (5th Cir. 2009).
- *Romain v. Frankenmuth Mut. Ins. Co.*, 762 N.W.2d 911 (Mich. 2009).
- *United States v. Zajac*, 748 F.Supp.2d 1340 (D. Utah 2010).
- *Wolters v. Lakey*, 456 B.R. 687 (D. Kan. 2011).
- *Howard v. Howard*, 336 S.W.3d 433 (Ky. 2011).
- *Donatelli v. D.R. Strong Consulting Eng'rs, Inc.*, 261 P.3d 664 (Wash. Ct. App. 2011).
- *In re Woods*, 465 B.R. 196 (B.A.P. 10th Cir. 2012).
- *Blockbuster Investors LP v. Cox Enters., Inc.*, 724 S.E.2d 813 (Ga. Ct. App. 2012).

Intermediate

Rewrite the following passages to put all citations in footnotes and otherwise improve the style:

- Having initially remanded the question of attorney's fees to the Circuit Court following its decision in *Greenwald Cassell Assocs., Inc. v. Department of Commerce*, 15 Va. App. 236, 421 S.E.2d 903 (1992), the Court of Appeals' subsequent review of that remand in *Greenwald Cassell Assocs., Inc. v. Guffey*, 19 Va. App. 179, 450 S.E.2d 181 (1994) provides an ample basis to determine the appropriateness and thoroughness of the appellate review conducted.
- In certain narrow exceptions, a court may consider patents and publications issued after the filing date. *In re Koller*, 613 F.2d 819, 824 (C.C.P.A. 1980). For example, in deciding an appeal from the denial of an application, the Federal Circuit relied upon an article published in 1988, five years after an application's filing date, to conclude that the level of skill in the art in 1983 was not sufficiently developed to enable a scientist to practice the invention claimed. *In re Wright*, 999 F.2d 1557, 1562 (Fed. Cir. 1993). Similarly, in *Gould v. Quigg*, 822 F.2d 1074 (Fed. Cir. 1987), the same court upheld a

decision to permit the testimony of an expert who relied on a subsequent publication to opine on the state of the art as of the applicant's filing date. *Id.* at 1079. The publication was not offered to supplement the knowledge of one skilled in the art at the time to render it enabling. *Id.* In addition, later publications have been used by the Court of Customs and Patent Appeals numerous times as evidence that, as of the filing date, a parameter absent from the claims was or was not critical, *Application of Rainer*, 305 F.2d 505, 507 n.3 (C.C.P.A. 1962), that a specification was inaccurate, *Application of Marzocchi*, 439 F.2d 220, 223 n.4 (C.C.P.A. 1971), that the invention was inoperative or lacked utility, *Application of Langer*, 503 F.2d 1380, 1391 (C.C.P.A. 1974), that a claim was indefinite, *Application of Glass*, 492 F.2d 1228, 1232 n.6 (C.C.P.A. 1974), and that characteristics of prior-art products were known, *Application of Wilson*, 311 F.2d 266 (C.C.P.A. 1962). Nonetheless, none of these exceptions "established a precedent for permitting use of a later existing state of the art in determining enablement under 35 U.S.C. § 112." *Koller*, 613 F.2d at 824 n.5.

Advanced

Rewrite the following passage, putting all citations in footnotes. Improve the flow of the text. Decide what case names you might want to weave into your narrative — and how you can best accomplish this.

III. Attorney's Fees

In reality, Ohio law is in conflict as to whether attorney's fees may be claimed as compensatory damages (which would provide the foundation for punitive damages). Of course, Ohio law has long permitted recovery of attorney's fees, even in the absence of statutory authorization, where punitive damages are proper and first awarded. *Roberts v. Mason*, 10 Ohio St. 277 (1859); *Columbus Finance, Inc. v. Howard*, 42 Ohio St. 2d 178, 183, 327 N.E.2d 654, 658 (1975); *Zoppo v. Homestead Ins. Co.*, 71 Ohio St. 3d 552, 558, 644 N.E.2d 397, 402 (1994). However, the important question for our purposes is whether obtaining punitive damages is the only way in which to recover attorney's fees, or if attorney's fees can be recovered "before" punitive damages and used as the requisite compensatory foundation (actual damages) necessary for recovery of punitive damages.

Several cases hold that attorney's fees cannot be recovered unless punitive damages are first awarded. *See Olbrich v. Shelby Mut. Ins. Co.*, 469 N.E.2d 892 (Ohio App. 1983); *Ali v. Jefferson Ins. Co.*, 5 Ohio App. 3d 105, 449 N.E.2d 495 (1982); *Stuart v. Nat'l Indemn. Co.*, 7 Ohio App. 3d 63, 454 N.E.2d 158 (1982); *Convention Center Inn v. Dow Chemical Co.*, 484 N.E.2d 764 (Ohio Com. Pl. 1984). However, a close reading of the Ohio Supreme Court's decision in *Zoppo* suggests that such a requirement might not be necessary:

> Attorney fees may be awarded as an element of compensatory damages where the jury finds that punitive damages are warranted. *Columbus Finance, Inc. v. Howard*, 42 Ohio St. 2d 178, 183, 327 N.E.2d 654, 658 (1975).

Zoppo, 71 Ohio St. 3d at 558.

Furthermore, in the earlier decisions of *Spadafore v. Blue Shield*, 21 Ohio App. 3d 201 (1985), an Ohio appellate court held that damages "flowing from" bad faith conduct may include:

lost time at work and . . . mileage and other travel costs due to the
additional [testimonial] examination which was held out of town. . . .
An obvious loss to [the plaintiff] was the cost of the lawsuit to enable
recovery of his claim. . . .

Id. at 204. Other courts have alluded to the possibility of litigation expenses
and/or attorney's fees as compensatory damages. *See, e.g., LeForge v. Nationwide Mut. Ins. Co.*, 82 Ohio App. 3d 692 (1992) ("reasonable compensation for the . . . inconvenience caused by the denial of the insurance benefits"); *Eastham v. Nationwide Mut. Ins. Co.,* 66 Ohio App. 3d 843 (1990)
("evidence of . . . costs in this case, including expenses incurred in collecting (on the coverage) attorney fees, lost interest . . ."); *Motorists Mut. Ins. Co. v. Said*, 63 Ohio St. 3d 690, 703–04 (1992) (Douglas, J., dissenting) ("litigation expenses are primary compensatory damages in bad faith claim") (overruled in part by the *Zoppo* decision).

Moreover, in *Motorists Mut. Ins. Co. v. Brandenburg*, 72 Ohio St. 3d 157,
648 N.E.2d 488 (1995), the Ohio Supreme Court upheld a trial court's
award of attorney's fees to the insureds who were forced to defend their
right to coverage (against the insurance company) in a declaratory judgment
action. The court acknowledged the "anomalous result" that might arise
when an insured is required to defend his/her right to recover under an insurance policy, but cannot recover the damages incurred thereby. *Id.* at 160.

§ 29. Weave quotations deftly into your narrative.

Because our legal system relies on precedent, legal writers quote with great
frequency. We quote from statutes, cases, treatises, law reviews, and dictionaries. We quote from depositions and from live testimony. Yet most legal writers quote poorly, and many if not most of their readers skip the quotations.

Novices sometimes drop into the text direct quotations without any
lead-in at all. They pepper their discussions with others' language, seemingly to avoid thinking about or coping with the problem of paraphrasing what
someone else has said. Their style is disjointed and distracting.

A step beyond the novice is the intermediate writer who tries to incorporate quotations with stereotyped lead-ins such as these:

- The statute reads in pertinent part:
- The court stated as follows:
- According to *Federal Practice and Procedure*:
- As one noted authority has explained:
- *Black's Law Dictionary* states:
- The witness testified to the following facts:

These phrases are deadly. They're enough to kill a good quotation.

Then what, you may ask, are you to do? After all, those are the standard
quotation introducers. The answer is that you should tailor the lead-in to the

quotation. Say something specific. Assert something. Then let the quotation support what you've said. Good lead-ins resemble these:

- The statute specifies three conditions that a trustee must satisfy to be fully indemnified:
- Because the plaintiff had not proved damages beyond those for breach of contract, the court held that the tort claim should have been dismissed:
- In fact, as the court noted, not all written contracts have to be signed by both parties:
- The *Central Airlines* court recognized that the facts before it involved a lawyer who neither willfully nor negligently misled the opposing party:
- The power to zone is a state power that has been statutorily delegated to the cities:
- The court found that Nebraska's export laws are stricter than its in-state regulations:

By the way, is it acceptable to put a colon after a complete sentence? You bet.[7] More writers ought to be doing it.

If you follow this principle for introducing quotations, your writing won't contain boring passages like this one:

> Although the general rule is that the trial court has discretion concerning declaratory judgments, the court in *Joseph v. City of Ranger*, 188 S.W.2d 1013 (Tex. Civ. App.—Eastland 1945, no writ), held that the Declaratory Judgment Act was never intended to permit the piecemeal adjudication of a pending case. In that case, the court held:
>
> > We believe the court is not authorized to enter a declaratory judgment, unless the controversy between the parties thereto will be ended, or when such judgment will serve a useful purpose. In this case the declaratory judgment as entered by the court will not end the controversy, for the reason there are a number of other issues involved in the case that will have to be determined before a final judgment can be entered therein. It was never the purpose of the Declaratory Judgment Act to allow a case to be tried piecemeal. . . . There was no necessity for a declaratory judgment, and such judgment will serve no useful purpose. The parties were all before the court. They had joined issues upon all questions involved in the lawsuit. There was nothing to prevent the court from proceeding to trial upon all the issues and from rendering a final judgment in the case.
>
> *Id.* at 1014–15.

Instead, you'll brighten your writing with passages like the following one, in which the reader wants to see whether the lead-in is accurate:

---

7. *See Garner's Modern American Usage* 675–76 (3d ed. 2009); Wilson Follett, *Modern American Usage* 423–24 (1966); Bergen Evans & Cornelia Evans, *A Dictionary of Contemporary American Usage* 100 (1957).

Although the general rule is that the trial court has discretion concerning declaratory judgments, this Court has held that the Declaratory Judgment Act was never intended to permit courts to adjudicate cases bit by bit:

> [T]he court is not authorized to enter a declaratory judgment, unless the controversy between the parties thereto will be ended, or when such judgment will serve a useful purpose. . . . It was never the purpose of the Declaratory Judgment Act to allow a case to be tried piecemeal.

But if the reader wants to test the writer's accuracy, isn't this a bad thing? No: it's a way of getting the reader to focus on the quotation (as opposed to embarking on it as a matter of faith). Notice also that in the passage just quoted, the lead-in ends emphatically and the phrase *bit by bit* ties in nicely to the quotation (*piecemeal*).

If you consistently follow this principle, your writing—when it comes to quotations—will be markedly better than the vast bulk of what legal writers produce.

Exercises

Basic

In the following passage, edit the lead-in to the quotation. Make the second sentence sharper and more informative. To do this, you'll need to figure out (1) what the point of contrast is with the first sentence (that is, what the *But* is contrasting with) and (2) what the point of the quotation is. Keep your revised lead-in under 15 words.

> This Court held that the plaintiff (Julia) was entitled to damages for loss of consortium and affirmed that portion of the judgment. But the Court also held as follows:
>
>> [A] claim for negligent infliction of mental anguish that is not based on the wrongful-death statute requires that the plaintiff prove that he or she was, among other things, located at or near the scene of the accident, and that the mental anguish resulted from a direct emotional impact upon the plaintiff from the sensory and contemporaneous observation of the incident, as contrasted with learning of the accident from others after the occurrence. Julia has not met either of these requirements and therefore may not recover for mental anguish.
>
> The same reasoning applies equally here because . . .

Intermediate

In a single legal publication, find two examples of well-introduced quotations. Highlight them. Provide the full citation for your source. If you're part of a writing group or class, circulate a copy to each colleague.

Advanced

In a single legal publication, find two examples of poorly introduced quotations. Photocopy the pages containing the lead-in and the follow-up to each quotation, and edit each passage to supply a new lead-in that asserts something about the quoted material. Provide the full citation for your source. If you're part of a writing group or class, circulate a copy to each colleague.

§ 30. Be forthright in dealing with counterarguments.

Legal writers too often enfeeble their arguments by ignoring their weaknesses — or their seeming weaknesses. Some writers simply assume that dealing with these weaknesses is itself a sign of being weak. Others are simply so committed to their own arguments that they become blinded to their soft spots. Still others think that they should hold back until it is time to rebut the opponents' arguments. All these views give little or no credit to the reader's intelligence. They also show a surprising naiveté about the nature of argumentation.

If you want to write convincingly, you should habitually ask yourself why the reader might arrive at a different conclusion from the one you're urging. Think of the reader's best objections to your point of view, and then respond to them directly.

Let's assume that in one section you've made your main point. Then you'll need to ask yourself, "Why would a judge decide against me?" Deal with any possible snags in your argument. That way, you'll show yourself to be thorough and frank. Essentially, a well-constructed argument looks something like this:

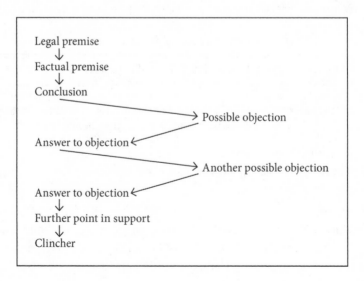

An argument using this structure makes for convincing reading. And it's hard to rebut.

Take, for example, the impeachment proceedings of 1998–99. If you had argued President Clinton's position, you would have needed to concede that the president's conduct was anything but exemplary. You'd simply say that it didn't rise to the level of an impeachable offense. If you had argued Kenneth Starr's position, you would have needed to concede that the constitutional threshold ("high crimes and misdemeanors") requires significant wrongdoing and that distasteful behavior in itself wouldn't be enough. You'd urge that perjury and obstruction of justice — even if the subject is as personal as sex — did meet the threshold. Whichever position you might have argued, explicit recognition of the other side's point would be crucial. Without it, you'd undermine your own credibility.

Don't set out your opponent's points at great length before supplying an answer. Instead, undercut your opponent's counterarguments swiftly. Try addressing the counterarguments in the middle part of each argument — not at the beginning and not at the end. Then knock each one down.

Exercises

Basic

Identify a judicial opinion that is written in such a way that the losing party would probably be satisfied that the court has dealt fairly with the points it raised. If you're part of a writing group or class, be prepared to explain why that is so.

Intermediate

Identify a newspaper editorial that does not deal squarely or fairly with counterarguments. If you're part of a writing group or class, be prepared to (1) explain what the counterargument is and (2) speculate about why the writer ignored the counterargument.

Advanced

See intermediate exercise. Rewrite the editorial to make it more credible.

PART THREE

Principles Mainly for Legal Drafting

The field known as "legal drafting" includes all the various types of documents that set forth rights, duties, and liabilities in the future: contracts (everything from assignments to licensing agreements to warranties), wills, trusts, municipal ordinances, rules, regulations, and statutes. Lawyers commonly think of drafting as being more "technical" than other types of legal writing. Perhaps it is. It certainly differs from most other types of writing you might think of:

- *People will read it adversarially, so it's important to be unmistakable.*
- *It deals with future events.*
- *It's typically a committee product — over time.*
- *It's boring to read (and the writer doesn't even care about being lively).*
- *It's rarely read straight through, so it needs to be easy to consult.*

Although some drafters' habits migrate to other areas — where they typically don't belong — the problems discussed in §§ 31–40 are predominantly those of transactional and legislative drafters.

Yet every lawyer occasionally gets involved in legal drafting of some sort — even if it's only a short letter agreement — and every lawyer should practice these principles.

§ 31. Draft for an ordinary reader, not for a mythical judge who might someday review the document.

Today the prevailing attitude, unfortunately, is that lawyers should draft contracts, legal instruments, and statutes with the judicial reader in mind. Draft for the legal expert, the thinking goes, not for the ordinary reader.

But this approach is wrongheaded for at least five reasons. First, lawyers who draft for judges tend to adopt a highly legalistic style, since judges have legal training. Yet because these lawyers aren't litigators, they almost never interact with judges. They don't know how much most judges detest legalese. Second, judges never see most drafted documents — only a small fraction of 1% ever get litigated. Third, this approach contemplates only the disaster that might occur if litigation were to erupt. It does nothing to prevent the litigation from arising. In other words, the approach focuses exclusively on the back-end users, with no concern for the front-end users who must administer and abide by the document. Fourth, the further removed a document is from plain English, the more likely the parties are to ignore it in their everyday dealings. It won't effectively govern their relationship. Fifth, the further removed a document is from plain English, the more divergent the views will be about its meaning — even among judges.

There is nothing newfangled about drafting for ordinary readers. It's what the drafting experts have been saying for a long time, whether the document is a contract or a statute. This list is only a sampling:

- **1843:** "[Most legal documents can be written] in the common popular structure of plain English."[1]
- **1887:** "[Good drafting] says in the plainest language, with the simplest, fewest, and fittest words, precisely what it means."[2]
- **1902:** "Latin words and, where possible without a sacrifice of accu-

---

1. George Coode, *On Legislative Expression* (1843).
2. J. G. Mackay, *Introduction to an Essay on the Art of Legal Composition Commonly Called Drafting*, 3 Law Q. Rev. 326, 326 (1887).

racy, technical phraseology should be avoided; the word best adapted to express a thought in ordinary composition will generally be found to be the best that can be used. . . ."[3]

- **1938:** "The simplest English is the best for legislation. Sentences should be short. Long words should be avoided. Do not use one word more than is necessary to make the meaning clear. The draftsman should bear in mind that his Act is supposed to be read and understood by the plain man."[4]

- **1976:** "[M]ore often than might be expected, [the lawyer's] . . . duty to be complete and exact will require only short and ordinary words, and short, or at least simple, sentences. The language of lawyers need not, as Coode remarked of the statutes, be 'intricate and barbarous.' "[5]

- **1988:** "The most competent version of language and legal drafting . . . is that version which enables the message to be grasped readily, without difficulty and confusion. This is none other than plain language — language which gets its message across in a straightforward, unentangled way, that lets the message stand out clearly and does not enshroud or enmesh it in convolution or prolixity."[6]

- **1996:** "From the draftsman's point of view, complexity intensifies the risk of error in the drafting and the risk of different interpretations in the reading: both chum for litigators. The commercial attorney, therefore, must work to achieve a result as simple as possible."[7]

- **2012:** "[T]he choice between precision and clarity is usually a false choice. If anything, plain language is *more* precise than traditional legal and official writing because it uncovers the ambiguities and gaps and errors that traditional style, with all its excesses, tends to hide. So not only is plain language the great clarifier, it improves the substance as well."[8]

There's a related point here. Drafters often lapse into the poor habit of addressing their provisions directly to someone other than the reader for whom the document is ostensibly written. Take, for example, this provision in a fee agreement, which, though purportedly directed to a prospective client, certainly wasn't written with the client in mind:

---

3. Lord Thring, *Practical Legislation* 81 (1902).

4. Alison Russell, *Legislative Drafting and Forms* 12 (4th ed. 1938).

5. J. K. Aitken, *The Elements of Drafting* 55–56 (5th ed. 1976).

6. Robert D. Eagleson, "Efficiency in Legal Drafting," in *Essays on Legislative Drafting* 13, 13 (David St. Kelly ed., 1988).

7. Peter Siviglia, *Writing Contracts* 73 (1996).

8. Joseph Kimble, *Writing for Dollars, Writing to Please: The Case for Plain Language in Business, Government, and Law* 40 (2012).

> Client understands that any estimates provided by the Firm of the magnitude of the expenses that will be required at certain stages of any litigation asserting a cause of action are not precise, and that the kinds and amounts of expenses required are ultimately a function of many conditions over which the Firm has little or no control, particularly the extent to which the opposition files pretrial motions and engages in its own discovery requests, whether in the nature of interrogatories, depositions, requests for production, or requests for admission, or any other type of discovery allowed by the rules of procedure in the forum in which the dispute is pending.

Who's the real audience there? Perhaps the fee-dispute committee of the local bar, or perhaps the grievance committee. And for most clients, it's a major turnoff. A leaner version informs the client more effectively because the point is clearer:

> Our estimates are just that: estimates. Conditions outside our control, especially the other side's pretrial motions and discovery requests, may raise or lower expenses.

Interestingly, lawyer groups—dozens of them—that have compared those two passages have said that if they were sitting on a grievance committee, they would be much less favorably disposed to the lawyer who wrote the first version.

Write for your immediate readers—the ones to whom you're directing your communications. Don't write for some remote decision maker who probably won't ever see, let alone interpret, the document. If you write well for the front-end users, you're less likely to have trouble down the line.

Exercises

Basic

Revise the following sentences so that they aren't so obviously directed to the judicial interpreter:

- Nothing expressed or implied in this Agreement is intended or shall be construed to give to any person or entity, other than the parties and the Buyer's permitted assignees, any rights or remedies under or by reason of this Agreement.
- The Corporation and the Executive explicitly agree that this Agreement has been negotiated by each at arm's length and that legal counsel for both parties have had a full and fair opportunity to review the Agreement so that any court will fully enforce it as written.
- The employee explicitly acknowledges and agrees that the agreement not to compete, set forth above, is ancillary to an otherwise enforceable agreement and is supported by independent, valuable consideration as required by Texas Business and Commerce Code § 15.50. The employee further agrees that the limitations as to time, geographical area, and scope of activity to be restrained are reasonable and do not impose any greater restraint than is reasonably necessary to protect the goodwill and other business interests of the employer.

Intermediate

In a formbook, identify a legal document that no one apart from an expert would likely understand. If you're part of a writing group or class, be prepared to discuss (1) the extent to which people other than experts might need to be able to understand the document and (2) at least three characteristics of the document that make it particularly difficult.

Advanced

Revise one or two provisions (about 200 words total) from the document you identified for the intermediate exercise. Produce before-and-after versions. If you're part of a writing group or class, circulate a copy to each colleague.

§ 32. Organize provisions in order of descending importance.

Experienced legal readers will expect you to lead with your most important points and to arrange other points in order of descending importance. This principle might seem so obvious as to be unnecessary. Yet some legal drafters habitually bury critical information.

Remember that plain English is concerned with readers — what they need to know and when they need to know it. You can't be content to let readers fend for themselves. You'll need to organize documents so logically and clearly that future reference to any specific point is easy. Although the nature of the particular document will influence the structure, the following guidelines generally enhance readability:

- Put the more important before the less important.
- Put the broadly applicable before the narrowly applicable.
- Put rules before exceptions.

If you're drafting a contract, the first substantive provisions should be the parties' main obligations to each other. And if you're drafting a statute, put the main requirements up front — everything else flows from them.

Consider the following, a statute dealing with discriminatory housing practices. As you read it, try to figure out the drafter's method of organizing the material:

Boston Fair Housing Commission — Title VIII — Enforcement, Penalties

AN ACT empowering the Boston Fair Housing Commission to impose civil penalties and enforce by judicial power the provisions of Title VIII.

Be it enacted by the Senate and House of Representatives in General Court assembled, and by the authority of the same, as follows:

SECTION 1. The following words used in this Act shall have the following meanings:

"Aggrieved person" means any person who claims to have been injured by a discriminatory housing practice or believes such person will be injured by a discriminatory housing practice that is about to occur.

"Commission" means the Boston Fair Housing Commission.

"Housing accommodations" means any building, structure or portion thereof which is used or occupied or is intended, arranged or designed to be used or occupied as the home, residence or sleeping place of one or more human beings and any vacant land which is offered for sale or lease for the construction or location thereon of any such building, structure or portion thereof.

"Person" includes one or more individuals, partnerships, associations, corporations, legal representatives, trustees, trustees in bankruptcy, receivers, and the commonwealth and all political subdivisions and boards or commissions thereof.

"Source of income" shall not include income derived from criminal activity.

SECTION 2. Subject to the provisions of section five, classes protected by this Act shall include race, color, religious creed, marital status, handicap, military status, children, national origin, sex, age, ancestry, sexual orientation and source of income.

SECTION 3. All housing accommodations in the city of Boston shall be subject to this Act, except as hereinafter provided. Nothing in this Act shall apply to housing accommodations which are specifically exempted from coverage by this Act, Title VIII of the Civil Rights Act of 1988, as amended, 42 U.S.C. Sections 3601 et seq. or chapter one hundred and fifty-one B of the General Laws. Nothing in this Act shall apply to the leasing or rental to two or fewer roomers, boarders, or lodgers who rent a unit in a licensed lodging house.

SECTION 4. Nothing in this Act shall prohibit a religious organization, association or society, or any nonprofit institution or organization operated, supervised, or controlled by or in conjunction with a religious organization, association, or society, from limiting the sale, rental or occupancy of housing accommodations which it owns or operates for other than a commercial purpose to persons of the same religion, or from giving preference to such persons, unless membership in such religion is restricted on account of race, color, marital status, handicap, military status, children, national origin, sex, age, ancestry, sexual orientation or source of income.

SECTION 5. In the city of Boston, discriminatory housing practices are prohibited; provided, however, that no practice shall be prohibited hereunder unless such practice is also prohibited by the federal Fair Housing Act or chapter one hundred and fifty-one B of the General Laws.

SECTION 6. Any person who violates the provisions of this Act as to discriminatory housing practices shall, pursuant to the provisions of section seven, be subject to orders, temporary, equitable and legal, including compensatory damages, punitive damages or civil penalties and attorney's fees and costs.

Lawyers who read that statute invariably say the same thing: § 5 should be moved to the fore. Once you make this change — as well as using headings and fixing various sentence-level problems — the statute is vastly improved:

Boston Fair Housing Commission — Title VIII — Enforcement, Penalties

This Act creates civil penalties for discriminatory housing practices.

The Legislature enacts the following:

1. Definitions.

1.1 "Housing accommodation" means any building, structure, or portion of a building or structure that is used or occupied or is intended, arranged, or designed to be used or occupied as the home, residence, or sleeping place of one or more human beings, including any vacant land that is offered for sale or lease for the construction or location of such a building or structure.

1.2 "Person" includes one or more individuals, partnerships, associations, corporations, legal representatives, trustees, trustees in bankruptcy, and receivers, as well as the commonwealth and all political subdivisions and boards or commissions of the commonwealth.

1.3 "Source of income" does not include income derived from criminal activity.

2. Discriminatory Practices Prohibited. In the city of Boston, discriminatory housing practices are prohibited to the greatest extent that they are prohibited by the federal Fair Housing Act or Chapter 151(B) of the General Laws. Classes protected by this Act include those based on race, color, religious creed, marital status, handicap, military status, parental status, national origin, sex, age, ancestry, sexual orientation, and source of income.

3. Scope of Prohibition; Exemptions. All housing accommodations in the city of Boston are subject to this Act. But nothing in the Act applies to housing accommodations that are specifically exempted from coverage by 42 USC §§ 3601 et seq. or Chapter 151(B) of the General Laws. Nothing in the Act applies to the leasing or rental to two or fewer roomers, boarders, or lodgers who rent a unit in a licensed lodging house.

4. Religious and Nonprofit Organizations. Nothing in this Act prohibits a religious organization or any nonprofit organization operated or supervised by a religious organization from limiting the sale, rental, or occupancy of housing accommodations that it owns or operates for other than a commercial purpose to persons of the same religion, or from giving preference to those persons, unless membership in the religion is restricted on account of race, color, marital status, handicap, military status, parental status, national origin, sex, age, ancestry, sexual orientation, or source of income.

5. Penalties. Any person who violates this Act is subject to court orders — temporary, equitable, and legal — including compensatory damages, punitive damages, and civil penalties, as well as attorney's fees and costs.

So weigh the relative importance of the ideas you're writing about — especially their importance to an intelligent reader. Then let your document reflect sensible judgment calls.

One last thing about organizing legal documents. Try to make whatever you write — and every part within it — self-contained. Your readers shouldn't have to remember other documents or sections, or flip back to them, to make sense of what you're saying.

Exercises

Basic

Reorganize the following paragraph from a commitment letter for the purchase of unimproved land. (A commitment letter is a lender's written offer to grant a mortgage loan.) Group the sentences according to whether they (1) specify the purpose of the letter, (2) state a buyer commitment, or (3) clarify the limitations of the letter. Then rewrite the passage in four paragraphs. Create a new introductory paragraph, and then create three paragraphs numbered 1, 2, and 3.

> No sale or purchase agreement nor contract of sale is intended hereby until ABC Company (Buyer) and Lucky Development Company (Seller) negotiate and agree to the final terms and conditions of a Sale-and-Purchase Agreement. Buyer shall exercise its best efforts toward securing such commitments from high-quality department and specialty stores as are essential to establishment, construction, and operation of a regional mall. For the 111.3 acres of land in the Benbow House Survey, Abstract 247, the total consideration to be paid by Buyer to Seller, in cash, shall be equal to the product of Five and 50/100 Dollars ($5.50) multiplied by the total number of square feet within the boundaries of the land, in accordance with the terms and conditions that shall be contained in a subsequent Sale-and-Purchase Agreement mutually acceptable to and executed by Buyer and Seller within sixty (60) days from the date hereof. Buyer shall exercise its best efforts to enter into the Sale-and-Purchase Agreement within the stated time period. In the event Buyer and Seller cannot come to final agreement on the terms and conditions of a Sale-and-Purchase Agreement within sixty (60) days from the date hereof, this letter of commitment shall be null and void and neither party shall have any liabilities or obligations to the other.

Intermediate

Reorganize and rewrite the following paragraph from an oil-and-gas lease. If you feel the need, break the passage into subparagraphs and add subheadings.

> 9. The breach by Lessee of any obligations arising hereunder shall not work a forfeiture or termination of this Lease nor cause a termination or reversion of the estate created hereby nor be grounds for cancellation hereof in whole or in part unless Lessor shall notify Lessee in writing of the facts relied upon in claiming a breach hereof, and Lessee, if in default, shall have sixty (60) days after receipt of such notice in which to commence the compliance with the obligations imposed by virtue of this instrument, and if Lessee shall fail to do so then Lessor shall have grounds for action in a court of law or such remedy to which he may feel entitled. After the discovery of oil, gas or other hydrocarbons in paying quantities on the lands covered by this Lease, or pooled therewith, Lessee shall reasonably develop the acreage retained hereunder, but in discharging this obligation Lessee shall not be required to drill more than

one well per eighty (80) acres of area retained hereunder and capable of producing oil in paying quantities, and one well per six hundred forty (640) acres of the area retained hereunder and capable of producing gas or other hydrocarbons in paying quantities, plus a tolerance of ten percent in the case of either an oil well or a gas well.

Advanced

In a statute book or contract formbook, find a document (no more than ten pages) with provisions that aren't in a well-organized order of descending importance. Give it what professional editors call a "macro-edit"—that is, edit for organization without worrying much about sentence-level problems. If you're part of a writing group or class, circulate a copy of your cleanly edited version to each colleague. Be prepared to explain your edits.

§ 33. Minimize definitions and cross-references. If you have more than just a few definitions, put them in a schedule at the end — not at the beginning.

You'll find that most contracts begin with definitions. That's all right if the document contains three or four of them. But if it has several pages of them, the definitions become a major obstacle. And believe it or not, you'll sometimes encounter documents (such as municipal bonds) that begin with more than 30 pages of definitions.

Although you might think of definitions as clarifiers, they are often just the opposite — especially when bunched up at the outset of a corporate document. Take, for example, what is known as a "stock-purchase agreement." The first section (which runs for ten pages) begins this way, in the middle of page one:

> *"Accounts Payable"* means trade payables, plus Affiliate (as defined below) payables due in connection with Intercompany Agreements (as defined below) that will not be terminated prior to Closing (as defined below) pursuant to Section 6(h) below, less vendor credit receivables.
> *"Accounts Receivable"* means trade receivables, plus Affiliate (as defined below) receivables due in connection with Intercompany Agreements (as defined below) that will not be terminated prior to Closing (as defined below) pursuant to Section 6(h) below, plus miscellaneous receivables less the reserve for doubtful accounts.
> *"Active Employees"* means:
> (i) AFPC Employees (including but not limited to Union Employees (as defined below)) as defined below;
> (ii) Seller Guarantee Employees as defined below;
> (iii) Shared Service Employees as defined below;
> who remain in the employ of, or become employed by, AFPC on the date

of Closing (as defined below), including but not limited to employees who are on the active payroll of AFPC, Seller Guarantor or Anaptyxis Corporation immediately prior to the Closing (as defined below) and who, although not performing direct services, are deemed to be Active Employees under AFPC's, Seller Guarantor's, or Anaptyxis Corporation's standard personnel policies, such as employees on vacation.

"AFPC" has the meaning set forth in the recitals above.

"AFPC Employees" means employees of AFPC immediately prior to the Closing (as defined below).

"AFPC Facilities" means the plants, operations, and equipment owned or leased by AFPC and located in Jacksonville, Florida; Madison, Wisconsin; Virginia Beach, Virginia; Asheville, North Carolina; Sacramento, California; Canyon, Texas; Hot Springs, Arkansas; Morristown, New Jersey; Springfield, Illinois; and Yakima, Washington. The singular *"AFPC Facility"* means any one of the foregoing AFPC Facilities, without specifying which one.

"AFPC Pension Plan" means the General Employee Retirement Plan of Anaptyxis Foam Products Company and Participating Companies.

"AFPC Severance Plan" has the meaning set forth in Section 7(d)(v) below.

"AFPC Shares" means all of the shares of the Common Stock, par value one hundred dollars and no/100 cents ($100.00) per share, of AFPC. The singular *"AFPC Share"* means any one of the AFPC Shares, without specifying which one.

"Affiliate" means, with respect to each of the Parties (as defined below), any legal entity that, directly or indirectly, (1) owns or otherwise controls, (2) is owned or otherwise controlled by, or (3) is under common control with, the aforesaid Party.

"Affiliated Group" means the affiliated group of corporations within the meaning of Section 1504(a) of the Code (as defined below) of which Anaptyxis Corporation is the common parent.

And we're not even halfway through the *A*'s. The list finishes with the term *Union Welfare Plans* (sensibly enough never telling us that the singular *Union Welfare Plan* refers to any one of the specified plans, without specifying which one).

Corporate lawyers often become immune to this stuff after learning the material. They get used to having the definitions up front. But this approach violates § 32 — about organizing from most to least important. In time, you might even conclude that these definitions are nothing but a ruse, by and large, for stripping the important information from relevant provisions and sticking it somewhere else, for the purpose of willful obscurity.

Of course, definitions aren't always intended to obfuscate. Sometimes they're placed in context — but again they're often unnecessary. Maybe these definitions get in the way a little, and maybe nonlawyers will laugh at them, but they don't usually cause ambiguity. They're just a symptom of paranoia:

> **11. Indemnification.** Each party hereto will indemnify and hold harmless (the "Indemnifying Party") the other party (the "Indemnified Party") from all loss and liability (including reasonable expenses and attorney's fees) to which the Indemnified Party may be subject by reason of the breach by the

> Indemnifying Party of any of its duties under this Agreement, unless such loss or liability is also due to the Indemnified Party's negligence or willful misconduct.

Delete the definitions, use the fairly ordinary legal word *indemnitor*, and you'll shorten the passage by more than 25%:

> **11. Indemnification.** Each party will indemnify the other party from all loss and liability (including reasonable expenses and attorney's fees) to which the other party may be subject if the indemnitor breaches its duties under this Agreement, unless the loss or liability is also due to the indemnified party's negligence or willful misconduct.

The revised version is clearer on a first read-through. And it's every bit as clear on a second, third, or fourth.

If you work with securities disclosure documents, there's some hope. The Securities and Exchange Commission has urged — if not mandated — that prospectuses and other securities documents minimize definitions.[9] Most disclosure documents today put definitions, if there are any, at the end.

So what can you do if you're not working in securities law? The first step is to put all the definitions in a schedule at the end of your document. Call it Schedule A. The second step — a much more ambitious one that you may have to postpone until you achieve some degree of seniority — is to rewrite the document to cut the definitions in half. That is, rewrite it so that it doesn't need all those definitions. Simply say what you mean at the very place where you're discussing something. In time, you'll revise the document further. And one day you'll find that you're down to fewer than half a dozen definitions.

Then you can move them up front again, if you like. You won't be creating a ghastly parade of terms at the outset. And if you have fewer than six, they're likely to be only the most important terms. Getting to that point will involve much toil and trouble. But it will be worthwhile for virtually all your readers — whoever they may be.

As for cross-references, the question is whether they are genuinely intended to help the reader. If so, they are beneficial. But they can become instruments of sadistic torture. Let's say you want to know whether you can e-file a pleading in a state trial court, but you're not certain whether your case qualifies as a commercial action. Good luck discovering the answer:

> "For purposes of this rule, 'commercial action' shall mean an action in which at least one claim of the types described in subparagraph (1) of paragraph (B) of subdivision (b) of section 6 of chapter 367 of the laws of 1999, as amended by chapter 416 of the laws of 2009 and chapter 528 of the laws of 2010, as amended, is asserted."

---

9. *See* Garner, *Securities Disclosure in Plain English* §§ 62–64, at 99–102 (1999).

Note that the drafter has referred to the legislature's session laws, as opposed to the statute sections as codified, just to make finding the answer more onerous. A more readable version would incorporate the elements of the cross-referenced statute:

> "For purposes of this rule, a 'commercial action' is one in which (1) neither party is a natural person, (2) the dispute concerns a business transaction, or (3) the lawsuit involves a claim of subrogation, contribution, or indemnity."

This version gives you what you need without your needing to hunt elsewhere.

The world record for obscure cross-referencing must go to § 509(a) of the Internal Revenue Code, which states:

> For purposes of paragraph (3), an organization described in paragraph (2) shall be deemed to include an organization described in section 501(c)(4), (5), or (6) which would be described in paragraph (2) if it were an organization in section 501(c)(3).[10]

To understand this provision, you must hold in mind the contents of six different sections nearly simultaneously. Some tax lawyers say that even after studying it at length, they're not entirely sure what the provision means.

Exercises

Basic

In the literature on legal drafting, find additional authority for the idea that good drafters minimize definitions.

Intermediate

In a formbook or statute book, find a contract or statute in which definitions account for at least 40% of the length. If you're part of a writing group or class, be prepared to discuss your views on (1) why the drafter resorted to so many definitions, (2) the extent to which you consider the definitions a help or a hindrance, and (3) whether any of the definitions are downright silly.

Advanced

In a formbook or ordinance book, find a short contract or ordinance in which definitions account for at least 20% of the length. Rewrite it without definitions. If you're part of a writing group or class, be prepared to discuss any difficulties you had.

---

10. I.R.C. § 509(a).

§ 34. Break down enumerations into parallel provisions. Put every list of subparts at the end of the sentence — never at the beginning or in the middle.

Statutes and contracts typically contain lists, often long ones. These lists are the main cause of overlong sentences. Break them up — set them apart — and when you're calculating readability, the pieces won't count as a single sentence.[11]

Although it's sometimes useful to have a 1-2-3 enumeration within a paragraph of ordinary expository writing, in legal drafting it's almost always better to set off the enumerated items. No one should have to trudge through this kind of marshy prose:

> In the event that by reason of any change in applicable law or regulation or in the interpretation thereof by any governmental authority charged with the administration, application or interpretation thereof, or by reason of any requirement or directive (whether or not having the force of law) of any governmental authority, occurring after the date hereof: (i) the Bank should, with respect to the Agreement, be subject to any tax, levy, impost, charge, fee, duty, deduction, or withholding of any kind whatsoever (other than any change which affects solely the taxation of the total income of the Bank), or (ii) any change should occur in the taxation of the Bank with respect to the principal or interest payable under the Agreement (other than any change which affects solely the taxation of the total income of the Bank), or (iii) any reserve requirements should be imposed on the commitments to lend; and if any of the above-mentioned measures should result in an increase in the cost to the Bank of making or maintaining its Advances or commitments to lend hereunder or a reduction in the amount of principal or interest received or receivable by the Bank in respect thereof, then upon notification and demand being made by the Bank for such additional cost or reduction, the Borrower shall pay to the Bank, upon demand being made by the Bank, such additional cost or reduction in rate of return; *provided, however*, that the Borrower shall not be responsible for any such cost or reduction that may accrue to the Bank with respect to the period between the occurrence of the event which gave rise to such cost or reduction and the date on which notification is given by the Bank to the Borrower.

Drain the marshes, add some headings and subheadings (see § 4), and you have a presentable piece of writing, even though the material is fairly complex:

8.3 Payment of Reductions in Rates of Return

(A) *Borrower's Obligations.* The Borrower must, on demand, pay the Bank additional costs or reductions in rates of return if the conditions of both (1) and (2) are met:

(1) the law or a governmental directive, either literally or as applied, changes in a way that:

---

11. *See* Rudolf Flesch, *The Art of Plain Talk* 36–37 (1946); *see also* Rudolf Flesch, *The Art of Readable Writing* 226–27 (1962).

> (a) increases the Bank's costs in making or maintaining its advances or lending commitments; or
> (b) reduces the principal or interest receivable by the Bank; and
> (2) any of the following occurs:
>> (a) the Bank becomes—with respect to the Agreement—subject to a tax, levy, impost, charge, fee, duty, deduction, or withholding of any kind whatever (other than a change that affects solely the tax on the Bank's total income);
>> (b) a change occurs in the Bank's taxes relating to the principal or interest payable under the Agreement (other than a change that affects solely the tax on the Bank's total income); or
>> (c) a reserve requirement is imposed on the commitments to lend.
> **(B)** *Exceptions to Borrower's Obligations.* The Borrower is not responsible for a cost or reduction that accrues to the Bank during the period between the triggering event and the date when the Bank gives the Borrower notice.

A fix like that is mostly a matter of finding enumerated items, breaking them out into subparts, and then working to ensure that the passage remains readable.

You'll need to use this technique almost every time you see parenthesized romanettes (i, ii, iii) or letters (a, b, c) in the middle of a contractual or legislative paragraph. Spotting the problem is relatively easy in a paragraph like this one:

> **5.4** *Termination Fees Payable by Pantheon.* The Merger Agreement obligates Pantheon to pay to OJM an Initial Termination Fee if (a) (i) OJM terminates the Merger Agreement because of either a Withdrawal by Pantheon or Pantheon's failure to comply (and to cure such noncompliance within 30 days' notice of the same) with certain Merger Agreement covenants relating to the holding of a stockholders' meeting, the solicitation of proxies with respect to the Pantheon Proposal, and the filing of certain documents with the Secretary of State of the State of Delaware, (ii) Pantheon terminates the Merger Agreement prior to the approval of the Pantheon Proposal by the Pantheon stockholders, upon Pantheon having received an Acquisition Proposal and the Pantheon Board having concluded that its fiduciary obligations under applicable law require that such Acquisition Proposal be accepted, or (iii) either party terminates the Merger Agreement because of the failure of Pantheon to obtain stockholder approval for the Merger Agreement and the transactions contemplated thereby at a duly held stockholders' meeting, and (b) at the time of such termination or prior to the meeting of the Pantheon stockholders there has been an Acquisition Proposal involving Pantheon or certain of its significant subsidiaries (whether or not such offer has been rejected or withdrawn prior to the time of such termination or of the meeting).

Breaking down the list into parallel provisions, with cascading indents from the left margin, clarifies the provision:

> **5.4** *Termination Fees Payable by Pantheon.* The Merger Agreement obligates Pantheon to pay to OJM an initial termination fee of $250 million if both of the following conditions are met:

(A) any of the following occurs:

    (1) OJM terminates the merger agreement because Pantheon's board withdraws its support of the merger or because Pantheon fails to comply (and fails to properly cure its noncompliance within 30 days of receiving notice) with its merger-agreement covenants relating to the holding of a stockholders' meeting, the solicitation of proxies on the Pantheon proposal, and the filing of certain documents with the Delaware Secretary of State;

    (2) Pantheon terminates the merger agreement before the Pantheon stockholders approve the Pantheon proposal, upon Pantheon's having received a business-combination offer involving at least 15% of Pantheon's stock and the Pantheon board's having concluded that its fiduciary obligations under applicable law require acceptance of that proposal; or

    (3) either party terminates the merger agreement on grounds that Pantheon has failed to obtain stockholder approval for the merger agreement and the related transactions at a duly held stockholders' meeting; and

(B) at the time of the termination or before the meeting of the Pantheon stockholders, there has been a business-combination offer involving at least 15% of Pantheon's stock or of its significant subsidiaries (whether or not the offer has been rejected or withdrawn before the termination or the meeting).

There's another point here: you can't have the main verb come after the list. The core parts of the English sentence are the subject and the verb (and sometimes an object). One key to writing plain English is ensuring that your readers reach the main verb early on. That way, the structure of the sentence becomes transparent.

One of the worst habits that drafters develop is putting long lists of items in the subject so that the main verb is seriously delayed. This postponement of the action results in what linguists call "left-branching" sentences: ones with lots of complex information that branches out to the left side of the verb. The metaphor is that of a tree. As you read from left to right, and remembering that the tree's trunk is the verb, imagine a sentence configured in this way:

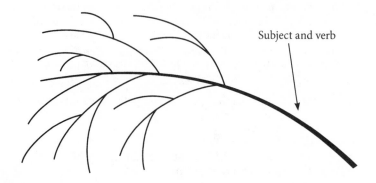

Subject and verb

That's going to be fiendishly difficult to get through.

But imagine the tree reconfigured:

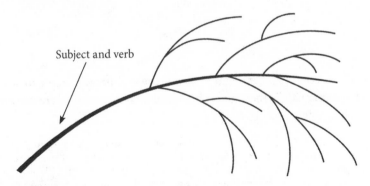

Subject and verb

If all this talk of trees sounds too botanical, look at actual examples of sentences done both ways. Here's a typical left-brancher:

> Except as may otherwise be provided in these rules —
> (a) every order required by its terms to be served;
> (b) every pleading subsequent to the original complaint unless the court orders otherwise because of numerous defendants;
> (c) every paper relating to discovery required to be served upon a party unless the court orders otherwise;
> (d) every written motion other than one that may be heard ex parte; and
> (e) every written notice, appearance, demand, offer of judgment, designation of record on appeal, and similar paper
> — must be served on each of the parties to the action.

The language after the enumeration — sometimes called "unnumbered dangling flush text"—is uncitable. That can be a problem. Once you put the enumeration at the end, however, the problem is cured: every subpart is citable. Here's the same sentence done as a right-brancher, with the enumeration at the end. Notice the newly added foreshadowing language (*the following papers*):

> Except as these rules provide otherwise, the following papers must be served on every party:
> (a) an order required by its terms to be served;
> (b) a pleading filed after the original complaint, unless the court orders otherwise because of numerous defendants;
> (c) a discovery paper required to be served on a party, unless the court orders otherwise;
> (d) a written motion, other than one that may be heard ex parte; and
> (e) a written notice, appearance, demand, offer of judgment, designation of record on appeal, or similar paper.

This is only a special application of the principle announced in § 7: keep the subject and verb together toward the beginning of the sentence.

Here's the upshot: find the operative verb in the sentence and move it toward the front, putting your lists at the end of the sentence. Even with fairly modest lists, this technique can enhance readability.

Exercises

Basic

Revise the following paragraph to put the enumerated items in separate subparagraphs. At the same time, be sure that you don't create unnumbered dangling flush text.

> **7.7 Insurance.** Borrower shall provide or cause to be provided the policies of insurance described in *Exhibit I*, together with such other policies of insurance as Lender may reasonably require from time to time. All insurance policies (i) shall be continuously maintained at Borrower's sole expense, (ii) shall be issued by insurers of recognized responsibility which are satisfactory to Lender, (iii) shall be in form, substance and amount satisfactory to Lender, (iv) with respect to liability insurance, shall name Lender as an additional insured, (v) shall provide that they cannot be canceled or modified without 60 days' prior written notice to Lender, and (vi) with respect to insurance covering damage to the Mortgaged Property, (A) shall name Lender as a mortgagee, (B) shall contain a "lender's loss payable" endorsement in form and substance satisfactory to Lender, and (C) shall contain an agreed value clause sufficient to eliminate any risk of coinsurance. Borrower shall deliver or cause to be delivered to Lender, from time to time at Lender's request, originals or copies of such policies or certificates evidencing the same.

Intermediate

Revise the following passage to cure the left-branching problem:

> If at any time the Federal Energy Regulatory Commission should disallow the inclusion in its jurisdictional cost of gas, cost of service, or rate base any portion of the cost incurred because of this gas purchase or the full amount of any costs incurred by Buyer for any field services or facilities with respect to any well subject hereto, whether arising from any term or provision in this Agreement or otherwise, including but not limited to price and price adjustments, the prices provided for herein, then Seller agrees that the price will be reduced to the maximum price for gas hereunder which the Federal Energy Regulatory Commission will allow Buyer to include in its jurisdictional cost of gas, cost of service, or rate base and Seller shall promptly refund with interest all prior payments for gas purchased hereunder which exceed the amount Buyer is permitted to include in said cost of gas, cost of service, or rate base.

Advanced

In a contract formbook, find a 200-plus-word paragraph that contains a series of romanettes (i, ii, iii). Rewrite the paragraph to set off the listed items, and make any other edits that improve the style without affecting the meaning. If you're part of a writing group or class, circulate a copy of the before-and-after versions to each colleague. Be prepared to discuss your edits.

§ 35. Delete every *shall.*

Shall isn't plain English. Chances are it's not a part of your everyday vocabulary, except in lighthearted questions that begin, "Shall we . . . ?"

But legal drafters use *shall* incessantly. They learn it by osmosis in law school, and law practice fortifies the habit. Ask a drafter what *shall* means, and you'll hear that it's a mandatory word — opposed to the permissive *may.* Although this isn't a lie, it's a gross inaccuracy. And it's not a lie only because the vast majority of drafters don't know how shifty the word is.

Often, it's true, *shall* is mandatory:

> Each corporate officer in attendance shall sign the official register at the annual meeting.

Yet the word frequently bears other meanings — sometimes even masquerading as a synonym of *may.* Remember that *shall* is supposed to mean "has a duty to," but it almost never does mean this when it's preceded by a negative word such as *nothing* or *neither:*

- Nothing in this Agreement *shall* be construed to make the Owners partners or joint venturers.
- Neither the Purchaser nor any Employer *shall* discriminate against any employee or applicant for employment on the basis of race, religion, color, sex, national origin, ancestry, age, handicap or disability, sexual orientation, military-discharge status, marital status, or parental status.
- Neither party *shall* assign this Agreement, directly or indirectly, without the prior written consent of the other party.

Does that last example really mean that neither party has a duty to assign the agreement? No. It means that neither party is allowed to (that is, *may*) assign it.

In just about every jurisdiction, courts have held that *shall* can mean not just *must*[12] and *may*[13] but also *will*[14] and *is.*[15] Even in the U.S. Supreme Court, the holdings on *shall* are major cause for concern. The Court has

---

12. *See, e.g., Bell Atlantic–N.J., Inc. v. Tate,* 962 F. Supp. 608 (D.N.J. 1997).

13. *See, e.g., Northwestern Bell Tel. Co. v. Wentz,* 103 N.W.2d 245 (N.D. 1960).

14. *See, e.g., Cassan v. Fern,* 109 A.2d 482 (N.J. Super. 1954).

15. *See, e.g., Local Lodge No. 1417, Int'l Ass'n of Machinists, AFL-CIO v. NLRB,* 296 F.2d 357 (D.C. Cir. 1961).

- held that a legislative amendment from *shall* to *may* had no substantive effect;[16]
- held that if the government bears the duty, "the word 'shall,' when used in statutes, is to be construed as 'may,' unless a contrary intention is manifest";[17]
- held that *shall* means "must" for existing rights, but that it need not be construed as mandatory when a new right is created;[18]
- treated *shall* as a "precatory suggestion";[19]
- acknowledged that "[t]hough 'shall' generally means 'must,' legal writers sometimes use, or misuse, 'shall' to mean 'should,' 'will,' or even 'may'";[20]
- held that when a statute stated that the Secretary of Labor "shall" act within a certain time and the Secretary didn't do so, the "mere use of the word 'shall' was not enough to remove the Secretary's power to act."[21]

These examples, which could be multiplied, show only a few of the travails that *shall* routinely invites. And the 92 pages of reported cases in *Words and Phrases*—a useful encyclopedia of litigated terms—show that the word *shall* is a mess.[22] As Joseph Kimble, a noted drafting expert, puts it: "Drafters use it mindlessly. Courts read it any which way."[23]

Increasingly, official drafting bodies are recognizing the problem. For example, most sets of federal rules—Civil, Criminal, Appellate, and Evidence—have recently been revamped to remove the *shall*s.[24] (In stating requirements, the rules use the verb *must*.) The improved clarity is remarkable. Meanwhile, many transactional drafters have adopted the *shall*-less style, with the same effect. (In stating contractual promises, they typically use *will*.) You should do the same.

---

16. *Moore v. Illinois Cent. Ry.*, 312 U.S. 630, 635 (1941).
17. *Railroad Co. v. Hecht*, 95 U.S. 168, 170 (1877).
18. *West Wis. Ry. v. Foley*, 94 U.S. 100, 103 (1877).
19. *Scott v. United States*, 436 U.S. 128, 146 (1978) (Brennan, J., dissenting).
20. *Gutirrez de Martinez v. Lamagno*, 515 U.S. 417, 434 n.9 (1995) (adding that "certain of the Federal Rules use the word 'shall' to authorize, but not to require, judicial action," citing Fed. R. Civ. P. 16(e) and Fed. R. Crim. P. 11(b)).
21. *United States v. Montalvo-Murillo*, 495 U.S. 711, 712 (1990).
22. 39 *Words and Phrases* 173–259 (2011), plus pp. 37–43 in 2012 pocket part.
23. Joseph Kimble, *The Many Misuses of "Shall,"* 3 Scribes J. Legal Writing 61, 71 (1992). *See also* Antonin Scalia & Bryan A. Garner, *Reading Law: The Interpretation of Legal Texts* 112–15 (2012).
24. *See* Garner, *Guidelines for Drafting and Editing Court Rules* § 4.2(A), at 29 (1996).

Exercises

Basic

Edit the following sentences for clarity, replacing the *shall*s:

- Escrow Agent shall be entitled to receive an annual fee in accordance with standard charges for services to be rendered hereunder.
- Each member shall have the right to sell, give, or bequeath all or any part of his membership interest to any other member without restriction of any kind.
- The occurrence of any one or more of the following shall constitute an event of default: (a) Borrower shall fail to pay any installment of principal or interest on an advance . . .
- After completion of Licensee's work, Licensee shall have the duty to restore the License Area to its former condition, as it was before the Licensee's entry into the License Area.
- The sender shall have fully complied with the requirement to send notice when the sender obtains electronic confirmation.

Intermediate

In the following extract from a licensing agreement, count the various ways in which duties are stated. Edit the passage for consistency.

7.3 **Ownership and Use of the Marks and Copyrights.** Licensee shall not claim any title to or right to use the Marks except pursuant to this Agreement. Licensee covenants and agrees that it shall at no time adopt or use any word or corporate name or mark that is likely to cause confusion with the Marks.

7.4 **Compliance with the Law.** Licensee will use the Marks and copyright designation strictly in compliance with all applicable and related legal requirements and, in connection therewith, shall place such wording on each Licensed Item or its packaging as Licensee and Licensor shall mutually agree on. Licensee agrees that it will make all necessary filings with the appropriate governmental entities in all countries in which Licensee is selling the Licensed Item or using the Marks to protect the Marks or any of Licensor's rights.

7.5 **Duty of Cooperation.** Licensee agrees to cooperate fully and in good faith with Licensor for the purpose of securing, preserving, and protecting Licensor's rights in and to the Marks. Licensee must bear the cost if Licensee's acts or negligence have in any way endangered or threatened to endanger such rights of Licensor.

Advanced

In a contract formbook, find a document in which *shall* appears inconsistently. On a photocopy, highlight every *shall*, as well as every other verb or verb phrase that seems to impose a requirement — such as *must, will, is obligated to, agrees to, undertakes to,* and *has the responsibility to.* If you're part of a writing group or class, bring a highlighted copy to each colleague. Be prepared to discuss (1) how serious the inconsistencies are, (2) how they might have come about, and (3) how easy or difficult it would be to cure the problem in your document.

§ 36. Don't use provisos.

Legal-drafting authorities have long warned against using *provided that*.[25] The phrase has three serious problems: (1) its meaning is often unclear, since it can create a condition, an exception, or an add-on; (2) its reach is often unclear, especially in a long sentence; and (3) it makes the sentence sprawl and creates more margin-to-margin text. You're better off never using the phrase. You can always find a clearer wording.

Since *provided that* has as many as three meanings, the phrase has long been known to cause ambiguities.[26] It has been said to be equivalent to *if*,[27] *except*,[28] and *also*.[29]

But that's only the beginning of the problem. Another frequent source of litigation arises over what the phrase modifies. Does it go back ten words? Twenty? A hundred? That depends on how long the sentence is. Believe it or not, there's a canon of construction about provisos, and the test is anything but clear: a proviso modifies only the immediately preceding language (whatever that is),[30] but it may be held to reach back still further to effectuate

---

25. *See, e.g.,* Thomas R. Haggard, *Legal Drafting in a Nutshell* 129–31 (1996); G. C. Thornton, *Legislative Drafting* 79–81 (4th ed. 1996); Bryan A. Garner, *Garner's Dictionary of Legal Usage* 727 (3d ed. 2011); Barbara Child, *Drafting Legal Documents* 322 (2d ed. 1992); Michèle M. Asprey, *Plain Language for Lawyers* 107–09 (1991); E. L. Piesse, *The Elements of Drafting* 67–71 (J. K. Aitken ed., 7th ed. 1987); Reed Dickerson, *The Fundamentals of Legal Drafting* § 6.9, at 128–29 (2d ed. 1986); Robert C. Dick, *Legal Drafting* 92–100 (2d ed. 1985); John A. Bell, *Prose of Law: Congress as a Stylist of Statutory English* 10–12 (1981); Reed Dickerson, *Materials on Legal Drafting* 194 (1981); Elmer A. Driedger, *The Composition of Legislation* 86, 110–20 (1956).

26. 2 Emory Washburn, *A Treatise on the American Law of Real Property* 26 (5th ed. 1887) ("The word 'proviso' or 'provided,' itself, may sometimes be taken as a condition, sometimes as a limitation, and sometimes as a covenant"). *See* Antonin Scalia & Bryan A. Garner, *Reading Law: The Interpretation of Legal Texts* 154 (2012).

27. *See, e.g., Barbara Oil Co. v. Patrick Petroleum Co.,* 566 P.2d 389, 392 (Kan. Ct. App. 1977) ("A proviso in a contract creates a condition . . .").

28. *See, e.g., Bounds v. State Workmen's Compensation Comm'r,* 172 S.E.2d 379, 383 (W. Va. 1970) ("[T]he statute, by the proviso, creates an exception . . .").

29. *See, e.g., Attorney General ex rel. Mann v. City of Methuen,* 129 N.E. 662, 665 (Mass. 1921) ("[A] proviso in statutes, contracts, or wills not infrequently introduces new or independent matter . . .").

30. *See, e.g., Grupo Protexa, S. A. v. All Am. Marine Slip,* 954 F.2d 130, 140 (3d Cir. 1992) ("[T]he language [in a proviso] qualifies the duty imposed by the language preceding the proviso . . ."); *Hos-*

the drafters' manifest intention.[31] This type of guidance is of little practical value.

Finally, there's the problem of the blocklike appearance that provisos commonly create. You can double or even triple the length of a sentence with a couple of ill-placed provisos. Drafters frequently do this.

Let's look at a passage that illustrates all three problems. The first two words in the passage mean *if*, but after that the sense of the provisos gets more confusing:

> *Provided that* the Issuing Bank or Escrow Agent has received an Inspection Report, the Purchase Price will be released upon the earliest occurrence of one of the following: (i) receipt by the Escrow Agent or the Issuing Bank of a letter from the Buyer, the Buyer's freight forwarder, if any, or the Buyer's shipper certifying that the Glenn Mill is loaded on one or more cargo vessels and in transit to Brazil; or (ii) the expiration of a period of one hundred twenty (120) calendar days following the Delivery Date; *provided, however, that* any events or circumstances beyond Buyer's reasonable control which prevent the disassembly, packing or shipment of the Used Steel Mill and/or Incomplete Mill, including both events of force majeure and causes imputable to Seller, shall extend the aforementioned period for the same number of days that such event or circumstance persists, and *provided, further, that* if such a period should be extended by such events or circumstances more than one hundred eighty (180) calendar days beyond the Delivery Date, either party may rescind this Agreement by written notice to the other, with a copy to the Escrow Agent or the Issuing Bank in accordance with section 11, hereof, whereupon the portion of the Purchase Price being held in the Escrow Account will be released to the Buyer or the letter of credit will be canceled, as the case may be, and title to and possession of the Glenn Mill will revert to Seller without the need for further action.

In fact, the middle proviso creates an exception, and the third (as you might have recognized) creates what lawyers call a "condition subsequent" to the exception. But then there's the question of what the second proviso modifies: does it go back to the beginning of the sentence, or only to (i) and (ii), or only to (ii)? If you took the time to puzzle it out, you'd finally conclude that it

---

pital Ass'n v. Axelrod, 565 N.Y.S.2d 884, 886 (App. Div. 1991) ("[G]enerally, a proviso limits the clause or terms immediately preceding it"), *appeal denied*, 577 N.E.2d 1059 (N.Y. 1991); *Schneider v. Forcier*, 406 P.2d 935, 938 (Wash. 1965) (en banc) ("Referential and qualifying words and phrases, where no contrary intention appears, refer solely to the last antecedent. Thus a proviso is construed to apply to the provision or clause immediately preceding it"); *Essex v. Washington*, 176 P.2d 476, 481 (Okla. 1946) ("[A proviso] qualifies and restricts that which immediately precedes it").

31. *See, e.g., Hill v. Board of Educ.*, 944 P.2d 930, 332 (Okla. 1997) ("[A] proviso need not be confined to the immediately preceding subject where it clearly appears to have been intended to apply to some other matter"); *Sanzone v. Board of Police Comm'rs*, 592 A.2d 912, 919 (Conn. 1991) ("While sometimes a proviso is said to limit only the language immediately preceding it, the better rule is that the proviso limits the entire section or, as the case may be, subsection within which it is incorporated").

modifies only (ii), which is the only preceding language that mentions a period of time. Finally, did you notice how unappealing the long paragraph is?

If you eliminate the provisos and use subparagraphs (see § 34), the ambiguities are removed. Equally important, the passage becomes much more readable:

> If the Issuing Bank or Escrow Agent receives an Inspection Report, the Purchase Price must be released upon the earlier of
>
> (A) the date when the Escrow Agent or the Issuing Bank receives a letter, from either Buyer or Buyer's freight forwarder or shipper, certifying that the Glenn Mill is loaded on one or more cargo vessels and is in transit to Brazil; or
> (B) 120 days past the Delivery Date, with the following qualifications:
>> (1) this 120-day period will be extended for as long as any event or circumstance beyond Buyer's reasonable control — including force majeure and causes imputable to Seller — prevents disassembling, packing, or shipping the Used Steel Mill or Incomplete Mill;
>> (2) if, under (1), the period is extended for more than 180 days beyond the Delivery Date, either party may rescind this Agreement by giving written notice to the other and by forwarding a copy to the Escrow Agent or the Issuing Bank, in accordance with section 11; and
>> (3) if either party rescinds under (2), the portion of the Purchase Price held in the Escrow Account will be released to Buyer or the letter of credit canceled; title to and possession of the Glenn Mill will then automatically revert to Seller.

According to the system for computing average sentence length (again, see the beginning of § 34), the average in that particular passage is now down to 33 words — as opposed to the 250-word sentence in the original.

You'll see the same phenomenon again and again: you can always improve on a proviso. Here are three more examples:

- Neither party may assign this Agreement without the prior written consent of the other party; *provided, however, that* Publisher may assign its rights and obligations under this Agreement without the prior written consent of Author to any person or entity that acquires all or substantially all of the business or assets of Publisher.
- If Pantheon's annual requirements for aluminum closure sheet fall below the 9-million pound minimum, Pantheon will purchase and Alu-Steel will supply all of Pantheon's volume requirements; *provided, however, that* Pantheon may have reasonable trial quantities supplied by an alternate source.
- If in the absence of a protective order Bryson is nonetheless compelled by court order to disclose protected information, Bryson may disclose it without liability hereunder; *provided, however, that* Bryson gives Pantheon written notice of the information to be disclosed as far in advance of its disclosure as practicable and that Bryson use its best efforts to obtain assurances that the protected information will be accorded confidential treatment; and

provided further, that Bryson will furnish only that portion of the protected information that is legally required.

The first two examples are easily remedied by relying on *But* as a sentence starter — a perfectly acceptable and even desirable method of beginning a sentence (see § 6):

- Neither party may assign this Agreement without the prior written consent of the other party. But without the Author's prior written consent, Publisher may assign its rights and obligations under this Agreement to any person or entity that acquires all or substantially all of Publisher's business or assets.
- If Pantheon's annual requirements for aluminum closure sheet fall below the 9-million-pound minimum, Pantheon will purchase and Alu-Steel will supply all of Pantheon's volume requirements. But Pantheon may have reasonable trial quantities supplied by an alternate source.

A grammatically acceptable but less appealing method would be to start those revised sentences with *However*.[32]

The third example requires only slightly more ingenuity to improve the wording:

- If a court orders Bryson to disclose protected information without entering a protective order, Bryson may disclose it without liability if

  (A) Bryson gives Pantheon written notice of the information to be disclosed as far in advance of its disclosure as practicable;

  (B) Bryson uses best efforts to obtain assurances that the protected information will be accorded confidential treatment; and

  (C) Bryson furnishes only the portion of the protected information that is legally required.

Notice how the revision makes it clear that there are three requirements with which Bryson must comply. That wasn't as clear in the original.

By the way, relatively few transactional lawyers have ever heard the chorus of warnings about provisos. Long-standing members of the bar, having practiced for 25 years or more, often use provisos throughout their work. You might well ask how this is possible if the principle about avoiding them is so well established. The answer is that despite recent improvements, legal drafting has long been neglected in American law schools. And the literature on legal drafting is little known. You'll find that most transactional lawyers can't name even one book on the subject. So it's hardly surprising that even the most basic principles of good drafting are routinely flouted. Only recently have law schools begun to correct this problem by offering more drafting courses.

---

32. *See* William Strunk Jr. & E. B. White, *The Elements of Style* (4th ed. 2000); Bryan A. Garner, *Garner's Modern American Usage* 428–29 (3d ed. 2009); Sheridan Baker, *The Complete Stylist* 55–56 (2d ed. 1972).

Exercises

Basic

Revise the following passages to eliminate the provisos:

- The quantity of product whose delivery or acceptance is excused by force majeure will be deducted without liability from the quantity otherwise subject to delivery or acceptance; *provided, however, that* in no event will Buyer be relieved of the obligation to pay in full for product previously delivered.

- Contractor will be reimbursed for travel and subsistence expenses actually and necessarily incurred by Contractor in performing this Contract in an amount not to exceed $2,000; *provided that* Contractor will be reimbursed for these expenses in the same manner and in no greater amount than is provided in the current Commissioner's Plan.

- The Borrower may, at any time and from time to time, prepay the Loans in whole or in part, without premium or penalty, upon at least one business day's notice to the Lender, specifying the date and the amount of the prepayment; *provided, however, that* each such prepayment must be accompanied by the payment of all accrued but unpaid interest on the amount prepaid to the date of the prepayment.

Intermediate

Revise the following passages to eliminate the provisos:

- If Seller's production of the product is stopped or disrupted by an event of force majeure, Seller must allocate its available supplies of the product to Buyer based upon the same percentage of Seller's preceding year's shipments of products to Buyer in relation to Seller's total shipments for the product, *provided, however, that* to the extent that Seller does not need any tonnage that is available in excess of the allocation of products to Buyer, it must make that tonnage available to Buyer.

- This Agreement will terminate upon the termination of the Merger Agreement under § 6.1 or two years from the effective date of this Agreement, whichever occurs earlier; *provided that* if the Merger Agreement is terminated under § 6.1(d), 6.1(g), or 6.1(h) of that agreement and at the time of termination there has been an acquisition proposal as described in § 14 of that agreement, then this Agreement will not terminate until four months after the termination of the Merger Agreement or payment to the parent company of a termination fee under § 6.2, whichever occurs earlier.

- When the Lease term expires, if Renton has fully complied with all its obligations under the Lease, Renton will be entitled to a 20% interest in the profits of Jamie Ridge in the form of a nonmanaging membership interest, and the right to lease or buy for nominal consideration approximately 1.6 acres, in an area designated by Jamie Ridge, for the purpose of operating a garden nursery, *provided that* any such lease or sale would be contingent upon the nursery's purpose being permitted under all applicable laws, and *provided further that* the area designated for the nursery would be burdened by a restrictive covenant prohibiting any other use thereof.

Advanced

In a federal statute or regulation, find a passage containing at least two provisos. Rewrite the passage to eliminate the provisos and otherwise improve the style. If you're part of a writing group or class, circulate a copy of the before-and-after versions to each colleague.

§ 37. Replace *and/or* wherever it appears.

With experience you'll find that you don't need *and/or*. But more than that, you'll find that *and/or* can be positively dangerous.

About half the time, *and/or* really means *or*; about half the time, it means *and*. All you need to do is examine the sentence closely and decide what you really mean. If a sign says, "No food or drink allowed," it certainly doesn't suggest that you may have both. And if a sign says, "Lawyers and law students are not allowed beyond this point," even though the message is bizarre it doesn't suggest that a lawyer may proceed alone.

But let's look at real sentences from transactional documents. In the following examples, *and/or* means *or*:

- Licensee provides no warranty as to the nature, accuracy, *and/or* [read *or*] continued access to the Internet images provided under this Agreement.
- The Foundation will promptly furnish Sponsor with a disclosure of all intellectual property conceived *and/or* [read *or*] reduced to practice during the project period.
- Each party will inform the other if it becomes aware of the infringement by a third party under any claim of a patent that issues on joint inventions *and/or* [read *or*] sole inventions. If litigation occurs under any joint invention *and/or* [read *or*] sole invention, and both parties are necessary parties to the litigation, then each party will pay its own costs.

Here, though, it means *and*:

- All applicable state and federal taxes will apply to cash awards received *and/or* [read *and*] options exercised by Zerton.
- Licensee agrees to indemnify Owner for any claims for brokerage commissions *and/or* [read *and*] finder's fees made by any real-estate broker for a commission, finder's fee, or other compensation as a result of the License.
- The deliverables are the Sponsor's property, and the Sponsor may use *and/or* [read *and*] duplicate them in its normal business operations.

The danger lurking behind *and/or* is that the adversarial reader can often give it a skewed reading. Consider the employment application that asks, "Are you able to work overtime and/or variable shifts?" If the applicant can work overtime but not variable shifts, the answer would be yes. The next question reads, "If the previous answer was 'No,' please explain." The applicant need not fill this out, since the previous answer was yes. She gets hired, goes to work, and is soon asked to work variable shifts. She says no and gets fired. A wrongful-termination lawsuit soon follows. Is that a far-fetched case? No. It's one of many actual lawsuits spawned by the use of *and/or*.

Courts, by the way, have routinely had extremely unkind words for those who use *and/or*.[33] Don't give them cause for more grumbling.

Exercises

Basic

Edit the following sentences to remove *and/or*:

- AmCorp and Havasu have the sole right to use inventions covered by this Agreement and to obtain patent, copyright, and/or trade-secret protection or any other form of legal protection for the inventions.
- Immediately upon notice from Licensor, Licensee must discontinue the printing and/or manufacture of licensed items at every print shop and/or the making of those items.
- No change, waiver, and/or discharge of this Agreement is valid unless in a writing that is signed by an authorized representative of the party against whom the change, waiver, and/or discharge is sought to be enforced.
- The settlement is binding on all the creditors and/or classes of creditors and/or on all the stockholders or classes of stockholders of this Corporation.

Intermediate

Find three cases in which courts have criticized the use of *and/or*. Quote and cite the relevant passages.

Advanced

In state statutes or regulations, find three sentences in which *and/or* appears. Retype them, providing citations, and then edit them to remove *and/or* without changing the original drafter's meaning. If you're part of a

---

33. *Sandman v. Farmers Ins. Exch.*, 969 P.2d 277, 281 (Mont. 1998) ("[T]he use of this much-maligned and overused conjunctive–disjunctive reflects poor draftsmanship and generally should be avoided"); *California Trout, Inc. v. State Water Resources Control Bd.*, 255 Cal. Rptr. 184, 194 n.8 (Ct. App. 1989) ("'And/or' is taboo in legislative drafting"); *Klecan v. Schmal*, 241 N.W.2d 529, 533 (Neb. 1976) ("[T]he use of 'and/or' in a statute is not to be recommended as it leads to uncertainty"); *In re Bell*, 122 P.2d 22, 29 (Cal. 1942) (noting that *and/or* "lends itself . . . as much to ambiguity as to brevity [and] cannot intelligibly be used to fix the occurrence of past events"); *Employers Mut. Liab. Ins. Co. v. Tollefsen*, 263 N.W. 376, 377 (Wis. 1935) (noting that *and/or* is a "befuddling, nameless thing, that Janus-faced verbal monstrosity").

writing group or class, circulate a copy of the before-and-after versions to each colleague. Be prepared to discuss your edits.

§ 38. Prefer the singular over the plural.

You'll find an age-old provision in statutes and contracts: "The singular includes the plural; the plural includes the singular." Only the second part of this formulation has ever really mattered. For example, if an ordinance says, "People may not set off fireworks within the city limits," the plural words *people* and *fireworks* create several problems. First, does the ordinance apply only to people who work in groups, but not to individuals? Second, even if it does apply to individuals, doesn't the phrasing imply that everyone gets a freebie? That is, only *fireworks* are forbidden, but if you shoot off just one . . . (Some would make it a big one.) Third, what constitutes a violation? If you set off 30 fireworks in 30 minutes, how many times have you violated the ordinance? Once or 30 times?

But if the ordinance says, "No person may set off a firework," it avoids all those problems. That's the beauty of the singular.

It's true that you'll occasionally need the plural. For example:

- Any dispute among employers may be resolved by the employers' grievance committee.
- The Company agrees to destroy all unauthorized reproductions in its possession.
- These rules are intended to streamline discovery.

If you're going to use a plural, however, double-check it: make sure that it really is necessary.

Exercises

Basic

Edit the following sentences to change the plural to singular when appropriate:

- Employees who have earned more than 25 credits are eligible for positions under § 7.
- The fire marshal is responsible for issuing all the permits listed in this section.
- All the shareholders of the corporation have only one vote.
- If the appealing parties have not satisfied the requisites for interlocutory appeals, their appeals will be dismissed.
- When issues not raised by the pleadings are tried by the express or implied consent of the parties, the issues must be treated in all respects as if they had been raised by the pleadings.

Intermediate

In a state-court rulebook, find a rule that is undesirably worded in the plural. Photocopy the rule and edit it to fix the problem you've identified. If you're part of a writing group or class, circulate a copy of your edited version to each colleague.

Advanced

In the literature on legal drafting, find additional authority for the idea that a singular construction typically works better than a plural one.

§ 39. Prefer numerals, not words, to denote amounts. Avoid word–numeral doublets.

To maximize readability, spell out the numbers one to ten only. For 11 and above, use numerals. They're more economical. Compare just how many characters you save by writing 73 as opposed to *seventy-three*. For the busy reader, even milliseconds add up.

But this numerals-vs.-words rule has four exceptions:

1. If a passage contains some numbers below 11 and some above — and the things being counted all belong to the same category or type — use numerals consistently: *Although we ordered 25 computer terminals, we received only 2.* (But *We received our 25 terminals over a three-month period.*)
2. For dollar amounts in millions and billions, use a combination of numerals plus words for round numbers (*$3 million*) and numerals for other numbers (*$3,548,777.88*).
3. For a percentage, use numerals with a percent sign: 9%, 75%.
4. Spell out a number that begins a sentence: *Two hundred fifty-three cases were disposed of in this court last year.* (You also might just recast a sentence like that one.)

An additional point: unless you're preparing mathematical figures in a column, omit ".00" after a round number.

As for word–numeral doublets — "one hundred thousand and no/100 dollars ($100,000)" — few lawyers know the origin of this ancient habit. Having put the question to more than fifty (50) lawyerly audiences, I've mostly heard wrong answers:

- Word–numeral doublets are a safeguard against typos.
- They increase readability.

- In checks, they help in cases of illegible handwriting.
- The illiterate can at least read the numbers.
- They prevent discrepancies in numbers.

The last is the most ludicrous: discrepancies aren't possible *unless* you write it twice.

In truth, word–numeral doublets arose centuries ago as a safeguard against fraudulently altered documents. That's why you write out checks in both words and numerals — the numerals by themselves would be too easy for a cheat to alter. And the practice proliferated in the days of carbon copies. When you had five or six carbons, the typewriter's impressions for digits often weren't legible on the last couple of copies. Hence the doubling helped ensure that all the carbons were legible.

But these rationales don't extend very far. There's no good reason why modern briefs, judicial opinions, statutes, or contracts should contain doublets — yet many of them do. The result is unappealing:

Not this:	But this:
WHEREAS, the Borrower has requested the Lender (a) to make a term loan to the Borrower in the aggregate principal amount of four million and no/100 dollars ($4,000,000.00); (b) to make available to the Borrower a revolving line of credit for loans and letters of credit in an amount not to exceed six million and no/100 dollars ($6,000,000.00); and (c) to make available to Borrower a capital expenditures line of credit for loans in an amount not to exceed one million and no/100 dollars ($1,000,000.00), which extensions of credit the Borrower will use for Borrower's working capital needs and general business purposes.	The Borrower has requested the Lender to extend three types of credit for working capital and general business purposes: - a term loan of $4 million - a revolving line of credit for loans and letters of credit of up to $6 million - a capital-expenditures line of credit for loans of up to $1 million
Licensee agrees to pay the Licensor two hundred thousand dollars ($200,000) within seven (7) days after the execution of this agreement.	The Licensee must pay Ciglerion $200,000 within seven days after this agreement is signed.

Not this:	But this:
The parties have stipulated for purposes of this Agreement that the fair market value of the Property is Three Hundred Eighty-Nine Thousand Six Hundred Sixty-Seven and 00/100 Dollars ($389,667.00).	The stipulated fair market value of the Property is $389,667.

Often you'll find passages in which the important numbers are written out once, while the trivial ones get doubled:

> If the sale transaction closes on or before December 31, 2010, (i) the purchase price will be reduced by $100,000; and (ii) on the second anniversary of the closing date, the City will receive the vehicles and equipment listed in Exhibit G. During the two (2) year period after the closing date, Pitmans will make its vehicles and equipment available to the City for routine emergency maintenance at the rate of fifty and no/100 dollars ($50.00) per hour.

Are the two-year period and the $50 rate really more susceptible to fraudulent alteration than the sum of $100,000?

The extremes to which this silly habit is taken are illustrated by a letter I recently received from a fellow lawyer. This acquaintance has an underdeveloped sense of humor, so I knew the letter was no joke. It began: "Dear Bryan: It was a real pleasure running into you and your two (2) daughters last week at the supermarket." Did he really suspect that I might alter the letter?

Quite apart from the recommendation in this section, be exceedingly careful about numbers in drafted documents. Your eye, of course, will be immediately drawn to the numerals. So the recommendation will help you. But whatever convention you follow, you'll find that it's important to double-check — even though you shouldn't double up — your numbers.

Exercises

Basic

Fix the numbering problems in the following passage:

> Before the entry of the final decree on June 5, 2010, the parties participated in four (4) hearings before three (3) Commissioners in Chancery, took three (3) additional sets of depositions of healthcare providers, and had at least twelve (12) *ore tenus* hearings. The court granted a divorce on the ground of separation in excess of one year, granted spousal support and Five Thousand Dollars ($5,000.00) in costs and attorney's fees to the wife, and equitably distributed the property.

Intermediate

In the literature on legal drafting, find two authoritative discussions on any aspect of word–numeral doublets, such as the idea that words control over numerals (and why). If you're part of a writing group or class, bring the authorities with you and be prepared to report on them.

Advanced

Find two cases in which courts have had to interpret documents that contain discrepancies in doubled-up words and numerals. Brief the cases and, if you're part of a writing group or class, be prepared to discuss them.

§ 40. If you don't understand a form provision — or don't understand why it should be included in your document — try diligently to gain that understanding. If you still can't understand it, cut it.

There's a recurring story in law offices. It goes something like this.

Two corporations are planning a joint venture. Each one, of course, is represented by a law firm. One firm — the one representing the larger corporation — prepares the first draft of the contract. Naturally, the lawyers rely on one of their forms. They just tweak it.

Henry, a third-year associate at Firm A, sends the draft contract over to Lindsay, a partner at Firm B. Being an experienced lawyer, Lindsay carefully works through the draft, noting possible additions, amendments, and negotiating points. After a few hours of reading, she comes across § 7.1, on page 31. It seems to be a remnant of some other deal — something not at all germane to the joint venture. She can't understand what it's saying. She talks to a couple of colleagues, who agree. So she calls Henry.

> "Henry, this is Lindsay."
>
> "Hi."
>
> "I've been working through your draft contract, and I expect to have my comments to you by next Tuesday. I don't see any serious impediments."
>
> "Glad to hear it," says Henry.
>
> "Oh, but there's one thing I want to ask you about now. Do you have a copy of the contract handy?"
>
> "Let me just get it." (Pause.) "OK."
>
> "Look at page 31. Section 7.1. What does that mean?"
>
> (Long pause.)
>
> "Now that you mention it, I'm not quite sure. I didn't draft that part of the agreement. I'm working on this deal with Barbara, a partner here at the firm. Let me talk with her about it. I'll get back to you."

Henry has just admitted to Lindsay that he didn't know the meaning of a provision in a document that he sent to her. It's a little embarrassing—but only a little. Now he has the difficult problem of raising the issue with Barbara. He'll have to finesse the discussion. Here goes:

> "Say, Barbara," he says, "Lindsay just called about our draft contract. She'll have her comments to us by next Tuesday."
> "Good," says Barbara. "Thanks for telling me."
> "Well, that's not all. She wants to know something about § 7.1, right here on page 31. See?"
> "What does she want to know?"
> "Well, she's asking what it means."
> "Did you tell her?"
> "No. Since I didn't draft that, I thought I should get your view of it."
> "I see. What do you *think* it means?"
> "To be honest, I can't tell. I've looked at it and can't figure it out."

As you can imagine, this hasn't been pleasant for Henry. He has had to admit both to Lindsay and to Barbara that he sent a contract out without knowing what one of its provisions means. Barbara, being a partner, knows what it means. And she says so in fairly clear language: "Henry, essentially § 7.1 does thus-and-so." A light goes on in Henry's brain. Now he sees it.

Back at his office, he calls Lindsay:

> "This is Henry again. I've talked with Barbara about § 7.1, and essentially that provision does thus-and-so."
> "Oh. That's what it's doing there. Let's just say it that way, then. 'Thus-and-so' is clear, but not this language you have at § 7.1. I don't have any problem with what you're trying to accomplish, but we need to say it so that my client and I can understand it."
> "You mean change the language?"
> "Of course. I can't understand § 7.1."
> "Well, I'll have to talk with Barbara about this."

And he does. In the end, Lindsay always wins this kind of discussion. But rather than use the newly clarified language, Firm A sticks to its bad old form—the one that even its third-year associates can't understand. That's the way of the world.

This scenario might seem far-fetched. In fact, though, some version of it plays out every day in dozens of law offices throughout the country.

What might be even more surprising is that official documents frequently contain provisions that are so obscure that no one knows how, when, or why they got inserted. In the mid-1990s, when a state supreme court revised its appellate rules for clarity, there were several sentences that befuddled everyone. Even procedural scholars wouldn't venture to guess why those sentences were there, or even what they meant. So did the court keep the sentences? Absolutely not. The revisers cut them, and rightly so.

If you don't understand a provision, it's probably one that will come back to harm you in some way — especially in a contract. So rather than leave something in, idly supposing there's a reason for it when no knowledgeable lawyer can say what that reason is, you're better off deleting it. But remember the part about diligence: you must sometimes sweat and fret awhile to discover a meaning before you can safely conclude that there isn't any.

Exercises

Basic

Decide whether you think the provisions described below have any real meaning. If you're part of a writing group or class, be prepared to defend your position.

- No savings and loan holding company, directly or indirectly, or through one or more transactions, shall . . . acquire control of an uninsured institution or retain, for more than one year after other than an insured institution or holding company thereof, the date any insured institution subsidiary becomes uninsured, control of such institution. [12 CFR § 584.4(b).]
- "Spouse" is defined as the person to whom the Cardholder is legally married or the person with whom the Cardholder is cohabiting as husband and wife and has been cohabiting for at least two years provided that where there is a legally undissolved marriage and the Cardholder is cohabiting with a person as husband and wife and has been so cohabiting for at least two years, the spouse is the person with whom the Cardholder has been cohabiting.
- The 911 provider shall not impose, or fail to impose, on Company any requirement, service, feature, standard, or rate that is not required of the incumbent local exchange company.

Intermediate

Interview a lawyer who (1) has practiced transactional law for at least ten years and (2) can recall a situation in which a provision relating to some other deal had meaninglessly crept into draft contracts where the provision didn't belong. Take specific notes on the interview. If you're part of a writing group or class, be prepared to report your findings.

Advanced

Find a reported case in which a party has had to argue that a sentence or paragraph is essentially meaningless. Write a case brief. Decide whether you agree with the court's resolution of the issue. If you're part of a writing group or class, circulate a copy of both the case and your case brief to each colleague.

PART FOUR

Principles for Document Design

What's the first thing a prospective employer notices about a résumé? Its overall appearance. And first impressions matter.

But document design is about much more than first impressions: it's about third and fourth impressions. After all, your reader may spend many hours with your work. If you know how to produce readable pages, you'll minimize readers' headaches and maximize the effortless retrieval of information.

So you must learn something about typography and page layout. Although lawyers formerly didn't have to trouble themselves with these things — because the options were severely limited in the days of typewriters — times have changed. Ignore document design at your peril. Although many judges, colleagues, and clients use some form of e-reader, you're wise to assume the primacy of print and to assume that it matters how your document will look if someone prints it.

§ 41. Use a readable typeface.

There's a lot more to learn about typography than most lawyers realize. Or want to realize. When someone starts talking about margins and white space and serifed typefaces, most lawyers tune out. And they tend to resent court rules containing specifications about type.[1]

Yet these matters are anything but trivial. As magazine and book publishers well know, design is critical to a publication's success. Of course, it won't make up for poor content. But poor design can certainly mar good content.

This is no time to get technical, so we'll keep it simple: use a readable serifed typeface that resembles what you routinely see in good magazines and books. (A serifed typeface is one that has small finishing strokes jutting from the ends of each character.) Here are some examples of various serifed typefaces that will serve you and your documents well:

We hold these truths to be self-evident. (Palatino)

We hold these truths to be self-evident. (Century Schoolbook)

We hold these truths to be self-evident. (Garamond)

We hold these truths to be self-evident. (Caslon)

We hold these truths to be self-evident. (Equity)

What you'll especially want to avoid is the traditional typeface for typewriters: Courier. It's blocklike and rather crude-looking:

We hold these truths to be self-evident. (Courier)

You won't find it in magazines or books. After all, no publisher would want to present such an unpolished look.

---

1. *See, e.g.*, Fed. R. App. P. 32.

Exercises

Basic

Find three sets of court rules that specify different typefaces or point size. Analyze the differences among them. If you're part of a writing group or class, be prepared to report your findings and to discuss which rule might result in more readable court papers.

Intermediate

Find two regulations (state or federal) that contain typeface specifications. Summarize those specifications and their purpose. If you're part of a writing group or class, circulate a one-page summary to each colleague.

Advanced

Find two nonlegal sources that discuss which typefaces are most readable. Retype the most pertinent passages and provide citations. If you're part of a writing group or class, circulate a copy to each of your colleagues and be prepared to discuss the recommendations.

or

Find authority for the proposition that a sans-serif typeface is often best for headlines, while a serifed typeface is best for text.

§ 42. Create ample white space — and use it meaningfully.

To the modern eye, densely printed pages are a huge turnoff. Readers find them discouraging if not downright repellent. So you'll need some methods to break up dense passages with white space. Many techniques discussed in this book contribute to white space, especially these:

- section headings (§ 4)
- frequent paragraphing (§ 26)
- footnoted citations (§ 28)
- set-off lists with hanging indents (§34)
- bullets (§ 43)

The white space around text is what makes a page look inviting and roomy. The lack of it makes the page look imposing and cramped.

By the way, which is easier for you to read: single-spaced or double-spaced text? Don't be so quick with your answer. If you're editing a manuscript, you'll want the page double-spaced. But if you're simply reading for comprehension, you probably won't. That's because double-spaced text has white space spread unmeaningfully throughout the page—between every two lines of type.

And there are three other disadvantages to double-spacing: (1) the document will be twice as long; (2) you'll encounter paragraphs and headings less frequently; and (3) you'll find it somewhat harder to figure out the document's structure. Book and magazine publishers know these things: when they produce polished, readable prose that is single-spaced, it's not necessarily because they're environmentalists.

Although court rules often require that lawyers' filings be double-spaced, you're generally better off single-spacing when you can—as in letters and memos. Just be sure that you create *meaningful* white space in the margins, between paragraphs, and between items in set-off lists.

What about the white space after a period? Should there be one forward-space or two? The answer may surprise you (as it surprised me, initially): all the reputable authorities mandate one space after a period:

- "The typewriter tradition of separating sentences with two word spaces has no place in typesetting. The custom began because the characters of monospaced typefaces used on typewriters were so wide and so open that a single word space—one the same width as a character, including the period—was not wide enough to create a sufficient space between sentences. Proportionally spaced fonts, though, contain word spaces specifically designed to play the sentence-separating role perfectly. Because of this, a double word space at the end of a sentence creates an obvious hole in the line." James Felici, *The Complete Manual of Typography* 80 (2003).

- "Put only one space, not two, following the terminal punctuation of a sentence." Kate R. Turabian, *A Manual for Writers of Research Papers, Theses, and Dissertations* rule A.1.3 (7th ed. 2007).

- "Like most publishers, Chicago advises leaving a single character space, not two spaces, between sentences and after colons used within a sentence." *The Chicago Manual of Style* rule 2.9 (16th ed. 2010).

- "I have no idea why so many writers resist the one-space rule. If you're skeptical, pick up any book, newspaper, or magazine and tell me how many spaces there are between sentences." Matthew Butterick, *Typography for Lawyers* 42 (2010).

For a detailed treatment of this point, see Matthew Butterick, *Typography for Lawyers* 41–44 (2010).

Exercises

Basic

Find a legal document in which ample white space appears. If you're part of a writing group or class, bring two or three photocopied pages for each colleague. Be prepared to discuss whether you think the writer used white space well or poorly, and why.

Intermediate

Find a legal document with insufficient white space. If you're part of a group or class, circulate a copy of the two most cramped-looking pages to each colleague. Be prepared to speculate on why the pages look the way they do.

Advanced

Redesign the pages that you found for the intermediate exercise.

§ 43. Highlight ideas with attention-getters such as bullets.

When you want to highlight important items in a list, there's hardly a better way than to use a series of bullet dots. They effectively take the reader's eye from one point to the next.

Consider the following paragraph from a legal memo. It's a midsize lump of sentences that buries the salient points:

> The most advisable form of entity for organization of activities related to ProForm in the United States depends on the purposes for the entity, and especially on whether there are short-term or long-term plans for the national affiliates to be used as vehicles for directly profiting Mr. LaRoche or other investors and sports personalities involved. In order to definitively respond to this item, we would need more information as to the business plans in the United States. For example, what are the business objectives of the affiliate in the United States? How exactly will the organization obtain its financial resources? Will it actually have revenues, and if so from what sources? Are merchandise sales contemplated, or will the organization limit itself to providing services? To what extent will the entity actually organize and administer athletic events, as opposed to merely promoting the new sport? To what extent will educational activities or facilitating cultural exchanges be parts of the entity's purposes? What other activities are planned?

But see what a bulleted list can do to make it snappier:

> What organizational structure to devise for the sport in the United States depends on the business objectives that Mr. LaRoche envisions. Perhaps the chief question is: Does he have short-term or long-term plans for hav-

ing the national affiliates directly profit himself or other investors and sports personalities? But to address even this question, we need more information about his business plans in the United States:

- What, specifically, are his business goals for the US affiliate?
- How will the entity be financed?
- Will it actually have revenues? If so, from what sources?
- Does Mr. LaRoche contemplate having the entity sell merchandise, or will he limit it to providing services?
- To what extent will the entity actually organize and administer athletic events as opposed to simply promoting the new sport?
- To what extent will educational activities, such as facilitating cultural exchanges, be part of the entity's purposes?
- What other activities are planned?

That sort of listing is vital to readability and punchiness. Advertisers, journalists, and other professional writers use bullets. So should you.

Because the mechanics of bullets aren't self-explanatory, here are several points — in bulleted fashion, of course — to keep in mind:

- Put a colon at the end of the sentence leading into the bulleted list. It serves as a tether for the bulleted items.
- Be sure to use "hanging" indents. That is, keep each bullet hanging out to the left, without any text directly underneath it.
- Adjust your tab settings so that you have only a short distance between the bullet dot and the first word. Normally, a quarter-inch is too much space — an eighth of an inch is about right.
- Make your items grammatically parallel (see § 8).
- Adopt a sensible convention for ending your items with semicolons or periods. (1) If each of your items consists of at least one complete sentence, capitalize the first word and put a period at the end of each item. (2) If each item consists of a phrase or clause, begin each item with a lowercase letter, put a semicolon at the end of all but the last item, and put a period at the end of the last. Place an *and* or an *or* after the last semicolon.

Exercises

Basic

Find one or more uses of bullets in the Federal Rules of Appellate Procedure. Consider (1) why you think the drafters used bullets in those places but not elsewhere and (2) to what extent the presentation follows the guidelines given in this section.

Intermediate

Find and photocopy a court rule containing a page with a list that would benefit from bullets. Retype the passage to improve it.

Advanced

In the literature on effective writing, find two discussions of bullets. If you're part of a writing group or class, be prepared to talk about what additional information you learned from those discussions.

§ 44. Don't use all capitals, and avoid initial capitals.

In the old days, typists had chiefly two ways — rather crude ways — to emphasize text. They could underline, or else they could capitalize all the characters. Typewriters afforded extremely limited options. Although computers have given writers many better options — boldface, italic, boldface italic, variable point sizes, and bullet dots, to name a few — many legal writers are stuck in the old rut of all-caps text.

The problem with using all capitals is that individual characters lose their distinctive features: the strokes that go above and below a line of text. (Typographers call these strokes "ascenders" and "descenders.") Capital letters, by contrast, are designed to be uniform in size. And when they come in battalions, the eye must strain a little — or a lot — to make out words and sentences. Modern readers think they scream:

> THESE SECURITIES HAVE NOT BEEN APPROVED OR DISAPPROVED BY THE SECURITIES AND EXCHANGE COMMISSION OR ANY STATE SECURITIES COMMISSION NOR HAS THE SECURITIES AND EXCHANGE COMMISSION OR ANY STATE SECURITIES COMMISSION PASSED UPON THE ACCURACY OR ADEQUACY OF THIS PROSPECTUS SUPPLEMENT OR THE ACCOMPANYING PROSPECTUS. ANY REPRESENTATION TO THE CONTRARY IS A CRIMINAL OFFENSE.

Even if you change to initial capitals, you can't say there's much improvement in readability. Initial caps create visual hiccups:

> These Securities Have Not Been Approved or Disapproved by the Securities and Exchange Commission or Any State Securities Commission Nor Has the Securities and Exchange Commission or Any State Securities Commission Passed upon the Accuracy or Adequacy of This Prospectus Supplement or the Accompanying Prospectus. Any Representation to the Contrary Is a Criminal Offense.

You'd be better off using ordinary boldface type:

> **Neither the SEC nor any state securities commission has approved these certificates or determined that this prospectus is accurate or complete. It's illegal for anyone to tell you otherwise.**

You might even consider putting the highlighted text in a box, like this:

> **Neither the SEC nor any state securities commission has approved these certificates or determined that this prospectus is accurate or complete. It's illegal for anyone to tell you otherwise.**

Although some statutes require certain types of language — such as warranty disclaimers — to be conspicuous, they typically don't mandate all-caps text. There's always a better way.

Exercises

Basic

Find a ghastly example of all-caps text in a brief or formbook. Then read it closely to see how many typos you can find. If you're part of a writing group or class, circulate a copy to each colleague.

Intermediate

In the literature on typography or on effective writing, find two authorities stating that all-caps text is hard to read. Type the supporting passage and provide a citation. If you're part of a writing group or class, circulate a copy to each colleague.

Advanced

Find a state or federal regulation requiring certain sections of certain documents to be in prominent type. Interview a lawyer who sometimes prepares these documents. Consider (1) how lawyers comply with the requirement—especially the extent to which they use all capitals, (2) whether capitals are actually required, and (3) whether you think there is a better way to comply with the requirement.

§ 45. For a long document, make a table of contents.

A two-page document doesn't need a table of contents. But anything beyond six pages — if it's well organized (see §§ 2, 3, 21, 31) and has good headings

(§ 4)—typically benefits from a table of contents. Your outline (§ 2) will be a good start. Yet even if you've neglected the outline, a table of contents can serve you well—as an afterthought. You'll benefit from rethinking the soundness of your structure after you've completed a draft.

Whatever the document, most readers will appreciate a table of contents. Some judges routinely turn first to the contents page of the briefs they read. Readers of corporate prospectuses often do the same—to get a quick overview of what the document discusses. Parties to a contract can use the contents page to find the information that concerns them.

If you're writing a brief, try creating a table of contents that looks something like the one below, by Jerome R. Doak of Dallas. Notice how every heading within the argument section is a complete sentence—an argumentative statement:

Table of Contents

If you're writing a securities-disclosure document such as a prospectus for an initial public offering—commonly called an "IPO"—your table of contents might look like the one below. Notice that this document uses topical headings, not argumentative ones:

Table of Contents

And if you're drafting a contract, try a table of contents like the one below. This one comes from an asset-purchase agreement. Again, the headings are topical instead of argumentative:

Asset-Purchase Agreement

An asset-purchase agreement like that one, of course, is usually the product of many hands over many years. You won't be expected to draft it from scratch—and almost certainly couldn't. But even when you're starting with a form, you should prepare a contents page. The process will help you understand the structure of the document. And your readers will thank you.

Exercises

Basic

In a contractual formbook, find a 10- to 20-page contract that has no table of contents. Make one for it. If you're part of a writing group or class, circulate a copy of your table to each colleague. Be prepared to discuss whether your outline would result in any major edits—especially edits that might cause the drafter to reorganize the document.

Intermediate

Find a state statute or regulation (10–25 pages) that has no table of contents. Make one for it. If you're part of a writing group or class, circulate a copy of your table to each colleague. Be prepared to discuss whether your outline would result in any major edits—especially edits that might cause the drafter to reorganize the document.

Advanced

Find a brief, an IPO prospectus, or an asset-purchase agreement that has a table of contents. Photocopy it, and then compare it with the relevant example in this section. Write a two- or three-paragraph essay comparing and contrasting the two. If you're part of a writing group or class, circulate a copy of your essay to each colleague, along with the table of contents you found.

PART FIVE

Methods for Continued Improvement

When will you have finished trying to improve your writing? That simply depends on how good a writer you want to be. If you aspire to be a top-notch writer, you'll never be finished.

§ 46. Embrace constructive criticism.

At first, all writers resist criticism. You probably tend to equate your writing with your intellect. You might instinctively believe that if someone criticizes your writing, it's an assault on the way your mind works. But if you don't learn to overcome this defensive instinct — if you insulate yourself from criticism — you'll find it difficult to improve.

What every writer needs to go through, at some point, is a series of good edits — not just edits, and not just heavy edits, but *good* edits. This means you'll need an experienced editor. In time, the edits will get lighter. But you'll never outgrow the need for a good editor. No writer ever does. Writing is a humbling affair.

You'll even find, with time, that you can get valuable comments from people who aren't professional editors. They might find a particular sentence awkward or a particular word jarring. You should listen to what they say. Don't simply discount their comments as uninformed blather.

Increasingly, writing pros are actually *paying* for nonprofessional advice. Testing legal documents on ordinary readers, just to see what might be going wrong, is a relatively recent practice that can dramatically improve quality. In the old days, if nonlawyers couldn't follow legal writing, many lawyers might have arrogantly claimed that the cause was the readers' sheer ignorance. Now, the more enlightened view is that misreadings more likely show the writer's sheer ineptitude.

It's possible to test the readability of all sorts of documents, from car warranties to apartment leases to court rules. It's even possible to test the persuasiveness of appellate briefs.[1]

But you must be willing to subject your writing to independent, objective scrutiny. The more secure you are as a writer, the more you'll seek out this scrutiny. It won't come naturally. You'll have to learn for yourself the value of seeking out criticism — and then heeding it.

---

1. *See* Garner, *The Winning Brief* § 99, at 454–57 (2d ed. 2004).

Exercises

Basic

Find a book chapter, a law-review note, or an article in need of a good edit. Retype a substantial section — at least one full page (but omit substantive footnotes) — in triple-spaced format. Then edit it by hand. If you're part of a writing group or class, circulate a copy of the marked-up version to each colleague.

Intermediate

Agree with a colleague that the two of you will do some mutual editing. Each of you will then write a three-paragraph persuasive essay. (Don't forget § 30.) Exchange the essays, edit them within a specified period, and then meet to discuss your edits. Each of you should agree to (1) listen open-mindedly to the other's edits and (2) refrain from making unduly negative remarks on your colleague's essay. Each of you should use your colleague's edits to revise the original.

Advanced

If you're part of a writing group or class, write a five-page essay defending a controversial legal position. Polish it. Make three copies (keep the original for yourself) and bring them to the meeting. The leader or instructor will divide the class into groups of three for purposes of exchanging papers. You'll then edit the essays from the other two people in your group, and they will edit yours. Try not to edit lightly. Write a note at the end of each paper you edit, noting both strengths and weaknesses; cover both style and content. (Say something positive if you can — and you always can.) When you return the following week, you'll have two sets of edits — possibly even three, if the leader or instructor has also edited your essay. Use the best edits (at least half) to revise the essay.

§ 47. Edit yourself systematically.

Imagine taking a golf lesson and having the instructor tell you to try a few things on your next swing: (1) keep your feet at shoulder width; (2) align the ball off your left heel; (3) bend your knees slightly; (4) start with your hands in front of the ball; (5) loosen your grip; (6) take the clubhead back low to the ground; (7) keep your left arm straight on the backswing; (8) keep your left heel on the ground throughout; (9) roll your right hand to the left at impact; (10) shift your weight from the right foot to the left just before impact; (11) clip the grass under the ball; (12) try not to move your head till the ball is struck. Finally, the instructor tells you, concentrate on hitting the ball smoothly instead of hard. Got that?

Professional golfers do most of those things naturally. For the pros, they're easy. Yet even the pros continue to need lessons because the fundamentals are easy to overlook. The golf swing is complex.

So is editing. It's at least as hard to explain what a good editor does when holding a pen as it is to explain what a good golfer does when holding a two-iron. Some years ago, I spent several days with John Trimble of the University of Texas — the author of the justly famous textbook *Writing with Style* (3d ed. 2011) — trying to identify precisely what a good editor does. Our goal was to devise an editorial protocol that almost anyone could carry out, step by step.

We found that, as editors, we work similarly. We both begin by clearing out the underbrush — sentence by sentence. We clean up the little, easily fixable problems. Then we go through the piece a second time, making more ambitious edits. This time, we concentrate especially on tightening slack wordings. Then we go through the piece again to rethink structure, transitions, and the ideas themselves. By now we're pretty familiar with the whole of what we're editing.

Having developed our protocol for LawProse seminars, we call it the Law-Prose Editing Method. Here it is:

The LawProse Editing Method

Level One: Basic Edits

1. Cut or reword pointless legalisms (§ 12).

2. Convert *be*-verbs (*is, are, was, were, be, been*) into stronger verbs (§ 13).

3. Convert passive voice into active unless there's a good reason not to (§ 9).

4. Change *-ion* words into verbs when you can (§ 15).

5. Check every *of* to see whether it's propping up a wordy construction (§ 14). If so, rephrase.

6. Check for misused words (§ 48), faulty punctuation (appendix A), and other mechanical problems.

7. Try to cut each sentence by at least 25% (§ 5).

8. Read aloud, accenting the final word or phrase in each sentence (§ 11). Does it read naturally?

Level Two: Edits to Refine

Ask yourself:

1. Does the central point emerge clearly and quickly (§ 22)?

2. Is there a strong counterargument that you haven't adequately addressed (§ 30)?

3. Can you spot a bridge at the outset of each paragraph (§ 25)?

4. For each block quotation, have you supplied an informative lead-in (§ 29)?

5. Can you dramatize your points better? Can you phrase them more memorably? Where you've enumerated points, should you set them off with bullets instead (§ 43)?

6. Have you found a way to subordinate citations so that they don't mar the page (and your analysis) (§ 28)?

7. Have you used real names for parties (unless there's a compelling reason not to) (§ 17)?

8. Have you achieved the right tone (§ 20)?

Because this method involves so many steps, it is artificial and laborious. But it's an excellent tool for self-teaching. It will almost certainly prompt you to carry out some edits that you'd otherwise overlook. And when you carry them out, they become yours. You start a good habit. You add to your repertoire as an editor.

Exercises

Basic

Take a short legal memo (2–5 pages) that you or someone else has written, and work through the LawProse Editing Method. First, if needed, type it word for word into the computer. Then work through the edits step by step. Create a new draft after each stage. If you're part of a writing group or class, make a copy of your before-and-after versions to each colleague.

Intermediate

In a real-estate formbook, find a short lease or other contract to which you can apply the LawProse Editing Method. First, type it word for word into the computer. Then work through the edits step by step. Create a new draft after each stage. If you're part of a writing group or class, make a copy of your before-and-after versions to each colleague.

Advanced

Take a substantial document that you've written — such as a term paper or law-review note — and work through the LawProse Editing Method. Be systematic: carry out only one type of edit at a time. If you're part of a writing group or class, be prepared to discuss what this experience was like for you — and what (if anything) you learned about editing.

§ 48. Learn how to find reliable answers to questions of grammar and usage.

Every practicing lawyer is, by the very nature of the job, a professional writer. Let's think for a moment about these two things: being a lawyer and being a professional writer.

What makes a lawyer a lawyer? The answer certainly isn't that the lawyer knows all the law in a given jurisdiction. That's impossible. What makes a lawyer a lawyer is knowing, when a legal question arises, how to find the answer — if there is one. Lawyers don't purport to give off-the-cuff answers without hitting the books. Anyone who does that probably won't remain a lawyer very long.

But if lawyers know about hitting the books on legal questions, what happens when a language question arises? Somebody asks whether it's acceptable (or even desirable) to start a sentence with *And* or *But*, whether it's wrong to end a sentence with a preposition, or some other grammatical or stylistic question. Where should the adverb go in relation to a verb phrase — inside or outside? Is splitting an infinitive always forbidden? Does *data* take a singular or a plural verb? What's the preferred plural of *forum*? Unfortunately, many lawyers aren't so fastidious about finding answers to these questions. They're likely to feel satisfied with a seat-of-the-pants approach. Yet even educated guesses about what the experts say are likely to be wrong.

That's why lawyers, of all people, need to know how to find the answers to questions of grammar and usage. Although most journalists generally know where to look, most lawyers are at a loss. Many might look in a book titled *English Grammar*, but most books bearing that title don't answer the questions. Others would look at a primer such as Strunk and White's *Elements of Style* (a superb weekend read), and still others would turn to the *AP Stylebook* or some other style manual. But on the finer points of grammar and usage, they'd come up empty.

The vast majority, though, wouldn't even crack a book: they'd give off-the-cuff answers based on half-remembered lessons from middle school. If they did this with legal questions, it would be prima facie legal malpractice. In writing, it's literary malpractice.

To avoid it, you'll need to own some dictionaries of usage. Very simply, these are guides to grammar, usage, and style arranged in alphabetical order — according to well-known terms of grammar and usage. So if you want to know whether you can justifiably begin a sentence with *And*, look under that word; with *But*, look there; on split infinitives, see "split infinitives"; on the placement of adverbs, see "adverbs"; on ending sentences with prepositions, see "prepositions."

If you're at all serious about writing, you'll need to own some usage guides. They'll arm you with knowledge when language questions arise.

Now before I tell you about various dictionaries of usage, a disclaimer is in order: I've written two of them. That's not really surprising, given that the dictionary of usage has long been my favorite literary genre. I'm not saying that you should go out and buy my books: you can have a good usage library without them. Have a look at what's available and judge for yourself.

Although hundreds of usage guides have appeared over the years, the following five are among the most helpful. They appear in chronological order:

- H. W. Fowler, *A Dictionary of Modern English Usage* (Ernest Gowers ed., 2d ed. 1965). More than anybody else, Fowler perfected the modern dictionary of usage. The first edition appeared in 1926. Although he was largely unconcerned with American English — and had a peculiarly British style — he still has many useful things to say to modern writers. Among the classic entries are "battered ornaments," "inversion," "polysyllabic humour," and "superstitions." The last of these is about the commonplace but false notions of what it means to write well.

- Theodore M. Bernstein, *The Careful Writer* (1965). For many years, Bernstein was an editor at the *New York Times*, and this book represents the culmination of his wisdom on writing and editing. With a light, wry touch, Bernstein provides guidance on such issues as "absolute constructions," "one idea to a sentence," "puns," and "rhetorical figures and faults." His introduction, entitled "Careful — and Correct," should be required reading.

- Wilson Follett, *Modern American Usage: A Guide* (Erik Wensberg ed., 2d ed. 1998). The book is a quite conservative guide to good usage. It has excellent essays on why good grammar matters, on journalese, and on the sound of prose. Follett was the first usage critic to take issue with the modern use of *hopefully* (to mean "I hope"). Originally published in 1966, this book was nicely updated in 1998.

- Bryan A. Garner, *Garner's Modern American Usage* (3d ed. 2009). This up-to-date usage guide quotes thousands of recent examples from newspapers, magazines, and books — with full citations. The most frequently cited grammatical bunglers are writers for the *New York Times*. Although the book treats the traditional usage problems and has, for example, a full discussion of how every punctuation mark is used, it contains hundreds of entries on word-choice problems that older books omit.

- Bryan A. Garner, *Garner's Dictionary of Legal Usage* (3d ed. 2011). This was the first dictionary of usage targeting legal writers. It discusses hundreds of usage problems that arise in law but not elsewhere. Among the entries worth consulting are "doublets, triplets, and synonym-strings," "indemnify," "plain language," "sexism," and "words of authority." There's even an entry called "lawyers, derogatory names for."

Whichever books you choose, keep them close at hand. Consult them. You'll come to appreciate their guidance.

No single usage guide has the final word. You'll learn to judge for yourself the value of one writer's guidance as compared to another's. And as you browse through them (that's inevitable), you'll learn all sorts of things that you never dreamed (or is it *dreamt?*) of.

If you want to improve your command of grammar and usage, browsing through dictionaries of usage is probably the easiest way — and the most enjoyable. You don't have to study the subject systematically. Just read a little bit each day, for a few minutes a day. Try a usage guide as idle-time reading for a few weeks, and you'll be on your way. That's the way it has worked for many excellent writers and editors. You could join their ranks. As for the question whether Internet search engines might serve just as well to answer usage questions, the answer is that they'll locate highly unreliable as well as reliable sources. Use them if you like — but warily. And meanwhile, become familiar with some authoritative paper sources.

Exercises

Basic

Correct the usage errors in the following sentences. Cite a usage guide that deals with the error in each sentence.

- When Margot arrived, Rodney told her that David had laid down because of his pain.
- Mrs. Clements testified that Kenneth was waiving the gun wildly and pointing it at Bill.
- Counsel testified that because the testimony would have harmed her case, she opted to forego it for reasons of trial strategy.

- Since the *Oneida* line of cases are now binding federal law in California, this Court is bound to follow them.
- The cost of any arbitration proceedings will be born by the party designated by the arbitrators.
- The gas would likely be inventory under the Idaho statutes defining the term, but these provisions might not apply since they do not effect Idaho taxable income.
- Texas law prohibits the unjustified interference with a parties' existing or prospective contractual relations.
- For the reasons stated in Jones's initial motion, Jones maintains that the Court's August 27 order precludes Fillmore from preceding on count six in this action.
- The laws of the State of Massachusetts (irrespective of its choice-of-law principals) govern the validity of this Agreement, the construction of its terms, and the interpretation and enforcement of the parties' rights and duties.
- Neither Mr. Robinson's affidavit nor Plaintiffs' deposition testimony carry the force of law.

Intermediate

Take two of the usage guides recommended here and find two others not mentioned. Be prepared to report on each guide's answers to the following questions:

1. Is it ever permissible to split an infinitive? If so, when?
2. Where should an adverb go in relation to a verb phrase? That is, not an infinitive but a verb phrase.
3. Is it grammatically correct to begin a sentence with *And*?
4. Which is correct: *self-deprecating* or *self-depreciating*?
5. What is elegant variation? Is it good or bad?
6. What is a fused participle? Is it ever acceptable to use one?
7. What is the difference between *historic* and *historical*?
8. What is the difference between *farther* and *further*?

Advanced

Prepare a bibliography of ten usage guides, including at least three of the ones listed in this section. Write a one-paragraph comment on each book's strengths and weaknesses.

§ 49. Habitually gauge your own readerly likes and dislikes, as well as those of other readers.

Most of us seem to have two sides of the brain that don't communicate with each other: the writerly side and the readerly side. The writerly side is stuffed with rules. Do this; don't do that. The readerly side generally isn't rule bound; it simply reacts positively or negatively to writing, often at a subconscious or semiconscious level. Over time, you can dramatically improve your writing by learning to monitor your readerly side: what do you like and dislike *as a reader*, and why?

Start with a clear head—not with all the rules that you've heard over the years. Then use your critical sense. If you respond favorably to an argument, ask yourself: "What did I like about the way the argument was presented?" If you respond unfavorably, ask yourself what you disliked about the presentation.

Every writer has a lot to learn from this process. If your instincts are sound—and they probably are—you can infer principles from these likes and dislikes. These principles will very likely be more reliable than the "rules" you remember from middle school.

For several years in judicial-writing seminars, I've asked judges to record their readerly likes and dislikes. I ask them to put aside what they think as writers and merely to record what they do and don't like about the legal material they read. Over time, the answers have been strikingly consistent. And because these answers are worth pondering, consider the list compiled from just one of these seminars, with almost every judge in the state of Delaware participating (see page 170). Notice that almost every quality mentioned in the left-hand column speeds up the delivery of information; almost every quality in the right-hand column, in one way or another, slows down the delivery.

Judges on Legal Writing

Likes	Dislikes
Brevity	Verbosity
Clarity	Obscurity
Logical flow	Clutter
Clear issues	Failure to frame the question
Interesting writing	Long paragraphs
Fluidity	Repetition
Informative headings	Too many footnotes
Clean overall appearance	Run-on sentences
Structured paragraphs	Disorganized style
Directness	Unnecessary material
Issue and answer in first paragraph	Unclear intentions
Practical writing	Boring writing
Trustworthiness	Latin terms; technical language
Succinctness	String citations

Likes	Dislikes
Flowing prose; good transitions	Poor grammar
Clear divisions of thought	Overstatement; hyperbole
Explanations	Passive voice: who did what?
Accuracy	Long decisions
Honest, sincere writing	Boilerplate
Supporting rationale	Complicated writing
No footnotes	Long-winded philosophical discourse
Decisiveness	Stream-of-consciousness
Originality in presenting ideas	Quotations
Concise sentences	Incompleteness
Clear, concise statement of facts	Witness-by-witness statement of facts
Outline style	Cases cited for the wrong proposition
Short words	Footnotes, especially giant ones
Clear conclusions	Long words
Conveying a sense of justice	Circuitous sentences
Instant clarity	Lengthiness
Storytelling	Lack of closure
Short, to-the-point style	Convoluted writing
Simple sentences	Spelling mistakes
Clever phrases	Disjointed ideas
Well-put phrases	Cuteness; unprofessional manner
Inspiring confidence about precise questions presented	Unnecessary detail
	Dancing around the issue
Understandable language	Uninformative writing
Common sense	Overuse of procedural labels
Immediate identification of issues	Writing you have to reread
Logical organization	Impossibly small type
Entertainment	Chattiness
Footnotes for string citations	Distortions of fact or law
Comprehensiveness	Overcontentiousness
Complex ideas stated simply and directly	Sentences broken up by citations
Footnotes properly and sparingly used	Lazy writing
Civil tone	"Clearly"

Note: This survey was part of an Advanced Judicial Writing workshop for the Delaware judiciary. Forty-two judges participated. The workshop took place in Rehoboth Beach in September 1996. The survey has been replicated at judicial seminars in more than 20 states, always with similar results.

Exercises

Basic

Interview two law professors who don't teach legal writing. Ask about their likes and dislikes in their on-the-job reading. Ask them to put aside what they do in their own writing and to focus exclusively on their readerly likes and dislikes. Prepare a composite similar to the one listed in this section. If you're part of a writing group or class, circulate a copy to each colleague.

Intermediate

Interview three practicing lawyers who have been members of the bar for at least ten years. Ask about their likes and dislikes in their on-the-job reading. Ask them to put aside what they do in their own writing and to focus exclusively on their readerly likes and dislikes. Prepare a composite similar to the one listed in this section. If you're part of a writing group or class, circulate a copy to each colleague.

Advanced

Do both the basic and intermediate exercises. Then write a short essay (1,000–1,500 words) reporting your findings.

§ 50. Remember that good writing makes the reader's job easy; bad writing makes it hard.

Psychologically, the main quality that distinguishes good writers from bad ones is this: good ones have cultivated an abiding empathy for their readers, while bad ones haven't. Good writers would no more write an opening sentence like the following one (from a memo) than they would shove people through a supermarket line:

> In an action pursuant to CPLR § 3213 upon a defaulted promissory note and guaranties, may the defaulting borrower's defense that the lender failed to fund interest due under the note from unrelated interest reserves pertaining to two other separate and distinct loans, each being evidenced by separate and distinct notes and guaranties, act as a bar to summary judgment?

It isn't decent. Often, too, this type of obscurity is a cover-up: the writer isn't sure what the case is really about.

Achieving simplicity—without oversimplifying—involves a paradox. Writers fear simplicity because they don't want to be considered simple-minded. In fact, though, there's no better way to strike your reader as an intelligent, sensible writer than to simplify. Psychologically, in other words, there's a gulf between writerly fears and readerly wants. You'll need to bridge it.

Exercises

Basic

Find a published judicial opinion that, in its opening paragraph, makes you feel stupid. Analyze why this is so. If you're part of a writing group or class, circulate a copy to each colleague and be prepared to discuss your example.

Intermediate

Find a published judicial opinion that, in its opening paragraph, makes you feel smart. Analyze why this is so. If you're part of a writing group or class, circulate a copy to each colleague and be prepared to discuss your example.

Advanced

Find a brief that, in its first few pages, makes you feel stupid. Rewrite the opener so that it would be immediately comprehensible to a generalist reader. If you're part of a writing group or class, circulate a copy of your before-and-after versions to each colleague.

APPENDIX A

How to Punctuate

Punctuation is an elaborate cuing system by which you signal readers how to move smoothly through your sentences. Used properly, punctuation helps you achieve emphasis and clarity. Used improperly, it does just the opposite. In fact, punctuation problems are often a symptom of bad writing. As one authority observes, "most errors of punctuation arise from ill-designed, badly shaped sentences, and from the attempt to make them work by means of violent tricks with commas and colons. . . ."[1] So learning punctuation is closely allied with learning to craft solid sentences. You can't have one skill without the other. Hence the guidance below.

1. Comma — 7 common uses, 5 common misuses
Using Commas

1.1 Use a comma when you join two independent clauses with a coordinating conjunction (such as *and, but, or, nor, yet,* or *so*).

- The United States is a common-law country, and its judges are common-law judges.
- About a dozen lawyers were in the room together, and the discussion was complete and candid.
- He entered a no-contest plea to possession of cocaine and drug paraphernalia, but the court withheld adjudication and sentenced him to one year on probation.

1.2 Use a comma after a transitional word or phrase (though not *And* or *But*), an introductory phrase (especially a long one), or a subordinate clause that precedes an independent clause.

- Significantly, Moore has not filed a cross-appeal. (Transitional word.)
- In the second *Reynolds* appeal, the majority opinion pointed out that experts frequently rely on comparable sales when appraising the value of property. (Introductory phrase.)
- When the court addresses the question of ambiguity, it must focus on the contractual language itself. (Subordinate clause.)

1.3 Use a pair of commas to mark the beginning and end of a nonrestric-

---

1. Hugh Sykes Davies, *Grammar Without Tears* 167 (1951).

tive phrase or clause — that is, either an appositive or a phrase or clause that gives incidental or descriptive information that isn't essential to the meaning of the sentence.

- A police officer, who is trained to overcome resistance, is likely to escalate force until the arrestee cannot escape without using deadly force. (Nonrestrictive clause.)
- Another authority, the court, has picked up some of the slack. (Nonrestrictive appositive.)
- The right allegedly violated in this case, freedom of speech as protected by the First Amendment, is one of our most fundamental constitutional rights. (Nonrestrictive appositive.)

1.4   Use a comma to separate items in a series — including the last and next-to-last.

- The term "reasonable doubt" is not designed to encompass vain, imaginary, or fanciful doubts. (Include the comma before *or*.)
- Jackson alleges that the October 2013 reassignment letter, the gag order, and the banishment order were implemented without affording her procedural due process. (Include the comma before *and*.)
- The scientific method has proved extraordinarily useful in matters involving radar, ballistics, handwriting, typewriting, intoxication, and paternity. (Include the comma before *and*.)

1.5   Use a comma to separate adjectives that each qualify a noun in parallel fashion — that is, when *and* could appear between the adjectives without changing the meaning of the sentence, or when you could reverse the adjectives' order without affecting the meaning.

- That is a simplistic, fallacious conclusion.
- Routine, hasty processing of criminal cases did not begin with plea bargaining at all.
- Wilson is a reserved, cautious person.

1.6   Use a comma to distinguish indirect from direct speech.

- Justice Scalia ended by saying, "The decision is an act not of judicial judgment but of political will."
- "Today, social workers provide a significant amount of mental-health treatment," wrote Justice Stevens.
- On the question of statutory interpretation, there is an apocryphal story about a celebrated Supreme Court Justice who remarked, "Because no legislative history is available on this point, we will have to look at the text of the statute."

1.7   Use commas to separate the parts of full dates and addresses, but (1) omit any comma before a ZIP code; (2) when writing just the month and the year, don't separate them with a comma (*July 2011*); and (3) when writing the month, day, and year, omit the comma after the year if you're using the date as an adjective (*the November 20, 2010 hearing*).

- Since July 15, 2011, Samuel Keeling has lived at 29 Cherry Street, Portland, Oregon 97203.

- Pollock wrote to them in April 2010 but never again.
- The court refused to reconsider its February 12, 2009 privilege order.

Preventing Misused Commas

1.8   Don't use a comma between a subject and its verb.

- **Not this:** The use of the terms "irrebuttable presumption" and "conclusive presumption," should be discontinued as useless and confusing. **But this:** The use of the terms "irrebuttable presumption" and "conclusive presumption" should be discontinued as useless and confusing.
- **Not this:** In that case, male teachers in a church-operated school, received a head-of-family salary supplement that was not provided to female heads of households. **But this:** In that case, male teachers in a church-operated school received a head-of-family salary supplement that was not provided to female heads of households.
- **Not this:** An insurance carrier or a union or union inspector, may be held liable under traditional tort concepts for the negligent performance of such an inspection. **But this:** An insurance carrier or a union or union inspector may be held liable under traditional tort concepts for the negligent performance of such an inspection.

1.9   Don't use a comma to set off a quotation that blends into the rest of the sentence.

- **Not this:** If one doctrine is more deeply rooted than any other in constitutional adjudication, it is that the Supreme Court, "will not pass on questions of constitutionality unless such adjudication is unavoidable." **But this:** If one doctrine is more deeply rooted than any other in constitutional adjudication, it is that the Supreme Court "will not pass on questions of constitutionality unless such adjudication is unavoidable."
- **Not this:** In lease cases, the related doctrine of constructive eviction has been held, "broad enough to include many different situations where the whole or a substantial part of the premises is rendered unfit for the purpose for which it was leased." **But this:** In lease cases, the related doctrine of constructive eviction has been held "broad enough to include many different situations where the whole or a substantial part of the premises is rendered unfit for the purpose for which it was leased."
- **Not this:** The Obama administration joined in the petition on grounds that the Second Circuit's decision would promote, "postemployment blacklisting." **But this:** The Obama administration joined in the petition on grounds that the Second Circuit's decision would promote "postemployment blacklisting."

1.10   Don't use commas to set off an adverb that needs emphasis.

- **Not this:** Defendants are, therefore, entitled to qualified immunity. **But this:** Defendants are therefore entitled to qualified immunity.
- **Not this:** We, nevertheless, wanted to bring this to the Court's attention. **But this:** We nevertheless wanted to bring this to the Court's attention.

1.11   Don't use a comma in the second part of a compound predicate — that is, when a second verb has the same subject as an earlier one.

- A good brief should address all the issues and analyze them intelligently. (No comma before the *and* because *brief* is the subject of *analyze*.)

- Quintanilla argued that Viveros had exculpatory information and charged the prosecutors with ignoring it. (No comma before the *and* because *Quintanilla* is the subject of *charged.*)
- After surgery to his knee in May 2009, Rowe was first given light-duty assignment as a production planner but then was laid off in March 2010. (No comma before the *but* because *Rowe* is the subject of *was laid off.*)

1.12 Don't use a comma as if it were a strong mark—a semicolon, colon, or period.

- **Not this:** One could view attendance at the football game as an alternative promise by Y, however, it seems readily apparent that this alternative is not a promise for which X has bargained. **But this:** One could view attendance at the football game as an alternative promise by Y; however, it seems readily apparent that this alternative is not a promise for which X has bargained. **Or this:** One could view attendance at the football game as an alternative promise by Y. But it seems readily apparent that this alternative is not a promise for which X has bargained. (The word *however*, within a pair of commas, cannot connect two independent clauses; a semicolon or period is needed.)
- **Not this:** The United Nations recognizes forced evictions as one of the root causes of international displacement of persons, "the two issues cannot be treated separately." **But this:** The United Nations recognizes forced evictions as one of the root causes of international displacement of persons: "the two issues cannot be treated separately." (The comma in the original sentence created a grammatical error known as a "comma splice"—joining two independent clauses with a comma.)

2. Semicolon—2 uses, 2 misuses

Using Semicolons

2.1 Use a semicolon to unite two short, closely connected sentences.

- In three-tier systems, the top court has tremendous discretion; it can usually decide which cases to hear and which to reject.
- One side must make an offer; the other side must accept it.
- A person who has been wronged often wants to win a fight; the sublimated courtroom fight may furnish the means of relief.

2.2 Use a semicolon to separate items in a list or series when (1) any single element contains an internal comma, (2) the enumeration follows a colon, or (3) the items are broken into subparagraphs.

- The individual defendants live in four cities: Austin, Texas; Bellingham, Washington; Boston, Massachusetts; and Denver, Colorado.
- The rationale is threefold: (1) since the declarant knows her own state of mind, there is no need to check her perception; (2) since the statement is of present state of mind, there is no need to check her memory; and (3) since state of mind is at issue, it must be shown in some way—and here, the declarant's own statements are the only way.
- To establish causation and intention in emotional-distress cases, the plaintiff is generally required to show that
  (1) the plaintiff was present when the injury occurred to the other person;

(2) the plaintiff was a close relative of the injured person; and

(3) the defendant knew that the plaintiff was present and was a close relative of the injured person.

Preventing Misused Semicolons

2.3   Don't use a semicolon where a colon is needed — especially after a salutation.

- **Not this:** Dear Sarah; . . . **But this:** Dear Sarah: . . .
- **Not this:** Two major reforms took place; the overhaul of no-fault insurance and the enhanced oversight of insurance companies. **But this:** Two major reforms took place: the overhaul of no-fault insurance and the enhanced oversight of insurance companies.

2.4   Don't use a semicolon where a comma will do — especially in a list with no internal commas.

- **Not this:** At common law, a corporation could be dissolved by an act of the legislature; the death of all members; the forfeiture of the franchise; or the surrender of the corporate charter. **But this:** At common law, a corporation could be dissolved by an act of the legislature, the death of all members, the forfeiture of the franchise, or the surrender of the corporate charter.
- **Not this:** The right of courts to refuse to enforce contract terms has been recognized for centuries; and fraud is one of the oldest doctrines used by the courts in this policing policy. **But this:** The right of courts to refuse to enforce contract terms has been recognized for centuries, and fraud is one of the oldest doctrines used by the courts in this policing policy.

3.   Colon — 4 uses, 1 misuse

Using Colons

3.1   Use a colon to link two separate clauses or phrases when you need to indicate a step forward from the first to the second — as when the second part explains the first part or provides an example.

- After two hours, they reconciled: the chef apologized, and the owner rehired him with a $10 raise.
- A trademark can be seen as an advertising idea: it is a way of marking goods so that they will be identified with a particular source.
- Even the stipulation did not extinguish Highland's uncertainty about what it was buying: the precise scope of PetroLink's compensatory and other duties remained in doubt.

3.2   Use a colon to introduce a list — especially one that is enumerated or broken down into subparagraphs.

- Each conspirator may be liable for the crimes of all other conspirators if two conditions are satisfied: (1) if the crimes were committed in furtherance of the conspiracy's objectives and (2) if the crimes were a natural and probable consequence of the conspiracy.
- The seller may do any of four things: (a) withdraw and terminate the contract, while remaining free to sell the property elsewhere; (b) force the

buyer to pay the price through an action for specific performance; (c) sue for actual damages; or (d) retain any down payment made by the buyer as liquidated damages.

- In the absence of an agreement to the contrary, the seller need not see that the goods reach the buyer but need only:
  - (a) put the goods into the hands of a reasonable carrier and make a reasonable contract for their transportation to the buyer;
  - (b) obtain and promptly tender any documents required by the contract or by trade usage to enable the buyer to take possession; and
  - (c) promptly notify the buyer of the shipment.

3.3   Use a colon to introduce a wholly self-contained quotation, especially a long one.

- Although some believe that lower courts are strictly bound by precedent, no matter how ill-fitting the result, Judge Learned Hand opposed this view:

  It is always embarrassing for a lower court to say whether the time has come to disregard decisions of a higher court, not yet explicitly overruled, because they parallel others in which the higher court has expressed a contrary view. I agree that one should not wait for formal retraction in the face of changes plainly foreshadowed. But nothing has yet appeared to satisfy me that the case at bar is of that kind. Nor is it desirable for a lower court to embrace the exhilarating opportunity of anticipating a doctrine that may be in the womb of time, but whose birth is distant; on the contrary, I conceive that the measure of its duty is to divine, as best it can, what would be the event of an appeal in the case before it.

- In response to a public outcry over the *Hinckley* case, Congress substantially codified the *McNaghten* rules in statutory form:

  It is an affirmative defense to a prosecution under any federal statute that, at the time of the commission of the acts constituting the offense, the defendant, as a result of a severe mental disease or defect, was unable to appreciate the nature and quality or the wrongfulness of his acts. Mental disease or defect does not otherwise constitute a defense.

- Molholt's May 1 report states: "My first hypothesis was that if persons who were near the plant at the time of the accident can be shown to have chronic immunosuppression ten years later, then they must have been exposed to at least 100 rems during the accident."

3.4   Use a colon after the salutation in correspondence. (A comma is acceptable in informal letters.)

- Dear Judge Reavley:
- Dear Ms. Grogan:

Preventing Misused Colons

3.5   Don't use a colon to introduce a quotation or list that blends into your sentence.

- **Not this:** The real issue is what has been called: "the most difficult problem in criminal procedure today." **But this:** The real issue is what has been called "the most difficult problem in criminal procedure today."

- **Not this:** In this sense, there is much wisdom in the apparently extreme aphorism of Jefferson that: "every constitution naturally expires at the end of 19 years." **But this:** In this sense, there is much wisdom in the apparently extreme aphorism of Jefferson that "every constitution naturally expires at the end of 19 years."
- **Not this:** The House Report stated that the purpose of the legislation was:

> to close the back door on illegal immigration so that the front door on legal immigration may remain open. The principal means of closing the back door, or curtailing future illegal immigration, is through employer sanctions. Employers will be deterred by the penalties in this legislation from hiring unauthorized aliens. And this, in turn, will deter aliens from entering illegally or violating their status in search of employment.

But this: The House Report stated that the purpose of the legislation was

> to close the back door on illegal immigration so that the front door on legal immigration may remain open. The principal means of closing the back door, or curtailing future illegal immigration, is through employer sanctions. Employers will be deterred by the penalties in this legislation from hiring unauthorized aliens. And this, in turn, will deter aliens from entering illegally or violating their status in search of employment.

4. Parentheses — 4 uses

4.1   Use parentheses to set off an inserted phrase, clause, or sentence that you want to minimize.

- If we increase the punishment, some people (not everybody) will stop doing the deed from fear of punishment.
- Once a child is born alive (assuming that the wife does not die in childbirth), the husband's shared freehold is converted into a life estate in his own right in his wife's freeholds.
- Sony and Toyota, if they were American companies, would have hundreds of lawyers on their payroll at their beck and call on Wall Street. (Maybe their American subsidiaries do.) Lawyers in the United States do things that are not done — or not done by lawyers — in Japan.

4.2   Use parentheses to introduce shorthand names.

- In the Controlled Question Technique ("CQT"), the test method that polygraph examiners use most often, an examiner asks three types of questions: neutral, control, and relevant. (The quotation marks within the parentheses are optional. An informal survey suggests that judges prefer them.)
- Sergeant Silk alleges that the City violated the Americans with Disabilities Act (ADA) by discriminating against him because of his sleep apnea. (Although quotation marks might be used — ("ADA") — they are less common and less desirable around well-known shorthand names.)
- Petitioners Southeast Crescent Shipping Company and Southeast Crescent Terminal Company (collectively "Southeast") are parties to a contract with the International Longshore Workers' Association, Local 1492 ("the Union").

4.3   Use parentheses around numbers or letters when you're listing items in text.

- This Court has reviewed orders not specified in the notice of appeal when (1) there is a connection between the specified order and unspecified order, (2) the intention to appeal the unspecified part is apparent, and (3) the opposing party is not prejudiced and has a full opportunity to brief the issues.
- Ohio law recognizes a claim for invasion of privacy in a case of (1) the unwarranted appropriation or exploitation of one's personality, (2) the publicizing of one's private affairs with which the public has no legitimate concern, or (3) the wrongful intrusion into one's private activities in a manner that outrages or shames a person of ordinary sensibilities.
- The court must determine the propriety of the remark by considering the following factors: (a) the nature and seriousness of the statement; (b) whether defense counsel invited it; (c) whether the district court sufficiently instructed the jury to disregard it; (d) whether defense counsel had the opportunity to respond to the improper statement; and (e) whether the weight of the evidence was against the defendant.

4.4   Use parentheses to denote subparts in a citation — or, in a case citation, to give information about the court and the year, an explanation about the holding or how the citation is relevant, or any explanation about how quoted text has been altered. Don't worry about nesting parentheses within parentheses, but do make sure that each opening mark has a corresponding closing mark.

- Fed. R. Crim. P. 41(d).
- 12 U.S.C. § 1821(d)(11)(A).
- *Fowlkes v. Thomas*, 667 F.3d 270 (2d Cir. 2012) (per curiam).

5.   Em-Dash (or Long Dash) — 3 uses, 1 misuse

Using Em-Dashes

5.1   Use a pair of em-dashes to set off an inserted phrase that, because of what it modifies, needs to go in the middle of a sentence.

- The Declaration of Independence, in its expressive force binding all "governments"—national, state, county, and city — doesn't declare itself to be "law."
- The plaintiffs here — two young children and their parents — have sued the city for violations of their constitutional rights.
- The argument is that testimony from Chancey — if she had given it — would have been enough to get those statements into evidence as prior recollections recorded.

5.2   Use a pair of em-dashes to set off a parenthetical phrase that you want to highlight.

- Accident law — the heart of the legal field we call torts — is basically the offspring of the 19th-century railroad.
- The enumerated rights found in the Constitution and in our Bill of Rights — the first ten amendments — are insufficient to found a system broad and comprehensive enough for a really free people.

- The majority — as Justice John Marshall Harlan pointed out in his dissent — brushed aside evidence of subhuman work conditions.

5.3   Use an em-dash to tack on an important afterthought or to add emphasis to what follows.

- In 1992, it was reported that about 100,000 private security guards toted guns — more than the combined police forces of the country's 30 largest cities.
- Overtime parkers now have to pay a big fine and run around the city to reclaim their cars — a colossal nuisance.
- The lawyers' special province is not peopled with human beings in their full humanity, but with types — that is, with human beings only as they fit into legal categories.

Preventing Misused Em-Dashes

5.4   Don't use more than two em-dashes in a sentence (and don't use more than one unless they are used as a pair).

- **Not this:** In the several matters involved in the *Noia* case, the Supreme Court denied certiorari four times — the first of these in 1948 — before it finally decided the case 15 years later — in 1963. **But this:** In the several matters involved in the *Noia* case, the Supreme Court denied certiorari four times — the first of these in 1948 — before it finally decided the case 15 years later, in 1963.
- **Not this:** Normally there is no difficulty in ascertaining who is entitled to the property — but if there is difficulty — for example, because it isn't known whether a missing beneficiary is alive or dead — the court may authorize the personal representative to distribute the estate on the assumption that a missing claimant is dead, or on some other reasonable assumption. **But this:** Normally there is no difficulty in ascertaining who is entitled to the property. But if there is difficulty — for example, because it isn't known whether a missing beneficiary is alive or dead — the court may authorize the personal representative to distribute the estate on the assumption that a missing claimant is dead, or on some other reasonable assumption.

6. En-Dash (or Short Dash) — 1 use, 1 misuse

Using En-Dashes

6.1   Use an en-dash as an equivalent of *to* (as when showing a span of pages), to express tension or difference, or to denote a pairing in which the elements carry equal weight.

- 233–34
- love–hate relationship
- contract–tort doctrines

Preventing Misused En-Dashes

6.2   Don't use an en-dash in place of a hyphen or an em-dash.

- **Not this:** The state–court action disposed of her wrongful–discharge claim. **But this:** The state-court action disposed of her wrongful-discharge claim.

- **Not this:** The court upheld the wage–and–hour laws. **But this:** The court upheld the wage-and-hour laws.
- **Not this:** A knowledgeable bench can smooth the road for a sound–or a persuasive-argument. **But this:** A knowledgeable bench can smooth the road for a sound — or a persuasive — argument.

7. Hyphen — 2 uses, 2 misuses

Using Hyphens

7.1   Use a hyphen to connect the parts of a phrasal adjective — that is, a phrase whose words function together to modify a noun.

- First-year law students are sometimes unready for their end-of-the-year doldrums. (*First-year* is a phrasal adjective modifying the noun phrase *law students; end-of-the-year* is a phrasal adjective modifying the noun *doldrums.*)
- The court applied the common-law mirror-image rule. (Both *common-law* and *mirror-image* are phrasal adjectives modifying *rule.* When used as a noun phrase, *common law* is unhyphenated.)
- The benefit-of-insurance clause and the waiver-of-subrogation clause were both held to be invalid because they conflicted with the plaintiff's marine-cargo insurance policy. (*Benefit-of-insurance* is a phrasal adjective modifying *clause; waiver-of-subrogation* modifies *clause; marine-cargo* modifies the noun phrase *insurance policy.*)

7.2   Use a hyphen when spelling out fractions.

- Three-fifths of those present concurred.
- One-third of the punitive damages were eliminated by remittitur.

Preventing Misused Hyphens

7.3   Don't use a hyphen after a prefix unless (1) the solid form might be confusing (e.g., *anti-intellectual*), (2) the primary word is capitalized, as when it's a proper noun (e.g., *non-Hohfeldian*), (3) the prefix is part of a noun phrase (e.g., *non-contract-law doctrine*), or (4) the unhyphenated form has a different meaning (e.g., *prejudicial* vs. *pre-judicial*).

- **Not this:** The co-defendant was a non-practicing attorney. **But this:** The codefendant was a nonpracticing attorney.
- **Not this:** The co-tenant was unable to collect the semi-annual payments, even with post-judgment garnishments. **But this:** The cotenant was unable to collect the semiannual payments, even with postjudgment garnishments.
- **Not this:** The nonMarxist point of view ultimately prevailed. **But this:** The non-Marxist point of view ultimately prevailed.

7.4   Don't use a hyphen (or even a pair of hyphens) in place of an em-dash or an en-dash.

- **Not this:** Frequently both sides will let a neutral third person - an arbitrator - make final decisions. **But this:** Frequently both sides will let a neutral third person — an arbitrator — make final decisions.
- **Not this:** The correctional complex--the latest trend in federal correc-

tions--is a series of several institutions on one enormous plot of land. **But this:** The correctional complex—the latest trend in federal corrections—is a series of several institutions on one enormous plot of land.

8. Quotation Marks—6 uses, 2 misuses

Using Quotation Marks

8.1 Use quotation marks when you're quoting a passage of 50 or fewer words. (Otherwise, set off and indent the quotation.)

- Vitalone's supervisor told him that he would be "out the door" if he complained one more time about Plourde. (The writer is quoting the supervisor.)
- Within earshot of both parents and pupils, Hennessy called the exhibition "disgusting" and the Cesaro painting "obscene" before leaving in the middle of class. (The writer is quoting Hennessy.)
- A quarter-century ago, Justice Powell wrote: "The Government, as an employer, must have wide discretion and control over the management of its personnel and internal affairs."

8.2 Use quotation marks when (1) referring to a word as a word or a phrase as a phrase (although italics are better if you do this frequently) or (2) providing a definition.

- The word "malice" contains an ambiguity.
- Both circuit courts turned to the legislative history to determine the meaning of the phrase "value as of the effective date of the plan."
- "Joinder" means "the uniting of parties or claims in a single lawsuit."

8.3 Use quotation marks when you mean "so-called" or "self-styled," or even "so-called-but-not-really."

- Certain forms of expression have been described as "illusory promises." (The quotation marks mean "so-called.")
- Jack Burke, a "cable troubleshooter," questioned Veazey about the message. (Here the quotes mean "self-styled"; Burke calls himself a "cable troubleshooter.")
- Immense effort has been made to discover the "origin" of the concept of consideration, to construct the "correct" definition of *consideration*, and to express in words the true consideration "doctrine" by means of which the enforceability of informal promises can be determined. But there is no specific and definite "origin" to be discovered; no particular definition can be described as the only "correct" one; and there never has been a uniform "doctrine" by which enforceability can be deductively determined. (The quotation marks show that the writer questions the accuracy of the words.)

8.4 Although quotation marks are traditionally used for titles of movies, songs, and poems (as well as articles), follow the standard form for legal citations. Consult the *Bluebook* (19th ed. 2010) or the *ALWD Citation Manual* (4th ed. 2010).

- In the screenplay "Concealed," Marty obtains information from an elderly retired city clerk who sells tomatoes.

- In his article entitled "Supply-Side Journalism," Seth Ackerman argues that the German welfare state has become so elaborate and labor costs so expensive that companies can't afford new workers.
- The wording was intended as an allusion to John Donne's poem "Death Be Not Proud."

8.5   Use single quotation marks for quoted words within quotations.

- In that case, the plaintiff saw the driver coming and attempted to flee, but he was unable to get out because "the door to the booth was 'jammed and stuck,' trapping the plaintiff inside." (The court's language goes from *the door* to *inside*, but the court has quoted testimony in the phrasing *jammed and stuck*.)
- Judge Charles E. Wyzanski Jr. has observed of Justice Holmes: "His starting point was an awareness that 'the provisions of the Constitution are not mathematical formulas having their essence in their form; they are organic living institutions transplanted from English soil.' " (Here the writer quotes Holmes's words in addition to Wyzanski's.)
- " '[T]he provisions of the Constitution are not mathematical formulas having their essence in their form; they are organic living institutions transplanted from English soil.' " (Here the writer quotes Wyzanski quoting Holmes, but without using any of Wyzanski's words. It would be better, if possible, to quote Holmes directly — to find the original source and verify the quotation. Otherwise, this form is necessary. The citation will be to Holmes "as quoted in" Wyzanski's book, or to Wyzanski "quoting Holmes.")

8.6   Place quotation marks correctly in relation to other punctuation: (1) periods and commas go inside; (2) colons and semicolons go outside; and (3) question marks and exclamation points go either inside or outside, depending on whether they're part of the quoted matter.

- The police officer testified that Jensen seemed "nervous," adding that at one point he seemed "jittery to the point of arousing a sense of alarm."
- The written review of Eversham's performance stated that "well-thought-out analysis was lacking"; that his understanding of financial analysis was "a major weakness"; and that he had a "tendency to bulldoze people."
- Did Pullman really attribute the decline to "poor sales projections"? **But:** Pullman asked, "Did I really say that?"

Preventing Misused Quotation Marks

8.7   Don't use quotation marks for a phrasal adjective.

- **Not this:** This "declining interest rate" scenario seems unlikely. **But this:** This declining-interest-rate scenario seems unlikely.
- **Not this:** According to the "fraud on the market" theory, if the market itself is defrauded by misrepresentations, then plaintiffs who relied on the integrity of the market price when buying securities have presumptively relied on those misrepresentations. **But this:** According to the fraud-on-the-market theory, if the market itself is defrauded by misrepresentations, then plaintiffs who relied on the integrity of the market price when buying securities have presumptively relied on those misrepresentations.

8.8 Don't use quotation marks merely to emphasize a word.

- **Not this:** There is not "any" evidence of this behavior. **But this:** There is not any evidence of this behavior.
- **Not this:** Although the Bertelsby Company "claims" to have been harmed, it has produced no evidence to date. **But this:** Although the Bertelsby Company claims to have been harmed, it has produced no evidence to date.

9. Ellipsis Dots — 3 uses

9.1 Use three ellipsis dots to denote that you've omitted something from within a sentence.

- "Statutes in most states . . . require the landlord to put the tenant in actual possession of the premises at the beginning of the leasehold term." (The quoter has deleted the phrase *with but a few exceptions*, which in the original was enclosed in a pair of commas.)
- "The immediate claimants have to be viewed . . . as members of classes whose contours are by no means self-evident." (The quoter has omitted the words *in other words*, which in the original were enclosed in a pair of commas.)
- "In presenting a few of the recognized authority techniques . . . , the author tried to group and phrase them in a way that shows how many distinct aspects of a case or of a doctrine there are." (The quoter has omitted the words *at page 77*, which in the original were enclosed in a pair of commas. The second comma is retained as specified in rule 1.2.)

9.2 Use four dots — three ellipsis dots plus a period — when you've omitted something at the end of a sentence. (A space goes before the first ellipsis dot.)

- "An arrest is neither a conviction of a crime nor even a final formal charge of a crime. . . ." (The original sentence continued with the words "but is merely an order holding a person in custody until he or she answers a complaint.")
- The court held that this "discrimination based on union activity constitutes an unfair labor practice. . . ." (The original sentence continued with the words "under NLRA §§ 8(a)(1) and (3), 29 USC §§ 158(a)(1) and (3).")
- "The 10-K reports of these companies made no reference to this investigation. . . ." (The original sentence continued with the words "but affirmatively asserted various other matters.")

9.3 Use four dots — a period plus three ellipsis dots — when you've omitted material following a sentence, but the quotation continues. (No space goes before the first dot [the period].)

- "Seeking the admission of video and photographs of a witness is hardly unusual. . . . [A]ttacking a witness's demeanor, if relevant, is a fully acceptable and expected litigation tactic." (The original passage reads: "Seeking the admission of video and photographs of a witness is hardly unusual. Although to seek the admission of this evidence solely so that the witness is made to appear 'evil' may cross the line, there is nothing

in the record that shows this purpose. On the contrary, attacking a witness's demeanor, if relevant, is a fully acceptable and expected litigation
tactic.")

- "The American court system is complex. Each state runs its own separate
  system of courts; no two state systems are exactly alike. . . . What makes
  matters even more mixed up is the double system of courts in this country: state and federal." (In the original passage, this additional sentence
  came where the ellipsis dots now appear: "The details of court structure
  can be quite technical and confusing, even to lawyers.")
- "The Council of State Governments has proposed, and a number of state
  legislatures have approved, three constitutional amendments. . . . These
  proposals, clearly a reaction against recent decisions of the Supreme
  Court, reflect a spirit of localism for whose counterpart we would have to
  look to the sectional struggles before the Civil War or even to the position
  of the states under the Articles of Confederation." (The quoter has omitted a complete sentence where the ellipsis appears.)

10. Apostrophe — 2 common uses, 2 common misuses

Using Apostrophes

10.1 Use an apostrophe to indicate the possessive case.

- The district court's refusal to give a requested jury instruction is reviewed for an abuse of discretion.
- She insisted that she had had no knowledge of the methamphetamine
  concealed in the truck's gas tank.
- The staffers' responsibility was to handle both agencies' telephone calls,
  including the three calls that originated from the Lopezes' home.

10.2 Use an apostrophe to mark the omission of one or more characters, especially in a contraction.

- You won't drive the nail straight if you don't hold it straight, and so also
  you won't achieve an effective system of law unless you give some heed to
  principles of legality.
- Many lawyers use these estate-planning solutions, and many who don't
  use them don't understand why they don't.
- Back in the late '80s, the claimant was stopped at two o'clock in the
  morning for driving under the influence.

Preventing Misused Apostrophes

10.3 Generally, don't use an apostrophe to form a plural. (But dot your i's
and cross your t's.)

- **Not this:** The evidence showed the applicant's intent to adopt a mark
  that suggests to purchaser's a successful mark already in use by another.
  But this: The evidence showed the applicant's intent to adopt a mark
  that suggests to purchasers a successful mark already in use by another.
- **Not this:** The Smith's will attend the Jones' open house. **But this:** The
  Smiths will attend the Joneses' open house.
- **Not this:** In the 2010's no zone is so intimate, personal, or private that it
  is immune from the staring eye of the law. **But this:** In the 2010s no zone

is so intimate, personal, or private that it is immune from the staring eye of the law.

10.4 Don't drop necessary apostrophes.

- **Not this:** Jean Forney then visited one of the hotels many shops. **But this:** Jean Forney then visited one of the hotel's many shops.
- **Not this:** Reynolds went immediately to the Johnsons house. **But this:** Reynolds went immediately to the Johnsons' house.

11. Question Mark — 1 use, 1 misuse

Using Question Marks

11.1 Use a question mark after a direct question.

- Does it make sense to talk about evolutionary change in the history of law?
- When is there no right answer to a question of law?
- In determining a contract's "plain meaning," should a court look to general linguistic usage in the nation or in the particular locality? Should the court consider meanings attached to words by people in a particular occupation, religion, or ethnic group? Which meaning should be used if M and X are not members of the same group? Should this question be resolved on the basis of which party had superior knowledge, charging that party with knowledge of the meaning that the other side might attach to the language?

Preventing Misused Question Marks

11.2 Don't use a question mark after an indirect question.

- **Not this:** She asked whether anyone present had seen the accident? **But this:** She asked whether anyone present had seen the accident.
- **Not this:** He wondered whether the weapon in question was the one he had confiscated from the athletic dorm? **But this:** He wondered whether the weapon in question was the one he had confiscated from the athletic dorm.

12. Exclamation Point — 1 use, 1 misuse

Using Exclamation Points

12.1 Use an exclamation point after an exclamatory word, phrase, or sentence — especially when quoting someone else.

- Before plunging into the sea, the captain shouted, "We're going over now!"
- Within seconds, there were cries: "Help! Man overboard!"

Preventing Misused Exclamation Points

12.2 Generally, don't use an exclamation point to express your own surprise or amazement.

- **Not this:** Yet they can't support this argument! **But this:** Yet they can't support this argument.

- **Not this:** Despite this overwhelming precedent, the court held otherwise!
  But this: Despite this overwhelming precedent, the court held otherwise.

13. Period — 3 uses

13.1 Use a period to end a sentence that is neither a question nor an exclamation.

- European legal scholars make much of the distinction between public and private law.
- But as many common-law scholars have pointed out, the distinction seems less and less relevant as time goes on.

13.2 Use a period to indicate abbreviations such as *Mr.*, *Ms.*, *Mrs.*, etc.

- This theory was first put forward by Dr. Jurgen Schafer.
- Though she had a PhD, she preferred to be called "Ms. Wheelock."

13.3 Put the period outside parentheses or brackets that enclose only part of a sentence, but inside parentheses or brackets that enclose a complete sentence.

- The Court has upheld a statute prohibiting local casinos from advertising in a way that encourages residents to visit the casinos (as opposed to encouraging tourists).
- A will has no effect on joint-tenancy property because the will is purely a testamentary conveyance (effective only at death, at which time the decedent's rights in the property evaporate).
- A plaintiff who establishes negligence but not malice also has to provide competent evidence of actual damages. (This changes the common-law rule that damages would be presumed by law for injury to reputation and did not require proof.) Actual damages may be awarded not only for economic losses but also for injury to the plaintiff's reputation in the community and for personal humiliation and distress.

14. Brackets — 3 uses, 1 misuse

Using Brackets

14.1 Use a pair of brackets in a quotation to enclose an editorial comment, correction, explanation, interpolation, substitution, or translation that was not in the original text.

- "The action arose *ex delicto* [in tort], not *ex contractu* [from a contract]." (The quoter has supplied translations.)
- Justice Rehnquist, for the Court, declared: "We hold that insofar as [the federal provisions] directly displace the States' freedom to structure integral operations in areas of traditional governmental functions, they are not within the authority granted to Congress." (The quoted matter originally used the word *they*; the quoter has substituted *the federal provisions*.)
- Maldanado is responsible for all "drugs [she] personally handled or anticipated handling and for drugs involved in additional acts that, being reasonably foreseeable by [her], were committed in furtherance of the conspiracy." (The quoted matter originally used the words *he* and *him* — the pronouns used in the statute; the quoter has substituted *she* and *her*.)

14.2 Use a pair of brackets around any character that you change in or add to quoted material.

- The search-warrant requirement arose from the Founders' understanding that "[p]ower is a heady thing, and history shows that the police acting on their own cannot be trusted." (In the quoted material, *Power* began the sentence and was uppercase.)
- The court also cautioned that any interpretation should guard against "chang[ing] the meaning, since this would go beyond mere interpretation." (In the quoted material, the phrase was "We caution that courts must not change the meaning. . . .")
- As Justice Rehnquist said in dissent in *Kassel*, the Court's present balancing approach "arrogate[s] to this Court functions of forming public policy, functions that, in the absence of congressional action, were left by the Framers of the Constitution to state legislatures." (The quoted matter used the word *arrogated*; the quoter has changed the word to *arrogates* to fit the syntax.)

14.3 Use a pair of empty brackets to show the deletion of part of a word.

- The Supreme Court has repeatedly held that an essential function of the warrant is to "assure[] the individual whose property is searched or seized of the lawful authority of the executing officer, his need to search, and the limits of his power to search." (The quoted material actually used the form *assures*.)
- When a case becomes moot, the federal courts "lack[] subject-matter jurisdiction over the action." (The quoted material actually used the singular *lacks* after the singular subject *a federal court*.)

Preventing Misused Brackets

14.4 Don't use brackets in place of ellipsis dots when one or more words have been deleted without any replacement language.

- **Not this:** "Although [] Jackson need not show a significant injury, he must have suffered at least some injury." **But this:** "Although . . . Jackson need not show a significant injury, he must have suffered at least some injury." (Several words have been deleted: *despite the foregoing arguments*.)
- **Not this:** "Several states provide by statute that compliance with applicable governmental statutes creates [] a presumption that the defendant exercised due care." **But this:** "Several states provide by statute that compliance with applicable governmental statutes creates . . . a presumption that the defendant exercised due care." (Several words have been deleted: *some legal implications, most importantly*.)

15. Slash (Virgule)—4 uses, 1 misuse

Using Slashes

15.1 Use a slash to separate the numerator from the denominator in a fraction.

- 1/4
- 15/365

15.2 Use a slash to separate alternatives (but remember to avoid *and/or*).

- The January/February issue is devoted to drafting better corporate documents.
- The employee/independent-contractor issue needs close consideration.
- The violent/nonviolent nature of the threat is often a determining factor.

15.3 In informal writing, use a slash as a shorthand signal for "per."

- 2,000/year
- $100/hour

15.4 In informal writing, use a slash to separate the elements in a date.

- 11/17/58
- 1/1/00

Preventing Misused Slashes

15.5 Don't use a slash when an en-dash or a hyphen would suffice.

- **Not this:** An essential element of the employer/employee relationship was lacking. **But this:** An essential element of the employer–employee relationship was lacking. (An en-dash works here because the employer and the employee aren't the same.)
- **Not this:** The lawyer/consultant worked for the company for no more than two months. **But this:** The lawyer-consultant worked for the company for no more than two months. (A hyphen works well here because *lawyer* and *consultant* refer to a single person.)

APPENDIX B

Four Model Documents

MEMORANDUM

TO: Weymouth Kirkland
          Howard Ellis
FROM: Steven C. Seeger
DATE: December 21, 1997
RE: Evidence: Admissibility of Police Reports Containing Hearsay

> The deep issue (§ 22) is a statement of the precise problem in 75 or fewer words.

Question Presented

In New York, a document is inadmissible when offered for its truth if it does not fall within an exception to the hearsay rule, or if it contains an opinion that the declarant would be unqualified to give in court. Two reports prepared by the McLean County Sheriff's Office state that the car driven by Heather Grimsby, who has sued our client, slid off the road because of icy road conditions. Are the reports admissible?

> The short answer completes the introduction begun by the deep issue. The writer concretely summarizes the answer, along with the obstacles ahead.

Short Answer

Probably. They seem to fall within both the business-records exception and the public-documents exception to the hearsay rule—as well as the still-valid but little-used common-law exception. The doubtful point will be the rules governing documents that contain opinions. But these rules do not necessarily make the documents inadmissible because either of two points is probably true: (1) the officer adequately observed the site and was qualified to form an opinion; or (2) the report does not rise to the level of an opinion.

Because we wish to introduce the reports into evidence, this memorandum will discuss three ascending hurdles that we must overcome to admit them: (1) authentication, (2) hearsay, and (3) opinions.

> In the discussion, the writer details each aspect of the problem—what steps must be taken, what other information needs to be gathered, and what counterarguments will have to be addressed.

Discussion

1. Authentication

We will need to authenticate the two police reports before the court can admit them into evidence. Fortunately, the procedure for authenticating official writings in New York is not complicated. A properly attested copy of an official record is self-authenticating as long as we satisfy five elements: (1) the document must purport to be a copy of an official record; (2) a certificate must be attached to the copy; (3) the certificate must state that the signatory is a public custodian of official records; (4) the certificate must state that the document is a true and accurate copy of an original, official record; and (5) the certificate must bear a presumptively authentic signature and seal.[1]

---

1   N.Y. Civil Practice Law and Rules ("C.P.L.R.") § 4540; *see also* Randolph N. Jonakait et al., *New York Evidentiary Foundations* 65 (1997).

Our copy of the police reports doesn't include an official certification. Because we hadn't yet done so, this morning I sent a letter (attached) requesting a properly attested copy of the reports so that the authentication requirement will not bar their admission.

2. Hearsay

As out-of-court statements offered for their truth, the police reports are inadmissible unless they fall within one of the exceptions to the hearsay rule. Fortunately, two possible exceptions arguably cover these reports—the business-records exception and the public-documents exception.

A. *Business-Records Exception*

The business-records exception is by far the most widely used avenue for admitting police records into evidence.[2] Section 4518 of the N.Y. C.P.L.R. sets out the basic requirements of the business-records exception:

> (a) *Generally.* Any writing or record, whether in the form of an entry in a book or otherwise, made as a memorandum or record of any act, transaction, occurrence or event, shall be admissible in evidence in proof of that act, transaction, occurrence or event, if the judge finds that it was made in the regular course of any business and that it was the regular course of such business to make it, at the time of the act, transaction, occurrence or event, or within a reasonable time thereafter. All other circumstances of the making of the memorandum or record, including lack of personal knowledge by the maker, may be proved to affect its weight, but they shall not affect its admissibility. The term "business" includes a business, profession, occupation and calling of every kind.

Based strictly on the text of the statute, three prerequisites are necessary for this exception: (1) the report must have been made in the regular course of business (i.e., it must reflect a routine, regularly conducted business activity); (2) it must have been the regular course of business to make such reports (i.e., it must be made according to established procedures); and (3) the person must have made the report at or near the time of the recorded event.[3] We must satisfy each of these requirements before the court will admit the police reports into evidence.

The first challenge will be selecting a witness who can lay the necessary foundation. As the New York Court of Appeals noted in *People v. Kennedy*,[4] the statute is "silent as to who, if anyone, must introduce a business record." At least one thing is clear: the exception does *not* require that we call the author of the business record.[5]

Relegating citations to footnotes (§ 28) lets the text flow without constant interruption.

---

2   *See, e.g., Federal Ins. Co. v. Ramirez,* 492 N.Y.S.2d 335, 338 (Sup. Ct. 1985) ("Police reports are admissible pursuant to the business-records exception to the hearsay rule.").
3   *See People v. Cratsley,* 653 N.E.2d 1162, 1166 (N.Y. 1995).
4   503 N.E.2d 501, 506 (N.Y. 1986).
5   *See Johnson v. Lutz,* 170 N.E. 517, 518 (N.Y. 1930) ("The purpose of the Legislature . . . was to permit a writing or record, made in the regular course of business, to be received in evidence, without the necessity of calling as witnesses all of the persons who had any part in making it."); *Kennedy,* 503 N.E.2d at 506 (same); *Gagliano v. Vaccaro,* 467 N.Y.S.2d 396 (App. Div. 1983) (holding that a police report prepared by a police officer who subsequently died was inadmissible, not because of the officer's unavailability, but

This flexibility is especially welcome in our case, given that Officer Howard cannot prevent us from offering his report as a business record. We must present someone familiar with the office routine who can testify that accident reports are routinely made and that it is a regular business practice of the department to make such reports.

If we can find a knowledgeable witness, I expect that we can meet all three requirements. Surely the preparation of accident reports is a regular practice of the sheriff's office, and I strongly suspect that they are prepared according to well-established procedures (as indicated by the use of a form, the type of information recorded, etc.). The reports were certainly made at or near the time of the event—all the reports show that they were prepared within an hour or two of the accident.

But the three requirements in the statutory text will not be the only obstacle. Many years ago, the Court of Appeals added an additional wrinkle to the business-records exception in *Johnson v. Lutz*.[6] The plaintiff there brought a wrongful-death action as a result of an automobile collision. To support his version of the accident, the defendant offered a report filed by an officer who had arrived at the scene shortly after the crash. The trial court admitted the report over the plaintiff's objection.

But at the start of a sentence or paragraph is an effective transition.

The Court of Appeals then confronted the question whether the police report fell within the business-records exception. The court concluded that the report "was not made in the regular course of any business, profession, occupation or calling" because it included the statements of third parties who were under no business duty to provide accurate information.[7] The court placed special importance on the fact that the police officer did not have personal knowledge of the events recorded in his report and that he obtained information from witnesses at the scene:

> The policeman who made it was not present at the time of the accident. The memorandum was made from hearsay statements of third persons who happened to be present at the scene of the accident when he arrived. It does not appear whether they saw the accident and stated to him what they knew, or stated what some other persons had told them.[8]

Even though the police officer was under a duty to record correct information, the court reasoned, the details of the accident came from bystanders who were under no business duty to report the accident accurately. The court ultimately held that the business-records exception does not cover police reports that are based on the observations of bystanders, reasoning that such informants lack the business duty of accuracy that is the very reason for reasoning that exception.[9]

Although the court in *Johnson* used the "made in the regular course of any business" language as its springboard, the problem in *Johnson* was really one of double

---

because the information was provided by unidentified bystanders); *see also* Michael M. Martin et al., *New York Evidence Handbook* 833 (1997); Robert A. Barker & Vincent C. Alexander, *Evidence in New York State and Federal Courts* 634 (1996).

6 170 N.E. 517 (N.Y. 1930).
7 *Id.* at 518.
8 *Id.*
9 *See id.* (observing that the exception "was not intended to permit the receipt in evidence of entries based upon voluntary hearsay statements made by third parties not engaged in the business or under any duty in relation thereto").

hearsay: the police report (hearsay) contained statements made by third parties (also hearsay). The business-records exception did not cover this additional level of hearsay because the informants were under no business duty to accurately describe how the accident happened. Because the informants had no business-related obligation to provide accurate information, their description of the accident lacked the special guarantee of reliability that justifies this and other hearsay exceptions.[10]

Topic sentences like this one lead the reader along the writer's train of reasoning.

➤ Lower courts have attempted to sharpen the rule of *Johnson* in more recent years, with varying degrees of success. The following is probably the most common recitation of the *Johnson* rule:

> Police reports may be admissible as business records if the police officer was a witness to the events disclosed in the record or if the person giving the police officer the information contained in the report was under a business duty to relate the facts. Otherwise the facts recited in a statement may be proved by a business record only if the statement qualifies as a hearsay exception, such as an admission.[11]

The *Johnson* case has proved to be a serious bar to the admission of police reports. In more than a dozen recent cases, courts have held that particular police reports were inadmissible because (1) the officer did not witness the accident, and (2) the reports contained statements by third parties who were under no business duty to provide accurate information.[12] To say the least, "it is now well settled that a police accident report, which is based upon information given to the investigating officer by [third parties], is not admissible as a business record . . . ."[13]

Still, the McLean County police reports should qualify as admissible evidence under a *Johnson* analysis. The press release from the McLean County sheriff's office does include a second layer of hearsay because it records statements made by several deputies: "Sheriff's Deputies state that Heather Grimsby . . . lost control of the vehicle she was driving due to the icy conditions." But this statement plainly falls within the business-records exception because the deputies, like the sheriff, were under a business duty to provide accurate information about the accident.[14]

The admissibility of the report prepared by Officer Howard (including the original report with the diagrams, and the supplemental report) is slightly more complicated. Unlike the press release from the sheriff's office, the report from Officer

---

10 *See id.* (not considering whether another hearsay exception, such as that relating to excited utterances, might have covered the statements made to the police officers).

11 *See Stevens v. Kirby*, 450 N.Y.S.2d 607, 611 (App. Div. 1982).

12 *See Liguori v. City of New York*, 672 N.Y.S.2d 916 (App. Div. 1998); *Antonik v. New York City Hous. Auth.*, 652 N.Y.S.2d 33 (App. Div. 1997); *Mooney v. Osowiecky*, 651 N.Y.S.2d 713 (App. Div. 1997); *Aetna Cas. & Sur. Co. v. Island Transp. Corp.*, 649 N.Y.S.2d 675 (App. Div. 1996); *Hatton v. Gassler*, 631 N.Y.S.2d 757 (App. Div. 1995); *Flores v. Pharmakitis*, 618 N.Y.S.2d 293 (App. Div. 1994); *Sansevere v. United Parcel Serv., Inc.*, 581 N.Y.S.2d 315 (App. Div. 1992); *Conners v. Duck's Cesspool Serv., Ltd.*, 533 N.Y.S.2d 942 (App. Div. 1988); *People v. Dyer*, 513 N.Y.S.2d 211 (App. Div. 1987); *Turner v. Spaide*, 485 N.Y.S.2d 593 (App. Div. 1985); *Auer v. Bienstock*, 478 N.Y.S.2d 681 (App. Div. 1984); *Stevens*, 450 N.Y.S.2d 607; *Murray v. Donlan*, 433 N.Y.S.2d 184 (App. Div. 1980); *Toll v. State*, 299 N.Y.S.2d 589 (App. Div. 1969).

13 *Mooney*, 651 N.Y.S.2d at 714.

14 *See People v. Jackson*, 338 N.Y.S.2d 760 (App. Div. 1972) (holding that a police report was admissible under the business-records exception even though the officer who prepared the report was not the officer who obtained the information); *see also* Michael M. Martin et al., *New York Evidence Handbook* 838 (1997).

Howard does not contain a second level of hearsay. The officer did not record or rely on the statements of third parties when preparing his report. In fact, all the parties had already left the accident site by the time Officer Howard arrived. The officer simply viewed the scene with his own eyes and recorded his personal observations. Because the patrolman did not rely on hearsay when preparing the business record, the report would not seem to present the sort of problem encountered by the Court of Appeals in *Johnson*.

I do have slight concern about the admissibility of this report because there is some rather loose language in the caselaw that a court could misconstrue. For example, the court in *Turner* offered the following recitation of the business-records exception: "Police reports are admissible as business records if the reporting officer *witnesses the accident* or if the person who relayed the information to the officer was under a business duty to do so."[15] Obviously, Officer Howard did not witness the accident, and he did not receive the information from a witness who was under a business duty to report information (or from anyone at all, for that matter). So a strict reading of *Turner* might lead a court to conclude that the report prepared by the officer is inadmissible.

> This memo shows unusually mature and thorough legal analysis.

But this language should not create a genuine problem. What matters under the business-records exception is not whether the officer viewed the accident per se, but whether the officer had personal knowledge of the events that he recorded. In other words, the relevant inquiry is whether the police officer gained knowledge of the subject of his report by direct observation or by talking with a collateral source. If the officer learned about the accident by discussing it with others, then the officer's report itself depends on hearsay, and thus the source of the information must also fall within an exception or else the report is inadmissible. If, on the other hand, the police officer directly observed the facts that he recorded, then there is no second level of hearsay, and thus there is no additional bar to the admission of the report.

The caselaw bears out the theory that the *Johnson* line of analysis is directed at whether the officer had personal knowledge of the events memorialized in the report. In *Bracco v. Mabstoa*,[16] an officer who arrived at the scene of a slip-and-fall accident recorded that the exit steps of the bus had slush on them and that the bus was on a steep incline.[17] The court allowed the police report into evidence even though the officer did not witness the accident, because the report was based on his personal observations.[18] Similarly, the court in *D'Arienzo v. Manderville*[19] allowed into evidence a police report that recorded the position of the cars immediately after an accident, even though the officer had not witnessed the collision itself: "[W]e note that the report was based on the personal observations of the scene by [the officer], not on

---

15 *Turner*, 485 N.Y.S.2d at 594 (emphasis added); *see also Conners*, 533 N.Y.S.2d at 942–43 (same); *Stevens*, 450 N.Y.S.2d at 611 (reciting the standard as whether the police officer "was a witness to the events disclosed in the record").

16 502 N.Y.S.2d 158 (App. Div. 1986).

17 *Id.* at 161.

18 *Id.* ("The references with respect to both the slush present on the steps and the position of the bus were, furthermore, derived from the personal observations of the . . . police officer and were not hearsay elicited from some unknown informant.").

19 484 N.Y.S.2d 171 (App. Div. 1984).

hearsay statements, and made by a person who was under a business duty to make the report."[20]

In light of this caselaw, the Howard report should satisfy the requirements of the business-records exception even though he did not witness the accident. The report is based entirely on the officer's direct observation of the crash site and does not rely on the statements of third parties. The Howard report, in other words, does not present the sort of double-hearsay problem encountered by the court in *Johnson*.

B. *Public-Documents Exception*

As an alternative, we could argue that the police reports satisfy the public-documents exception. Unlike the broad exception for business records, the statutory exception for public documents (§ 4520) is rather limited in New York:

> When a public officer is required or authorized, by special provision of law, to make a certificate or an affidavit to a fact ascertained, or an act performed, by him in the course of his official duty, and to file or deposit it in a public office of the state, the certificate or affidavit so filed or deposited is prima facie evidence of the facts stated.[21]

Admitting the police reports under this section may prove difficult.[22] By its terms, the statute applies only to "a certificate or an affidavit," which could be construed to exclude an investigative report.[23] But reports have been allowed under this provision in medical contexts.[24] A bigger problem might be that § 4520 applies only to records that are filed with "the state," which the court might construe to exclude political subdivisions. These issues may help explain why no New York court has addressed whether police reports fall within the guidelines of the statute.

C. *Common-Law Exception*

We may have more success if we argue that the reports satisfy the common-law exception, which was not superseded by statute.[25] Under the common-law exception, a public document is admissible "when a public officer is required or authorized, by statute or nature of the duty of the office, to keep records of acts or transactions occurring in the course of his official duty."[26] Not many cases address the common-law

[Margin note, left side:] Bridging words and phrases (§ 25) are especially important to show how the sections fit together.

---

20 *Id.* at 173; *see also Stevens*, 450 N.Y.S.2d at 611 ("The police reports . . . were inadmissible insofar as they contained hearsay statements relevant to ultimate issues of fact not within the personal knowledge of the sheriff deputies."); Robert A. Barker & Vincent C. Alexander, *Evidence in New York State and Federal Courts* 634 (1996) (observing that the contents of a business record are admissible if "the maker of the record had personal knowledge of the matter recorded").

21 N.Y. C.P.L.R. § 4520.

22 *See* Michael M. Martin et al., *New York Evidence Handbook* 833 (1997).

23 *But see Kaiser v. Metropolitan Transit Auth.*, 648 N.Y.S.2d 248, 250 (Sup. Ct. 1996) (observing that "the admissibility of a government investigatory report under this provision has not been definitively addressed in New York"); *Cramer v. Kuhns*, 630 N.Y.S.2d 128 (App. Div. 1995) (same).

24 *See Broun v. Equitable Life Assurance Soc'y of the U.S.*, 504 N.E.2d 379 (N.Y. 1986) (admitting an autopsy report); *People v. Brown*, 634 N.Y.S.2d 84 (App. Div. 1995) (admitting a report from the Medical Examiner's Office).

25 *See* N.Y. C.P.L.R. § 4543.

26 *People v. Michaels*, 667 N.Y.S.2d 646, 648 (Crim. Ct. 1997); *see also* Richard T. Farrell, *Richardson on Evidence* 688 (1995).

exception, and seemingly none has involved an accident report prepared by the police.[27] Yet the McLean County police reports appear to satisfy all the requirements—police officers are "public officers" who are "required or authorized" to keep records of important events in the community, such as automobile accidents. If we lay an adequate foundation, we should be able to admit the reports under this common-law exception.

3. Opinion

Even if the police reports fall within one of the exceptions to the hearsay rule, the court will not admit them if they are excluded by some other evidentiary bar. The New York rules regarding opinions impose a significant but not insurmountable barrier to the admission of the McLean County police reports.

Under New York law, a document is inadmissible if it contains opinions that the declarant would be unable to give on the witness stand.[28] Courts have not been shy about barring police reports under this rule. In fact, courts have repeatedly excluded police reports that contained opinions on the grounds that the officer could not have testified to that opinion in open court.[29] Such cases generally arise when a police report contains an officer's opinion about the cause of the accident. Such a report is admissible only if the opinion was based on "postincident expert analysis of observable physical evidence," and only if the officer was qualified to give the opinion.[30] At least two courts have excluded police reports containing opinions on ultimate issues of fact because that evidence invaded the jury's exclusive province to decide factual issues.[31]

The *Murray* case illustrates the approach that New York courts take.[32] The trial court allowed the plaintiffs to present a report prepared at the scene by an officer who concluded that the defendants were driving too fast and had failed to yield the right-of-way. The appellate court held that the admission of the report was error because the movants had failed to prove both that the officer was qualified to give the opinion and that his opinion was based on an expert analysis of physical evidence.[33]

---

27 *See Kozlowski v. City of Amsterdam*, 488 N.Y.S.2d 862 (App. Div. 1985) (holding that a report prepared by the Medical Review Commission of the State Commission of Corrections was admissible under the common-law exception); *People v. Brown*, 488 N.Y.S.2d 559 (Mad. Cnty. Ct. 1985) (holding that a police laboratory report fell within the common-law exception).
28 *Stevens*, 450 N.Y.S.2d at 611–12.
29 *See, e.g., Szymanski v. Robinson*, 651 N.Y.S.2d 826, 827 (App. Div. 1996); *Murray*, 433 N.Y.S.2d at 190.
30 *See Szymanski*, 651 N.Y.2d at 827; *Hatton*, 631 N.Y.S.2d at 758; *Conners*, 533 N.Y.S.2d at 943; *Murray*, 433 N.Y.S.2d at 190.
31 *See Van Scooter v. 450 Trabold Road, Inc.*, 616 N.Y.S.2d 129 (App. Div. 1994); *Stevens*, 450 N.Y.S.2d at 611–12.
32 433 N.Y.S.2d 184.
33 *Murray*, 433 N.Y.S.2d at 190; *see also Szymanski*, 651 N.Y.S.2d at 827 (holding that a police report, which concluded that the defendant's car had collided with the plaintiff's vehicle, was inadmissible because the movant offered no proof of the officer's qualifications); *Mancuso v. Compucolor, Inc.*, 567 N.Y.S.2d 694 (App. Div. 1991) (excluding a police report because the movant made no showing that the officer was qualified to testify as to the location of the accident); *Van Scooter*, 616 N.Y.S.2d at 130 (excluding a police report that opined that the accident was caused by the decedent's "inattention" because it invaded the province of the jury).

Although courts usually exclude police reports that contain opinions, a few courts have reached results that favor our position. In *Miller v. Alagna*,[34] the Appellate Division allowed a detective to testify that, in his opinion, the defendant's vehicle had not struck the plaintiff. The court concluded that the officer was qualified to give such "postincident expert analysis" based on his 21 years of training and experience as a police officer.[35] Although *Miller* dealt with live testimony, rather than a police report, the court's holding is helpful because it establishes that a police officer may be qualified to provide expert analysis of an accident scene based on years of service as an officer.[36]

Given these two cases, *Murray* and *Miller*, we can expect that the Grimsbys will argue that the police reports are inadmissible because they give opinions about the underlying facts. In particular, the plaintiffs could object to language in each report stating that Heather Grimsby lost control of the vehicle "due to the icy road condition." The Grimsbys could argue that, in this passage, the officer inserted an opinion about the underlying cause of the collision—evidence that must be excluded in the absence of proof that the officer adequately studied the scene and that he was qualified to give such an opinion.

We could respond in at least two ways. First, we could argue that this statement is not really an opinion but rather a reasonable inference based on concrete facts that the officer directly observed at the scene.[37] According to the accident reports, the highway was "ice covered" because of "freezing rain." The Grimsby vehicle, traveling downhill in such conditions, failed to properly navigate a curve in the road, rotated 180 degrees (at least), and went off the roadway backwards. In light of the hazardous weather conditions, the rotation and location of the car, and the curvature and declining elevation of the road, the conclusion that the driver lost control because of the icy road conditions seems more like a reasonable inference based on the facts than an opinion that would require extensive analysis by an expert.

Second, if the court were to conclude that the statement rises to the level of an opinion, we could argue that the officer adequately observed the scene and that he was qualified to render such an opinion. Proving that the officer adequately studied the site will be difficult because he is dead. But perhaps we could adequately support the point by focusing on the many details that he recorded. We could also present evidence that he was qualified to make such a conclusion based on his years of training and experience on the force.

Even if we persuade the court that the opinion was based on an expert analysis of the facts that the officer was qualified to give, we may have trouble because of his unavailability. In *In re Raymond Schaeffner*,[38] a purported creditor of an estate sought to admit into evidence a scientific report prepared by the local police department. The court concluded that the report qualified as a business record but barred its admis-

34 609 N.Y.S.2d 650 (App. Div. 1994).
35 *Id.* at 651.
36 *See also D'Arienzo*, 484 N.Y.S.2d at 173 (allowing the admission of a police report in which the officer concluded that the accident had occurred in the northbound lane).
37 *See Bogdan v. Peekskill Community Hosp.*, 642 N.Y.S.2d 478, 482 (Sup. Ct. 1996) (observing that "[f]actual findings and inferences which reasonably flow therefrom are admissible").
38 410 N.Y.S.2d 44 (Surr. Ct. 1978).

sion because "that portion of the report containing the detective's opinion must be stricken since the detective was unavailable for cross-examination."[39] If the plaintiffs argue this point, we may have the best success arguing that these isolated passages from the Surrogate's Court should not be accorded precedential value in the Supreme Court.

Conclusion

We have a good chance of admitting the McLean County police reports. The authentication of the reports will be simple, as long as we get a certified copy of the reports from their custodian. The hearsay rule should not be a barrier either, as long as we offer a foundation witness who can properly attest to each of the requirements. The rules regarding expert opinions may be a concern, but we may succeed if we argue that the reports do not contain opinions or, if they do, that the officer adequately studied the scene and was qualified to give an expert analysis of the cause of the accident.

Conclusion sums up and also suggests what the next steps are.

---

39 *Id.* at 48. *But see Hessek v. Roman Catholic Church of Our Lady of Lourdes*, 363 N.Y.S.2d 297 (Civ. Ct. 1975) (holding that a medical report was *admissible* even though the doctor was unavailable because a contrary holding "would be unconscionable").

**In the United States District Court
For the Eastern District of Texas
Sherman Division**

ACCESS YES!, INC. and SALLY BURTON, Plaintiffs, vs. PURLEY RESTAURANTS, INC. d/b/a THURGOOD'S, Defendant.	§ § § § § § § § § § § § § §	CIVIL ACTION NO.: 4:00-CV-368

**Defendant's Motion for
Summary Judgment and Brief in Support**

Summary

In ruling on this motion, the court faces two issues—all else being peripheral:

The deep issues state the dispositive points on page one.

- **Wheelchair Lift.** A building that predates the ADA (1992) must remove architectural barriers only if the changes can be made "without much difficulty or expense." Thurgood's restaurant, built in 1982, has a raised bar that is visible to and serves everyone in the restaurant. Burton, a wheelchair user, demands access to the bar through either a lift ($60,000 in annual lost revenues) or a ramp ($496,000 in annual lost revenues). Is such an accommodation required?

- **Toilet-Stall Renovation.** Burton also demands that Thurgood's enlarge the restrooms so that the toilet stalls—which are now individual tiled rooms—would have a larger axis for the turning of wheelchairs. This measure would force the restaurant to close for four to seven days ($40,000 to $70,000 in lost revenue) to gut and renovate the restrooms ($50,000 to $80,000 in cost, depending on structural loads). Is such an accommodation required under the ADA?

Plaintiff Sally Burton is the president of the corporate plaintiff, Access Yes!, a watch-dog group for people with disabilities. (The plaintiffs are collectively referred to here as "Burton.") Burton seeks to have Thurgood's remove various alleged architectural barriers from its restaurant in Plano, Texas. The restaurant was built a decade before the Americans with Disabilities Act ("ADA") was enacted. When built, the restaurant was in full compliance with all laws and regulations then in effect.

The ADA is principally directed to new construction, but it also requires existing facilities to remove architectural barriers to the extent that removal is "readily achievable"—that is, if it can be easily accomplished without much difficulty or expense.

All but two of Burton's complaints about the restaurant have been remedied: (1) increasing the size of a stall in the women's restroom, and (2) providing alternative access (other than steps) to a raised bar area. Neither of those remedies is readily achievable. The restroom stalls are permanently built in, and resizing them would mean completely gutting and rebuilding the entire restroom. Meanwhile, providing access to the bar would require a ramp 8 feet wide and 21 feet long. The restaurant would have to remove some 32 seats, at enormous cost to the restaurant, including extraordinary and ongoing lost revenue.

The ADA does not require access to the raised bar because the restaurant provides the same services and decor in other, accessible areas of the restaurant usable by everyone.

Since the restaurant has removed all the barriers to the extent readily achievable, and since removal of the remaining barriers is not readily achievable, Burton's claims fail as a matter of law.

The Material Facts

In the complaint, Access Yes! asserts that it represents persons who have disabilities and who use wheelchairs.[1] Its purpose is to "make businesses and governmental entities compliant with the Americans with Disabilities Act and. . . the Texas Accessibility Standards in the State of Texas."[2] Sally Burton, the president of Access Yes!,[3] is unable to walk and uses a wheelchair.[4]

The defendant, Thurgood's, owns and operates casual-dining restaurants, including the Plano restaurant at issue here.[5] Built in 1982, it has a bar area at its center.[6]

Burton originally complained that the restaurant had various architectural barriers. She had four complaints: (1) no striped access aisle and no clear, accessible route to the building from the designated handicapped parking spaces;[7] (2) no level landing at the front entry, and a threshold at the front entry that precluded entry by some people in wheelchairs;[8] (3) an inadequate turning radius in the handicapped stalls in

---

1 Pls.' Compl. ¶ 1.
2 Deposition of Sally Burton, p. 10, lines 7–10 (App. 51) (part of the transcript of the Deposition of Sally Burton is attached at Appendix pages 49–58 and is fully incorporated into this motion).
3 Burton Dep. p. 10, line 14 (App. 51).
4 Pls.' Compl. ¶ 4.
5 Deposition of Ronald Dumbarton, p. 8, lines 4–11 (App. 61) (part of the transcript of the Deposition of Ronald Dumbarton is attached at Appendix pages 59–66).
6 Dumbarton Dep. p. 9, lines 7–9 (App. 62); Decl. of Bert Savo ¶ 3 (App. 44).
7 Pls.' Compl. ¶ 7.
8 Id.

the restrooms, as well as inadequate hardware in those stalls;[9] and (4) a bar area inaccessible to persons in wheelchairs because using it means going up three stairs.[10]

Complaints #1 and #2 have since been resolved. First, Thurgood's has modified its parking area to provide more handicapped parking, has added a striped aisle or lane from the handicapped parking area to the front entrance, and has added both a curb cut and a ramp that is gently sloped and painted a color that contrasts with the parking lot and the sidewalk.[11] Burton acknowledges that the parking lot is now in compliance.[12] Second, Thurgood's has also altered the front door to provide a separate, fully accessible entrance that is wide and well marked.[13] Burton has agreed that the front entrance is now in compliance.[14]

Part of complaint #3 has been remedied. Thurgood's has changed the hardware in the handicapped stalls of the restrooms and has moved the water closet in each of those stalls so that it is an appropriate distance from each wall.[15]

But Thurgood's cannot mollify Burton on all aspects of complaint #3: it is impossible, as a practical matter, to increase the size of the handicapped stalls to enlarge the turning radius.[16] The restroom stalls are not the typical ones in which a metal partition is simply placed between several toilets.[17] Rather, each stall is a separate room within the restroom, constructed of permanent, floor-to-ceiling walls, with a vaulted ceiling that is made of hard cement plaster instead of wallboard.[18] And the ceiling has recessed lighting built into it.[19] Any attempt to increase the size of the handicapped stalls would require Thurgood's to completely gut and rebuild all its restroom facilities.[20] Such a project could require the restaurant to close for as many as four to seven days and would cost at least $50,000 to $80,000, depending on the structural loads encountered.[21] The restaurant would lose about $10,000 per day if it were required to close.[22]

As for complaint #4, Thurgood's has found it impossible, or at least not readily achievable, to provide independent wheelchair access to the raised bar area. Burton has suggested that a platform lift should be installed, asserting that this would solve the alleged problem.[23] But a platform lift would have to be operated by using a keyed switch that relies on positive, constant pressure.[24] Such a device would be of no use to someone who, for example, is in a mechanical wheelchair and cannot use his or

---

9 *Id.*
10 *Id.*
11 Savo Decl. ¶ 3 (App. 44).
12 Burton Dep. p. 32, line 16 through p. 33, line 14 (App. 52–53).
13 Savo Decl. ¶ 3 (App. 44–45).
14 Burton Dep. p. 34, lines 1–11 (App. 54).
15 Savo Decl. ¶ 3 (App. 44–45).
16 *Id.* at 3–4.
17 *Id.*; Affidavit of Bill Spears ¶ 8 (App. 3).
18 Savo Decl. ¶ 4 (App. 45); Spears Aff. ¶ 8 (App. 3).
19 Savo Decl. ¶ 4 (App. 45); Spears Aff. ¶ 8 (App. 3).
20 Savo Decl. ¶ 4 (App. 45); Spears Aff. ¶ 8 (App. 3); Declaration of William E. Mottle ¶ 3 (App. 24–25).
21 Mottle Decl. ¶ 3 (App. 24–25).
22 Declaration of John Attenborough ¶ 3 (App. 47–48).
23 Burton Dep. p. 53, lines 18–24 (App. 55).
24 Spears Aff. ¶ 12 (App. 4).

her hands to operate the keyed switch.[25] So platform lifts could not serve as the sole means of accessibility to a raised area in a public accommodation.[26] Lifts are also unsightly, sometimes difficult to maintain, and potentially unsafe.[27] A platform lift could pose a serious problem in a fire: if the platform lift were the only means of egress (as Burton has proposed), people with disabilities might not be able to leave quickly enough, since the lift must be operated by one person at a time.[28]

The other possible solution would be to construct a ramp to the bar area.[29] But a ramp—a means of egress under the city building code—would have to comply with that code as well as the ADA.[30] Under the combined requirements of the city code and the ADA, a ramp may have a slope no greater than one inch of rise for every foot of run.[31] Since the elevation to get to the bar is 21 inches,[32] a ramp to reach that height would need to be 21 feet long.[33] Also, there must be a flat, level landing, at least six feet long, at the base of the ramp, and five feet long at the top. Therefore, at least 32 feet of floor space would be needed to construct the ramp.[34] The only floor space that could conceivably be used for a ramp does not have enough space for a straight ramp of that length.[35] This means that the ramp would have to have a full turnaround, with an intermediate landing area that is at least five feet long.[36]

A ramp would also have to be at least 44 inches wide, according to the city code.[37] In this case, since the ramp would have to include a turnaround, it would be twice as wide as a straight ramp, meaning that it would be at least 88 inches wide. Allowing for eight inches of sidewalls (four inches for each section of the ramp), the ramp would use a floor space that is at least eight feet wide.[38] Given the necessary length and width of a legal ramp, any such ramp would take up one complete section of the restaurant's dining area, which now accommodates at least 32 patrons at a time.[39]

The cost of constructing the ramp itself would be at least $20,000.[40] And since each seat in the restaurant typically generates gross revenue of $15,500 per year, the restaurant could lose annual gross revenues of $496,000 (based on the average sales per seat).[41] Even if Thurgood's could install the platform lift as Burton has suggested, the installation would cost at least $35,000 and would cause the restaurant to lose at

---

25 *Id.* at 12–13.
26 *Id.*
27 Savo Aff. ¶ 5 (App. 45).
28 *Id.*
29 Spears Aff. ¶ 14 (App. 5).
30 *Id.*
31 *Id.* ¶ 15 (App. 5).
32 *Id.*
33 *Id.*
34 *Id.*
35 *Id.*
36 *Id.*
37 *Id.*
38 *Id.* ¶ 16 (App. 5–6).
39 *Id.*
40 Mottle Aff. ¶ 4 (App. 25).
41 Attenborough Decl. ¶ 3 (App. 47).

least four seats.[42] This loss in seating would result in annual lost sales of $62,000.[43] And since Thurgood's is a casual-dining restaurant with a multitude of serious competitors, taking away seats—which will increase customers' waiting time for a table—might well cause the restaurant to lose customers forever.[44] The effect on the business would be permanent—even catastrophic.[45]

Despite Burton's complaints, all the services offered at the bar are available to the general public throughout the restaurant.[46] For example, a patron in a wheelchair, even if not seated in the bar area, can have an alcoholic beverage and can see the television screens that are on display throughout the restaurant.[47] The video games that were formerly at the bar have been removed; they are no longer available anywhere in the restaurant.[48] Thurgood's ensures that the services available at the bar are made available throughout the restaurant, in all the seating areas.[49] The restaurant has never received a complaint, other than this one, from anyone with a disability who claimed not to be able to enjoy any of the goods and services there.[50]

Argument and Authorities

Argumentative writing begs for full sentences as headings, which advance the reasoning.

A. The ADA does not require full access to existing buildings.

Thurgood's acknowledges that the ADA requires public accommodations to remove architectural barriers under certain circumstances. Although the restaurant at issue is a public accommodation, not every architectural barrier must be removed.

Title III of the ADA generally grants rights to disabled customers to have access to businesses.[51] It became effective in 1992.[52] By that time, this restaurant was over ten years old. Directed mainly at new construction, the ADA also contains various requirements for existing buildings that are remodeled. But this isn't a case in which the design and construction of a new building is at issue. Nor is it a case in which a modification to a building has invoked the requirements of the ADA. This case involves only the issue of the extent to which an existing building must be modified to remove some of the building's attributes that are alleged to be architectural barriers.

The ADA does require existing buildings to remove some architectural barriers, but not all such barriers. A business must remove architectural barriers only if doing so is "readily achievable."[53] That is, a barrier in an existing building must be removed

---

42 Savo Decl. ¶ 5 (App. 45); Mottle Decl. ¶ 4 (App. 25).
43 Attenborough Decl. ¶ 3 (App. 47).
44 Declaration of James Allen ¶ 4 (App. 43).
45 *Id.*
46 *Id.* ¶ 3 (App. 42).
47 *Id.*
48 *Id.*
49 *Id.*
50 *Id.*
51 42 USC §§ 12181 et seq. (App. 67 et seq.).
52 *See, e.g.,* 42 USC § 12182, Hist. and Statutory Notes (App. 76).
53 42 USC § 12182(b)(2)(A)(iv) (App. 74).

only if the removal is "easily accomplishable and able to be carried out without much difficulty or expense."[54] The relevant regulations specify:

> A public accommodation shall remove architectural barriers in existing facilities . . . where such removal is readily achievable, i.e., easily accomplishable and able to be carried out without much difficulty or expense.[55]

This requirement to change existing buildings is designed to be, and must be interpreted as, less rigorous than the tests for accessibility to new buildings.[56]

B. The proposed modifications of the restrooms and the bar are not readily achievable.

In this case, the regulations show that the proposed changes in the restroom stalls and the elevated bar are not readily achievable. For instance, the ADA Accessibility Guidelines ("ADAAG"), promulgated by the U.S. Department of Justice, specifically approve, as an "alternative stall design," the type of handicapped stalls currently used at the restaurant.[57] The ADAAG and its related regulations are standards by which to measure compliance with the ADA.[58] Although the stalls might not comply with the ADA if they were being built today, they fully complied with the law that existed when they were built, and because they qualify as an alternative stall design, they comply with current law.[59]

The regulations also speak to the issue of the elevated bar:

> [I]n alterations, accessibility to raised or sunken dining areas, or to all parts of outdoor seating, is not required provided that the same services and decor are provided in an accessible space usable by the general public and are not restricted to use by people with disabilities.[60]

Here, the summary-judgment evidence shows that the services provided by the bar are available to everyone throughout the restaurant.[61]

The Department of Justice's section-by-section analysis of the ADA states even more clearly that a "public accommodation would generally not be required to remove a barrier to physical access posed by a flight of steps, if removal would require extensive ramping or an elevator."[62] In fact, the Department of Justice's analysis provides a strikingly relevant example:

---

54 42 USC § 12181(9) (App. 69); 28 CFR § 36.304(a) (App. 79).
55 28 CFR § 36.304(a) (App. 79).
56 U.S. Department of Justice's Section-by-Section Analysis of the ADA, 28 CFR pt. 36, app. B, § 36.304, at 608 ("28 CFR app. B") (App. 90).
57 Spears Aff. ¶ 9 (App. 3); ADA Accessibility Guidelines § 4.17.3 (28 CFR pt. 36, app. A, at 42 (p. 531 of 28 CFR)) (App. 85).
58 *See, e.g., DeFrees v. West*, 988 F.Supp. 1390, 1393 (D. Kan. 1997).
59 ADA Accessibility Guidelines § 4.17.3 (28 CFR pt. 36, app. A, at 42 (p. 531 of 28 CFR)) (App. 85).
60 *Id.* § 5.4 (28 CFR pt. 36, app. A, at 59 (p. 549 of 28 CFR)) (App. 87).
61 Allen Decl. ¶ 3 (App. 42).
62 28 CFR app. B § 36.304, at 609 (App. 91).

Thus, where it is not readily achievable to do, the ADA would not require a restaurant to provide access to a restroom reachable only by a flight of stairs.[63]

So the ADA would certainly not require a restaurant to provide such access to a bar when, as in this case, it is not readily achievable and the bar's services are available throughout the restaurant.

This is not a situation in which Thurgood's is attempting to thwart an obligation that can be easily met. Thurgood's has already shown its desire to accommodate the disabled and to comply with the ADA. All Thurgood's new restaurants are built to comply with the ADA.[64] And it has taken significant steps to ensure access to the restaurant at issue and to remove as many architectural barriers as possible.[65] But creating wheelchair access over the flight of steps to the bar, while increasing the size of the handicapped stalls in the restroom, is not practically possible—much less readily achievable.

This case is similar to *Slaby v. Berkshire*,[66] in which the plaintiffs were disabled members of a country club who could not gain access to the locker room and certain other areas that were reachable only by stairs. Although the country club made alternative lockers available, the plaintiffs demanded that the club install an elevator at a cost of $80,000. The court held that the elevator was not required. The analysis admittedly centered on a different section of the ADA (one dealing with elevators in two-story facilities), but the analysis is on point:

A court order to build an elevator is not necessary because . . . only 300 of the 10 million golfers in the United States use wheelchairs, and the adapted . . . facilities are sufficient to discharge the Club's obligations under the ADA.[67]

Similarly, in this case, Thurgood's has made sufficient alternative arrangements. And requiring the extreme expense of the requested modifications is unnecessary, would be ineffective, and is not required under the ADA.

The nature of Thurgood's business is also important.[68] Thurgood's is a restaurant, and Burton is, ultimately, complaining only about the bar. Those with disabilities can get through the door (the highest priority of the barrier-removal regulations).[69] Once they are through the door, all the restaurant's goods and services are available to them, including alcohol. Because of the nature of the facility, the drinks at the bar can easily be delivered, and often are delivered, to patrons at tables in other parts of the restaurant. The television screens at the bar are visible throughout the restaurant, and there are additional television screens throughout the facility. Hence, Burton is asking Thurgood's to undertake severe measures, at great cost, so that the disabled

---

63 *Id.*
64 Savo Decl. ¶ 7 (App. 46).
65 *Id.*
66 928 F.Supp. 613 (D. Md. 1996), *aff'd without opinion*, 110 F.3d 60 (4th Cir. 1997).
67 *Id.* at 616.
68 42 USC § 12181(9)(D) (App. 70).
69 28 CFR app. B § 36.304 (p. 610 of 28 CFR)) (App. 92).

will gain little or nothing. The ADA and its accompanying regulations simply do not require this.

C. Thurgood's provides its goods and services through alternative means.

Having proved that the requested barrier removal is not readily achievable, Thurgood's appreciates that it must make its goods and services available through alternative methods.[70] That is what makes the case unique: Thurgood's has always made liquor readily available to all the tables in the restaurant. No one is left out—except, of course, those who are underage or cannot be served alcohol for reasons unrelated to this case. Thurgood's "alternative" methods are, for all practical purposes, primary methods. People receive drinks at their tables all the time without showing a desire to go to the bar. Since relocation of the activity is an acceptable alternative means of access,[71] Thurgood's bar services comply with the law.

D. Burton's state-law claims also fail as a matter of law.

The Texas Accessibility Standards essentially mirror the federal standards, with which Thurgood's is in compliance. Therefore, Thurgood's is in compliance with the state standards, and Burton's claims must fail as a matter of law.

Burton has brought an add-on claim under § 121.003(a) of the Texas Human Resources Code, claiming to have been denied the full use and enjoyment of the restaurant. But she has not shown, and cannot prove, that she has been denied the full use and enjoyment of the facility. Burton has admitted that she has never been denied access to the restaurant because of a disability.[72] And once again, all the goods and services at the bar are available throughout the restaurant, to all patrons, including those with disabilities. Because the facility is accessible to and functional for people with disabilities,[73] it complies with the state and federal accessibility guidelines.[74] So Burton's claims under the Texas Architectural Barriers Act fail as a matter of law.

E. Thurgood's is entitled to summary judgment.

Thurgood's has shown that it is willing to comply—and has complied—with the ADA and state and local law in the design and construction of new facilities, and in the modifications it has made to the restaurant. It has also shown that the requested modifications to the restaurant and bar are not readily achievable. There are no genuine issues of any material fact. Because Thurgood's is entitled to judgment in its favor as a matter of law, the Court should dismiss this case.

---

70 42 USC § 12182(b)(2)(A)(v) (App. 74); 28 CFR § 36.305(a) (App. 80).
71 28 CFR § 36.305(b)(3) (App. 80).
72 Plaintiff Access Yes!, Inc.'s Responses to Defendant's First Set of Requests for Admissions, Requests 9 & 10 (App. 98).
73 *See* Tex. Rev. Civ. Stat. art. 9102, § 3(b).
74 Spears Aff. ¶ 17 (App. 6).

Conclusion

The ADA does not require Thurgood's to undertake the onerous steps that Burton is demanding. Likewise, ADAAG and the other regulations obviate the proposed measures. The crux of this case is whether Thurgood's should be forced to spend more than $35,000 and suffer lost business of about $62,000 per year to install a wheelchair lift that has proved ineffective in granting unassisted access to disabled people. Since the wheelchair lift will not fully work, the issue becomes whether Thurgood's should be forced to wipe out an entire section of its restaurant—at a loss of nearly $500,000 per year—to install a ramp over the stairs that lead to the bar. In its regulations, the Department of Justice tells us that a restroom, though accessible only by a flight of steps, need not be made accessible to wheelchairs if extensive ramping is necessary. Yet this case is about access to a bar whose goods and services are available to everyone throughout the restaurant. There is little if anything to be gained by installing a ramp to the bar (or a lift, for that matter), and the cost would be enormous. As for the handicapped stalls currently in the restrooms, they meet the Justice Department's approved alternative-stall design and are practically impossible to retrofit. Because the changes Burton demands are not readily achievable, they are not required under the ADA or state law.

Thurgood's respectfully asks the Court to enter summary judgment in its favor, ordering that Burton take nothing by way of this suit, dismissing this case with prejudice, awarding Thurgood's its costs and attorney's fees in an amount to be determined later, and awarding Thurgood's all other relief to which it is entitled.

Respectfully submitted,

The motion ends with a fairly detailed prayer, asking the judge to take specific action.

_____

Michael A. Logan
Michael L. Atchley
ATTORNEYS FOR DEFENDANT

APPENDIX B3: APPELLATE BRIEF

IN THE
UNITED STATES COURT OF APPEALS
FOR THE FIFTH CIRCUIT

No. 12-1026

JUAN ALVAREZ, M.D.,
Plaintiff–Appellant,

vs.

LAKESHORE MEDICAL CENTER, ROBERT L. SOMERSET, M.D., and
ROBERT L. SOMERSET, M.D., P.A.,

Defendants–Appellees.

Appeal from the United States District Court
for the Southern District of Texas,
Houston Division

Brief for Appellees

Statement of Jurisdiction

In the district court, federal-question jurisdiction existed under 28 U.S.C. § 1331 because the case arose under 42 U.S.C. § 1981 and 42 U.S.C. § 1320a-7b. The district court had jurisdiction over the pendent state-law claims under 28 U.S.C. § 1367(a).

Appellate jurisdiction exists under 28 U.S.C. § 1291 because this appeal is from the district court's final judgment.

Statement of the Issues

Issue 1: Waiver of Appellate Complaint

Under federal and local rules, an appellant waives its complaint unless its opening brief provides record references, reasons for reversal, and supporting authorities. In his opening brief, Alvarez omits all record references, fails to articulate any understandable reason for reversal, and cites as authority a single jurisdictional statute. Has Alvarez waived his appellate complaint?

Issue 2: No Evidence of Civil Conspiracy

Federal and state law precludes doctors from soliciting or receiving money for patient referrals. Alvarez claimed that Somerset and his P.A. violated this law during a conspiracy to oust Alvarez from the P.A. or from a local hospital. Alvarez's only proof was that (1) Somerset talked to another doctor about joint practice, and (2) Somerset's father worked as a consultant for another physician. Does this evidence raise fact issues on illegality and on the other essential elements of conspiracy?

Multiple issues bear topical headings, which characterize the case while keeping the issues separate yet quickly identifiable.

Statement of the Case

A. Course of Proceedings and Disposition in the District Court

In June 2004, Dr. Juan Alvarez, an anesthesiologist, sued Lakeshore Medical Center, Dr. Robert Somerset, and Somerset's professional association in a Texas state court.[1] Alvarez alleged that termination of his services contract with the P.A. gave rise to various tort, contract, and statutory claims under Texas law.[2]

About a year later, Alvarez dismissed all his claims against Lakeshore, the hospital where he had worked.[3] At the same time, he amended his petition, for the first time alleging claims arising under federal statutes.[4] Based on federal-question jurisdiction, Somerset and the P.A. then timely removed this case to federal district court.[5]

In early October 2005, Somerset and the P.A. reported in a case-management plan that they were preparing a summary-judgment motion.[6] Later that month, the trial court entered a docket-control order setting January 5, 2006, as the deadline for joining new parties.[7]

In March 2006—almost two years after filing suit and three months after the deadline to join new parties—Alvarez again tried to amend his pleadings.[8] This time, he sought to add a new RICO claim and a new defendant, Somerset's father.[9] The trial court denied that amendment as untimely and unfairly prejudicial to the defendants.[10] On appeal, Alvarez does not challenge the trial court's denial of his motion to amend.[11]

In April 2006, Somerset and the P.A. moved for summary judgment on all six of Alvarez's claims.[12] After a response, a reply, and supplemental briefing, the trial court granted summary judgment on all six claims.[13] While Alvarez's brief is less than clear, he appears to appeal the court's decision on only one of those claims—that of civil conspiracy.[14]

---

1 *See* R. 68; *see generally* R. 55–68.
2 *See* R. 57–64.
3 *See* R. 84–85 (signed order of dismissal).
4 *See* R. 41 & 47 ¶ 6 (alleging racial discrimination under 42 U.S.C. § 1981); R. 38 (alleging violation of federal Medicare law under 42 U.S.C. § 1320a-7b(b)).
5 *See* R. 74–77.
6 *See* R. 177, 169.
7 *See* R. 179.
8 *See* R. 224–26 (Alvarez's motion for leave to amend).
9 *See* R. 224–26 (Alvarez's first amended complaint in federal court).
10 *See* R. 439–42.
11 *See* R. 640 (notice of appeal, challenging only the September 24, 1996 final judgment); *see also* Brief of Appellant at 2.
12 *See* R. 411–38 (summary-judgment motion); R. 28–48 (petition).
13 *See* R. 624–37, 638.
14 *See* Brief of Appellant at 2 (issue statement mentioning only this claim), 5–6 (argument mentioning only this claim).

B. Statement of Facts

In November 2001, the P.A., of which Somerset was president and sole shareholder,[15] agreed to become the exclusive provider of anesthesiology services at Lakeshore, a privately owned hospital.[16] The contract between the P.A. and the hospital required that all anesthesiologists working there sign an attached Independent Contractor Agreement between the physician and the P.A.[17] This agreement, which Alvarez signed,[18] allowed either party to terminate the contract "with or without cause" after 90 days' written notice.[19]

> Restate the dispositive facts relied on. This is not the place for a full rendering.

Shortly after Alvarez began working, other doctors began complaining about his work.[20] Indeed, some surgeons even refused to work with him.[21] As a result, arranging and rearranging work schedules became difficult.[22] On October 1, 2003, the P.A. notified Alvarez in writing that (1) his contract would end on January 4, 2004, more than 90 days later, and (2) his clinical privileges at the hospital would be unaffected.[23]

On appeal, Alvarez has apparently abandoned five of his six claims. The one claim that he mentions in his brief is civil conspiracy. While this claim is not explained, his trial-court complaint alleges that Somerset, the P.A., and the hospital conspired to exclude him from practicing anesthesiology or to cause the unlawful termination of his contract.[24] The unlawful acts alleged to be at the heart of this supposed conspiracy were "unlawful payments" from other physicians who sought to practice with the P.A. and at the hospital.[25]

C. Summary of Argument

Alvarez has waived all his arguments on appeal by filing a brief that:
  (1) provides no record references;
  (2) articulates no plausible or understandable grounds for reversal; and
  (3) cites no relevant caselaw, statute, or other authority.
When an appellant broadly fails in this way to adhere to the basic briefing requirements of the federal and local rules, this Court consistently refuses to reach the merits of the appellant's position, concluding that the party has waived all arguments on appeal. In some cases, the Court has also awarded damages under Rule 38. At a minimum, then, this Court should conclude that Alvarez has waived his sole complaint on appeal.

If this Court decides, however, to consider Alvarez's unsupported arguments, Alvarez has failed on appeal, as he failed in the trial court, to raise any genuine fact issues on civil conspiracy—the sole claim referred to in his brief. Even if the uniden-

---

15 *See* R. 47 ¶ 4; R. 410 ¶ 1.
16 *See* R. 407; R. 48 ¶ 2.
17 *See* R. 405; R. 390.
18 *See* R. 380.
19 R. 386 ¶ 7.
20 *See* R. 409 ¶ 5.
21 *See id.*
22 *See id.*
23 *See* R. 377.
24 *See* R. 34–35.
25 R. 24.

tified federal and state statutes mentioned by Alvarez prohibit *soliciting*, as well as *receiving*, money for patient referrals, there is no evidence that either Somerset or the P.A. committed this unlawful act or any other—a required element of a civil-conspiracy claim.

Specifically, there is no legal or factual support for the notion that Somerset acted unlawfully by discussing with another physician the possibility of a buy-in to Somerset's practice. Similarly, the fact that another physician paid consulting fees to Somerset's father for his assistance does not show that either Somerset or the P.A. acted unlawfully. Based on this record, the district court correctly granted summary judgment against Alvarez on his conspiracy claim, concluding that he had failed to raise a genuine fact issue on whether Somerset or the P.A. had committed any unlawful act.

Finally, as Somerset and the P.A. argued in the district court, Alvarez has failed to raise a genuine fact issue on several other essential elements of a conspiracy claim. First, under Texas law, an entity such as a professional association cannot conspire with its own agent. Yet the only alleged conspirators were the P.A. and its agent Somerset. So Alvarez could not, and did not, show that two or more persons participated in the alleged conspiracy—an essential element of a conspiracy claim. Second, Alvarez could not, and did not, show the required meeting of the minds between the alleged participants, Somerset and the P.A. Third, the conduct challenged by Alvarez did not, as a matter of law, further the conspiracy's alleged object—whether that object was terminating Alvarez's contract or excluding him from practice at the hospital.

Because the record raises no genuine fact issue on Alvarez's civil-conspiracy claim, the district court correctly granted summary judgment to Somerset and the P.A. For any one of several alternative reasons, this Court should uphold that judgment.

Argument and Authorities

Standard of Review

This Court reviews a summary judgment de novo, applying the same criteria the district court used.[26] Under Rule 56, a defendant may seek summary judgment by pointing to the absence of a genuine fact issue on one or more essential claim elements.[27] The rule mandates summary judgment if the plaintiff then fails to make a sufficient showing on each of those elements.[28]

If the evidence is merely colorable, or is not sufficiently probative, summary judgment is proper.[29] As the Supreme Court has made clear, a nonmovant cannot

---

26 *See Topalian v. Erhman*, 954 F.2d 1125, 1131–32 (5th Cir. 1992); *Dorsett v. Board of Trustees*, 940 F.2d 121, 123 (5th Cir. 1991).

27 *See Matsushita Elec. Indus. Co. v. Zenith Radio Corp.*, 475 U.S. 574, 586–87 (1986); *Leonard v. Dixie Well Serv. & Supply, Inc.*, 828 F.2d 291, 294 (5th Cir. 1987).

28 *See Celotex Corp. v. Catrett*, 477 U.S. 317, 322–23 (1986).

29 *See Anderson v. Liberty Lobby, Inc.*, 477 U.S. 242, 249–50 (1986); *Ruiz v. Whirlpool, Inc.*, 12 F.3d 510, 513 (5th Cir. 1994).

raise a genuine fact issue merely by showing "some metaphysical doubt" about the facts.[30] If the record as a whole could not lead a rational fact-finder to decide for the nonmovant, then no genuine fact issue remains for trial.[31] As this Court has observed, summary judgment "affords a merciful end to litigation that would otherwise be lengthy and expensive."[32]

Issue 1: Waiver of Appellate Complaint

Under federal and local rules, an appellant waives its complaint unless its opening brief provides record references, reasons for reversal, and supporting authorities. In his opening brief, Alvarez omits all record references, fails to articulate any understandable reason for reversal, and cites as authority a single jurisdictional statute. Has Alvarez waived his appellate complaint?

Alvarez has failed to provide this Court with any reason or authority for reversing the district court's judgment. By failing to meet this Court's most basic briefing requirements, Alvarez has waived any possible argument on appeal and has succeeded only in wasting the Court's valuable time.

A. Alvarez's brief violates all three of the minimum briefing requirements.

1. *Alvarez's brief fails to cite the record.*

Alvarez has failed to cite any record references, thus violating the federal and local rules requiring them.[33] Rule 28(a)(6) plainly requires that an appellant's brief provide, along with its contentions, "citations to the . . . parts of the record relied on."[34] As Local Rule 28 makes equally clear, every assertion "regarding matter in the record shall be supported by a reference to the page number of the original record where the matter relied upon is to be found."[35] Yet Alvarez's scant brief—even when alleging facts—contains no references to the original record, which is almost four inches high.[36]

The most egregious lack of record support appears in the factual section, in which Alvarez includes a string of unsupported allegations about "moneys paid," "moneys solicited," a consulting agreement between two nonparties, and a supposed "effort to extort money from incoming anesthesiologists."[37] While announcing that the summary-judgment evidence of civil conspiracy "is clear," Alvarez conspicuously fails to cite even one page of that supposedly clear evidence.[38]

> Full-sentence point headings enhance advocacy.

---

30 *Matsushita*, 475 U.S. at 586; *see also Little v. Liquid Air Corp.*, 37 F.3d 1069, 1075 (5th Cir. 1994) (en banc).
31 *See Matsushita*, 475 U.S. at 587; *Schaefer v. Gulf Coast Regional Blood Ctr.*, 10 F.3d 327, 330 (5th Cir. 1994) (quoting *Liberty Lobby*, 477 U.S. at 248).
32 *Fontenot v. Upjohn Co.*, 780 F.2d 1190, 1197 (5th Cir. 1986).
33 *See* Fed. R. App. P. 28(a)(4), (6); Loc. R. 28.2.3.
34 Fed. R. App. P. 28(a)(6).
35 Loc. R. 28.2.3.
36 *See* Brief of Appellant at 1–7.
37 *Id.* at 4–5.
38 *Id.* at 4.

2. *Alvarez's brief provides no reason for reversing the trial court's judgment.*

The second failing of Alvarez's brief is its lack of any comprehensible reason for reversing the trial court's judgment. Instead of pointing out evidence establishing some unlawful act, Alvarez misstates the trial court's conclusions. For example, the court's opinion does not, as Alvarez contends, acknowledge evidence of "multiple solicitations" by Somerset or the P.A. from "various anesthesiologists."[39] Instead, the opinion merely notes that Somerset once discussed with Robins, another anesthesiologist, a possible buy-in to Somerset's practice—an arrangement that was never again discussed and that never occurred.[40] Meanwhile, the district court's conclusion on conspiracy remains eminently sound: Alvarez failed to produce any evidence of any unlawful act, including any kickback or bribe for a patient referral.[41]

3. *Alvarez's brief cites no authority supporting reversal.*

Finally, and perhaps most astonishingly, Alvarez's brief fails to cite any relevant caselaw, statute, or other authority to support his position on appeal. Indeed, the only citation of any kind appears in Alvarez's statement of jurisdiction.[42] Again, Alvarez has directly violated the federal appellate rule requiring an appellant to include within the argument "citations to the authorities [and] statutes. . . relied on."[43]

While vaguely mentioning "state and federal statutes" in his two-page argument, Alvarez fails to even *name* these statutes and provides no discussion or analysis of them.[44] Alvarez's entire brief, which consists of slightly over six pages, cites not a single case from any court or any jurisdiction. It is thus even less acceptable than the brief criticized by this Court in *Carmon v. Lubrizol Corp.*—a brief that, unlike Alvarez's, at least contained "cryptic" record citations and actually cited one case:

> Counsel for Carmon has caused this Court and the opposing party to waste time and resources, yet has filed nothing more than a five-page "slap-dash" excuse for a brief—a brief that fails to raise even one colorable challenge to the district court's judgment. The brief starts with a Statement of Facts consisting only of cryptic citations to the record, then proceeds to an Argument consisting of selective quotes from *Harris*, and finally concludes with the bald assertion that the district court erred by failing to apply the standard reaffirmed in *Harris*—a patently inaccurate statement.[45]

B. By omitting from his brief any argument, record citations, and authorities, Alvarez has waived his argument on appeal.

As this Court has made clear, Rule 28(a) "requires the argument section of the appellant's brief to contain not only the party's contentions but also its 'reasons there-

---

39 R. 626–27.
40 *See* R. 627.
41 *See* R. 626–27.
42 *See* Brief of Appellant at 1–2.
43 Fed. R. App. P. 28(a)(6).
44 *See* Brief of Appellant at 5–7.
45 *Carmon v. Lubrizol Corp.*, 17 F.3d 791, 795 (5th Cir. 1994).

for, with citations to the authorities, statutes and parts of the record relied on.'"[46] In the absence of such support, this Court consistently refuses to consider the merits of the argument.[47]

While Alvarez mentions, without record reference, that he filed certain papers in the trial court, this Court has rejected efforts by parties to preserve appellate issues by asking the Court to refer to "previously filed legal and factual arguments."[48] Indeed, in *Yohey v. Collins*, the Court denied such a request, even by a pro se appellant:

> Yohey has filed this appeal pro se. He requests, in part, the adoption of previously filed legal and factual arguments. . . . Yohey has abandoned these arguments by failing to argue them in the body of his brief. "Fed. R. App. P. 28(a)(4) requires that the appellant's argument contain the reasons he deserves the requested relief 'with citation to the authorities, statutes and parts of the record relied on.'" Although we liberally construe the briefs of pro se appellants, we also require that arguments must be briefed to be preserved.[49]

Moreover, the required arguments and authority must appear in the appellant's opening brief.[50] The noncompliant appellant cannot somehow "undo" the waiver by complying with the rules only later, in the reply brief, because such belated compliance would leave the appellee with no fair opportunity to respond.[51]

Further, this Court has sometimes concluded that the filing of a brief presenting "no plausible challenge to the district court's judgment" may result in damages under Rule 38 for filing a frivolous appeal or under 28 U.S.C. § 1927 for unreasonably and vexatiously multiplying the proceedings.[52] In *Carmon*, for example, such sanctions were imposed against the appellant for filing "a five-page 'slap-dash' excuse for a brief" that included inadequate record citations and inaccurate statements about the trial court's application of the law.[53]

At a minimum, Alvarez's inadequate brief supports the conclusion that Alvarez has waived his sole appellate complaint. Moreover, if the Court concludes that damages are warranted against Alvarez for filing a frivolous appeal, then Rule 38 empow-

---

46 *Randall v. Chevron U.S.A.*, 13 F.3d 888, 911 (5th Cir. 1994).

47 *See, e.g., id.* (declining to reach the merits "[i]n the absence of logical argumentation or citation to authority"); *Besing v. Hawthorne*, 981 F.2d 1488, 1492 n.9 (5th Cir. 1993) (refusing to address the merits because appellants had offered "no authority to support this theory, and they made no attempt to set forth any legal argument to persuade us of its correctness"); *Gulf States Land & Dev., Inc. v. Premier Bank N.A.*, 956 F.2d 502, 508 (5th Cir. 1992) (finding waiver under Rule 28(a) because appellants had "failed to specify their contentions or identify the particular provisions of [the] statutes under which their claims [arose]"); *Texas Mortg. Servs. Corp. v. Guadalupe Savs. & Loan Ass'n*, 761 F.2d 1068, 1073 (5th Cir. 1985) (citing cases for the principle that if appellant violates Rule 28(a) by failing to analyze and support its contentions, then waiver applies); *Kemlon Prods. & Dev. Co. v. United States*, 646 F.2d 223, 224 (5th Cir. 1981) (refusing to reach the merits because appellant's brief addressed neither the merits nor the district court's reasoning).

48 *Yohey v. Collins*, 985 F.2d 222, 224–25 (5th Cir. 1993).

49 *Id.* (citations omitted) (quoting *Weaver v. Puckett*, 896 F.2d 126, 128 (5th Cir. 1990), and *Price v. Digital Equip. Corp.*, 846 F.2d 1026, 1028 (5th Cir. 1988)).

50 *See Forsyth v. Barr*, 19 F.3d 1527, 1537 (5th Cir. 1994).

51 *See id.*; *Conkling v. Turner*, 18 F.3d 1285, 1305 (5th Cir. 1994).

52 *See Carmon*, 17 F.3d at 792–95; *Travelers Ins. Co. v. Liljeberg Enters., Inc.*, 38 F.3d 1404, 1413 (5th Cir. 1994).

53 *Carmon*, 17 F.3d at 795.

ers the Court, after reasonable notice, to award Somerset and the P.A. just damages and double costs.

Issue 2: No Evidence of Civil Conspiracy

> Federal and state law precludes doctors from soliciting or receiving money for patient referrals. Alvarez claimed that Somerset and his P.A. violated this law during a conspiracy to oust Alvarez from the P.A. or from a local hospital. Alvarez's only proof was that (1) Somerset talked to another doctor about joint practice, and (2) Somerset's father worked as a consultant for another physician. Does this evidence raise fact issues on illegality and on the other essential elements of conspiracy?

The sketchy argument in Alvarez's brief appears to be limited to a complaint about the district court's ruling on his civil-conspiracy claim, which—as Alvarez notes—is addressed on pages 10–12 of the court's opinion.[54] This claim is alleged in Count Five of Alvarez's First Amended Petition.[55] If this Court decides that it must reach the merits of Alvarez's largely inscrutable position, Alvarez has failed to raise any genuine fact issue on his civil-conspiracy claim.

Alvarez's brief includes two vague, unsupported arguments on his conspiracy claim—neither of which raises any genuine fact issue for trial.

A. Contrary to Alvarez's first argument, the district court properly enunciated the legal standard and properly rejected Alvarez's contentions on payments.

In the three sentences that constitute Alvarez's first argument, he misstates both the evidence and the trial court's conclusions about it, departs from his previous position on the alleged "illegal act," and then—on that shaky foundation—stacks his conclusion that the court has erred.[56]

The district court plainly did not, as Alvarez contends, "acknowledge evidence of multiple solicitations by one or both of the Somerset Defendants of money from various individual anesthesiologists."[57] Instead, the court explained that the only evidence involving *any* conduct by either defendant was evidence of one discussion between Somerset and Robins, another anesthesiologist, about a possible buy-in to Somerset's practice.[58] As the district court observed, "the arrangement was never again discussed," and "Dr. Robins made no payments to Somerset or to the Hospital."[59]

Moreover, the court did not find, as Alvarez imagines, that cash was paid to Somerset or the P.A. in "one or two instances," and the court did not "surmise," as Alvarez puts it, that these "one or two" payments could be otherwise explained.[60]

---

54 *See* Brief of Appellant at 6 (citing, without record reference, pages 10–12 of the district court's opinion); R. 626–28 (opinion).
55 *See* R. 34–35.
56 Brief of Appellant at 5–6.
57 *Id.* at 5.
58 R. 626–27.
59 R. 627.
60 Brief of Appellant at 5–6.

Instead, as the opinion makes clear, the court found that eight or nine months after signing a contract with the P.A., Dr. Loehr entered into a consulting agreement with Somerset's *father.*[61] As the court noted, however, no money was ever paid either to Somerset or to the P.A.[62]

Alvarez further claims that the trial court "failed to recognize" that soliciting, as well as receiving, money for patient referrals may constitute a statutory violation.[63] But again, Alvarez has misread the opinion. As the trial court observed, the federal Medicare statute "prohibit[s] the knowing and willful solicitation of an illegal remuneration, including a kickback, bribe, or rebate, in exchange for referring an individual to a person for the furnishing of any item of service."[64]

As much as Alvarez would like to find fault with the district court's opinion, the court's focus on payments came directly from Alvarez's argument on summary judgment. The opinion accurately states Alvarez's argument on one of the five essential elements of civil conspiracy and the defendants' response to that argument: "Defendants argue that they are entitled to summary judgment because Plaintiff cannot demonstrate the existence of any unlawful act. Plaintiff responds that the alleged payments of illegal moneys constitutes the unlawful act."[65] While Alvarez refuses to acknowledge it now, he consistently argued in the trial court that the actual *payment* of money constituted the requisite illegal act:

- "The purpose or object of the conspiracy . . . was to exclude Dr. Alvarez from the practice of anesthesiology at the Hospital; *the illegal act in furtherance of that stated purpose was acceptance of payments from incoming doctors* . . . ."[66]

- "Payments Made to the PA Are (1) Highly Relevant to A Determination of Summary Judgment And (2) Illegal."[67]

- "Payments by Incoming Physicians Are Highly Relevant."[68]

- "The making of such payments . . . is both illegal and highly relevant to a determination of whether Defendants are entitled to summary judgment in this case. Such payments show that . . . ."[69]

- "Payments To Defendants Are Illegal."[70]

- "Tangible evidence exists that the PA solicited and received improper cash . . . ."[71]

Bullet lists are excellent graphic devices for attracting readers' attention.

---

61 *See* R. 626.
62 *See id.*
63 Brief of Appellant at 5; *see* 42 U.S.C. § 1320a-7b(b); R. 626.
64 R. 626.
65 R. 627–28 (citation omitted).
66 R. 465 ¶ 34 (emphasis added).
67 R. 465 ¶ H.
68 R. 465 ¶ H(i).
69 R. 464–65 ¶ 35.
70 R. 464 ¶ H(ii).
71 R. 464 ¶ 36.

- "Any receipt of funds by Somerset Jr., directly or indirectly, or by the PA from another anesthesiologist . . . would be a violation of this section [of the federal Medicare statute]."[72]

- "Any receipt of funds by Somerset Jr., directly or indirectly, or by the PA from another anesthesiologist . . . would be a violation of this section [of a Texas healthcare statute]."[73]

- "Any receipt of funds by Somerset Jr., directly or indirectly, or by the PA from another anesthesiologist . . . would be a violation of this section [of a Texas penal statute]."[74]

Based on these statements, the trial court correctly articulated Alvarez's argument and then patiently explained why none of the summary-judgment evidence showed that Somerset or the P.A. received any unlawful payments.[75]

Even if Alvarez were allowed on appeal to suddenly argue that the illegal act was the *solicitation* of money—consisting of an isolated discussion between Somerset and Robins about a possible buy-in to Somerset's practice—that discussion could not serve as the illegal act underlying a civil conspiracy. Such a discussion is not a "willful solicitation of an illegal remuneration" in exchange for a patient referral,[76] and it does not violate any other pertinent statute. Indeed, physicians—like lawyers—frequently buy into an established practice without violating any statute or ethical rule.[77] If such buy-ins are legal, then the mere discussion of one certainly cannot be illegal.

B. Alvarez's second argument, about consulting fees to a third party, raises no fact issue on whether Somerset or the P.A. committed any unlawful act.

The three sentences that constitute Alvarez's second argument have nothing to do with any conduct by either Somerset or the P.A., but instead relate to a consulting agreement between two third parties—Somerset's father and another physician named Loehr.[78] In his brief, Alvarez neglects to mention that five months before granting summary judgment, the court had denied his belated motion to add Somerset's father as a defendant.[79]

Now, as in the trial court,[80] Alvarez ignores his failure to plead that Somerset's father played any role in the alleged conspiracy. In his complaint, Alvarez alleged that the only conspirators were Somerset, the P.A., and the hospital.[81] Yet the record contains no evidence that Somerset's father accepted any payments on behalf of those

---

72 R. 464 ¶ 36(a).

73 R. 463 ¶ 36(b).

74 R. 462–63 ¶ 36(c).

75 *See* R. 626; *id.* at 352–76 (excerpts from depositions of Somerset and other anesthesiologists who worked with the P.A., all of whom testified that they had paid no money to either Somerset or the P.A.).

76 42 U.S.C. § 1320a-7b(b); *see* R. 626.

77 *See Herbert v. Newton Memorial Hosp.*, 933 F.Supp. 1222, 1225–26 (D.N.J. 1996); *In re Enrique M. Lopez, M.D.S.C.*, 93 B.R. 155, 157 (Bankr. N.D. Ill. 1988).

78 *See* Brief of Appellant at 6.

79 *See* R. 224–26 (Alvarez's April 1996 motion for leave to amend); R. 177, 169 (October 1995 case-management plan, in which Somerset and the P.A. state that they are preparing a summary-judgment motion).

80 *See* R. 465–66.

81 *See* R. 35.

alleged conspirators. Nor is there any evidence that Somerset's father played any role in terminating Alvarez's contract or hospital privileges.

As in the trial court, Alvarez relies on sheer speculation when he suggests that the consulting fees paid by Loehr to Somerset's father were a "sham" or a "pretext for otherwise unlawful payments."[82] Meanwhile, Alvarez ignores the fact that the only evidence about this consulting arrangement—an excerpt from Loehr's deposition—shows that the purpose of the arrangement was for Somerset's father, in exchange for fees, to share his experience and provide advice about specific cases.[83]

As the Texas Supreme Court has explained, an alleged conspirator "is not liable for an act not done in pursuance of the common purpose of the conspiracy."[84] There is no evidence that these consulting fees were paid in furtherance of the alleged conspiracy's purpose—which, according to Alvarez, was to exclude him from practice with the P.A. or at the hospital.[85] Indeed, the record suggests the opposite: Loehr did not begin paying the consulting fees until eight or nine months *after* he had signed his own contract with the P.A.[86] The only reasonable inference is that Loehr's payments had nothing to do with displacing Alvarez or otherwise affecting his practice.[87]

C. Alvarez fails to even mention other missing elements of his claim—each of which provides an alternative basis for upholding the judgment.

This Court can affirm the summary judgment on any one of the several different grounds raised below.[88] Yet Alvarez fails to even mention the other challenged elements of his civil-conspiracy claim—elements that were raised by Somerset and the P.A. in the district court.

Under Texas law, the five essential elements of civil conspiracy are:

    (1) two or more persons;

    (2) an object to be accomplished;

    (3) a meeting of the minds on the object or course of action;

    (4) one or more unlawful, overt acts; and

    (5) damages as the proximate result.[89]

As discussed above, the trial court concluded that Alvarez had failed to raise a fact issue on the fourth element—an unlawful, overt act.[90] But other essential elements were lacking as well. Whether the alleged conspiracy's purpose was to exclude Alvarez from practice or to cause the unlawful termination of his contract,[91] the record

---

82 Brief of Appellant at 6.

83 *See* R. 443–45.

84 *Carroll v. Timmers Chevrolet, Inc.*, 592 S.W.2d 922, 928 (Tex. 1979).

85 *See id.*; R. 34–35; R. 465 ¶¶ 34–35.

86 R. 444–45.

87 R. 444.

88 *See Coral Petroleum, Inc. v. Banque Paribas-London*, 797 F.2d 1351, 1355 n.3 (5th Cir. 1986); *Davis v. Liberty Mut. Ins. Co.*, 525 F.2d 1204, 1207 (5th Cir. 1976).

89 *West v. Brazos River Harbor Navigation Dist.*, 836 F.Supp. 1331, 1339 (S.D. Tex. 1993) (citation omitted), *aff'd*, 32 F.3d 566 (table) (5th Cir. 1994).

90 R. 627–28.

91 R. 34–35; R. 465 ¶¶ 34–35.

Paragraphs start with a topic sentence that transitions from the previous one.

raises no genuine fact issues for trial on several different elements of his conspiracy claim.

1. *Alvarez failed to show that two or more persons participated.*

Alvarez's proof fails on the very first element of civil conspiracy: that two or more persons were involved. As courts applying Texas law have consistently held, an entity such as a professional association cannot conspire with itself.[92] Hence, a conspiracy claim cannot be based on a meeting of the minds between an entity and its agents.[93]

Alvarez could not, therefore, establish a legally cognizable conspiracy claim by showing that the P.A. had a "meeting of the minds" with Somerset—its president and sole shareholder.[94] Instead, to sustain a conspiracy claim, Alvarez needed evidence of a meeting of the minds between Somerset or the P.A., on the one hand, and the hospital, on the other. There is no such evidence.

Evidence of this essential element was similarly lacking in *West v. Brazos River Harbor Navigation District.*[95] There, a federal district court in Texas granted a summary-judgment motion on a conspiracy claim because the plaintiff had failed to show that two or more parties were involved in the supposed conspiracy. The plaintiff alleged a civil conspiracy to terminate his employment with the Brazos River Harbor Navigation District. He claimed that the conspirators were (1) the district; (2) people who were agents of the district; and (3) defendants not affiliated with the district.

The trial court granted summary judgment in favor of the nondistrict defendants because the plaintiff had produced no evidence of a meeting of the minds between them and anyone associated with the district.[96] As the court explained, summary judgment was appropriate for the district and its agents as well "because, as a matter of law, an entity such as the District cannot conspire with itself."[97]

Similarly, this record contains no evidence that the hospital played any role whatsoever either in terminating Alvarez's contract with the P.A. or in allegedly excluding him from practice. Because the P.A. could not conspire with itself, summary judgment on the conspiracy claim was appropriate for the P.A. and its agent Somerset.

2. *Alvarez failed to show a meeting of the minds.*

To show a meeting of the minds between the alleged conspirators, a plaintiff must prove actual intent to participate in the conspiracy and to achieve its object."[98]

---

92 *See West*, 836 F.Supp. at 1340; *Hankins v. Dallas Indep. Sch. Dist.*, 698 F.Supp. 1323, 1330 (N.D. Tex. 1988); *Zentgraf v. Texas A & M Univ.*, 492 F.Supp. 265, 272–73 (S.D. Tex. 1980).
93 *See West*, 836 F.Supp. at 1340.
94 *See id.*
95 *See id.*
96 *See id.*
97 *Id.*
98 *See Schlumberger Well Surveying Corp. v. Nortex Oil & Gas Corp.*, 435 S.W.2d 854, 857 (Tex. 1968); *Times Herald Printing Co. v. A. H. Belo Corp.*, 820 S.W.2d 206, 216–17 (Tex. App.—Houston [14th Dist.] 1991, no writ); *West*, 836 F.Supp. at 1338.

The evidence must establish that the parties charged with conspiracy knew about the conspiracy to injure the plaintiff and intended to participate in it.[99]

There is no proof that the hospital even knew about—much less intended to participate in—some alleged conspiracy to exclude Alvarez from practice or to terminate his contract with the P.A. Further, there is no evidence that the hospital knew about, or had a meeting of the minds with anyone else about, the two events that Alvarez attempts to rely on as evidence—Robins's discussion with Somerset about a possible buy-in and Loehr's payment of consulting fees to Somerset's father. So the record fails to show that the hospital knew about either the object of the conspiracy or the alleged illegal course of action supposedly undertaken to achieve that object.

Again, Somerset cannot have had a meeting of the minds with the P.A. of which he was president and sole shareholder.[100] Because the record fails to raise a genuine fact issue about whether there was a meeting of the minds on the object or course of action underlying the alleged conspiracy, summary judgment was proper on that essential element of a conspiracy claim.

3. *Alvarez failed to show that any allegedly unlawful conduct was in furtherance of any stated purpose.*

To establish civil conspiracy, the plaintiff must also show that the allegedly unlawful act was carried out in furtherance of the stated object or purpose.[101] As the Texas Supreme Court has explained: "An alleged conspirator is not liable for an act not done in pursuance of the common purpose of the conspiracy."[102]

a. The challenged conduct did not further the termination of the contract.

If the object of the alleged conspiracy was to terminate Alvarez's contract, as Alvarez has sometimes alleged,[103] the undisputed facts show that Somerset and the P.A. achieved this "object" through the entirely lawful means of giving 90 days' written notice under Alvarez's Independent Contractor Agreement.[104] So even assuming that the consulting fees and the discussion of a buy-in were illegal, this conduct neither advanced nor was even necessary to the stated object of the "conspiracy."[105]

In *Times Herald Printing*, the Houston Court of Appeals reached a similar conclusion based on similar facts.[106] In that case, a news service had entered into contracts to provide the plaintiff, a newspaper, with daily features. Later, the news service entered into an exclusive contract with the plaintiff's rival newspaper. After signing the exclusive contract, the news service gave the required notice and then canceled its contracts with the plaintiff.

---

99 *See Schlumberger*, 435 S.W.2d at 857.
100 *See West*, 836 F.Supp. at 1340; *Hankins*, 698 F.Supp. at 1330; *Zentgraf*, 492 F.Supp. at 273.
101 *See Carroll*, 592 S.W.2d at 928.
102 *Id.* (citation omitted).
103 *See* R. 34–35; R. 464 ¶ 35.
104 *See Juliette Fowler Homes, Inc. v. Welch Assocs.*, 793 S.W.2d 660, 665 (Tex. 1990).
105 *See Brown v. City of Galveston*, 870 F.Supp. 155, 161 (S.D. Tex. 1994); *Jackson v. Radcliffe*, 795 F.Supp. 197, 209–10 (S.D. Tex. 1992); *Times Herald Printing Co.*, 820 S.W.2d at 217.
106 *See Times Herald Printing*, 820 S.W.2d at 217.

The plaintiff sued the rival newspaper on several theories, including civil conspiracy. On that claim, the plaintiff alleged that its rival newspaper and the news service had conspired to terminate its contracts. According to the plaintiff, they had achieved this object through a series of allegedly unlawful acts. The court of appeals affirmed the trial court's directed verdict on this claim, explaining that the cancellation of the plaintiff's contracts with the news service "was 'accomplished' by lawful means"—the news service had "merely exercised its contractual rights to terminate them upon proper notice."[107]

Relying on *Times Herald Printing*, the district court in *Jackson v. Radcliffe* reached the same conclusion on facts nearly identical to those at issue here.[108] In *Jackson*, the plaintiff, a physician, had entered into an agreement allowing him to provide radiology services at a hospital. The hospital terminated the contract, providing the required 90 days' notice. The plaintiff sued, alleging that other radiologists had conspired to have his contract terminated because he had refused to pay a fee for patient referrals and to participate in a threatened hospital boycott.[109]

The federal district court granted summary judgment for the hospital and the radiologists on the civil-conspiracy claim. As the court observed, "lawful cancellation of a contract accomplished by lawful means is not evidence of an agreement to commit an unlawful act."[110] In terminating Alvarez's contract, Somerset and the P.A. have likewise acted lawfully. On that basis alone, summary judgment was proper on Alvarez's conspiracy claim.

b. The challenged conduct did not further Alvarez's exclusion.

The undisputed facts establish that even if the object of the alleged conspiracy was to exclude Alvarez from practice at the hospital (as Alvarez has sometimes alleged),[111] neither of the allegedly illegal acts furthered this supposed object. Indeed, Alvarez's medical staff membership and clinical privileges at the hospital remained intact, even after all the alleged conduct occurred.[112]

In a similar case, *Gonzalez v. San Jacinto Methodist Hospital*, a Texas court affirmed a summary judgment against Gonzalez, an anesthesiologist who had sued a hospital for breach of contract and tortious interference.[113] Gonzalez alleged that termination of his employment, after another physician had obtained an exclusive contract, interfered with his contractual rights to staff privileges under the hospital's bylaws.[114] The court disagreed, explaining that even after the plaintiff's employment had ended, his "staff privileges remain[ed] intact, subject only to his ability to find a way to get employment in the Hospital."[115] As the court noted, Gonzalez might get

---

107 *Id.*
108 *See Jackson*, 795 F.Supp. 197.
109 *See id.* at 202.
110 *Id.* at 210.
111 *See* R. 465 ¶ 34.
112 *See* R. 377.
113 *See Gonzalez v. San Jacinto Methodist Hosp.*, 880 S.W.2d 436 (Tex. App.—Texarkana 1994, writ denied).
114 *See id.* at 440–41.
115 *Id.* at 440.

work in the hospital's eye clinic, might work through the exclusive provider, or might even obtain the exclusive contract himself.[116]

If the object of the alleged conspiracy was to terminate Alvarez's staff privileges, then under the reasoning of *Gonzalez*, those privileges were never terminated, meaning that the alleged object was never achieved. Moreover, neither of the two allegedly illegal acts—Somerset's discussion with Robins, and Loehr's consulting arrangement with Somerset's father—was undertaken in furtherance of this alleged object.

No matter which alternative is considered the alleged conspiracy's purpose, none of the challenged conduct was carried out in furtherance of that purpose. So for still another reason, summary judgment was proper on the conspiracy claim.

Conclusion

Alvarez has waived his appellate complaint by filing a brief that provides no record references, articulates no grounds for reversal, and cites no relevant authority. Based on this waiver, the Court should refuse to reach the merits of this appeal.

Even if this Court considers the merits, the record creates no genuine fact issue on civil conspiracy. As the trial court concluded, the evidence fails to show that Somerset or the P.A. committed any unlawful act. Indeed, not even an inference of illegality arises from either Somerset's discussion of a possible buy-in or a third party's payment of consulting fees to Somerset's father. Further, Alvarez has failed to raise a fact issue on several other essential elements of conspiracy—that two or more persons participated, that there was a meeting of the minds, and that any challenged conduct furthered the alleged object.

Therefore, for any one of several independent reasons, this Court should affirm the summary judgment.

Respectfully submitted,

_____

Beverly Ray Burlingame
COUNSEL FOR APPELLEES,
ROBERT L. SOMERSET, M.D., and
ROBERT L. SOMERSET, M.D., P.A.

The conclusion goes well beyond the poor but common "For all the aforementioned reasons...." It is concrete and conclusive.

116 *See id.* at 439–40.

APPENDIX B4: CONSUMER CONTRACT

TIME WARNER *Connect* Agreement

Topical table of contents helps the consumer find the relevant terms quickly.

Table of Contents

Parties

In this Agreement, the terms "you" and "your" refer to _____

_____ ,

and the terms "we," "us," and "our" refer to TIME WARNER *Connect*. For other definitions, see § 16.

Background

A bullet list is an attractive way to lay out a short list of contract recitals.

- We are in the business of offering residents of clustered communities a package of services that includes local and long-distance telephone services, cable television, and alarm services.

- You are the owner of the multi-unit residential property (the "property") known as _____ (described in *Exhibit A*).

- Both you and we wish to make our services available to residents of the property in accordance with this Agreement's terms and conditions.

- Entertainment service will be provided by our authorized affiliate. We are acting as a marketing, sales, and billing agent for the affiliate.

- Alarm service will be provided by an alarm-service provider that we will select. We are acting as a referral and billing agent for the provider.

The parties agree as follows:

Terms and Conditions

1   **Services**

We will offer the following services to your residents during the term of this Agreement. Residents may choose to purchase some services and not others. Residents need not subscribe to any of our services. Residents choosing to receive a service may be required to sign a customer-service agreement and a service order.

1.1   **Local Telephone Service.** We will offer local telephone service and custom communications features to you and your residents. We will provide you and each customer with a telephone number and a local telephone book. We will also provide you and each customer with the following:

(A) access to 911 features provided to local-exchange-service end-users in the same 911 service area;

(B) access to operator and directory assistance; and

(C) at a customer's request, a directory listing in the local telephone directory.

1.2   **Long-Distance Telephone Service.** We will offer long-distance telephone services to you and your residents. All "1+" long-distance calls made by customers may be routed over the long-distance networks that we select to

-1-

carry long-distance traffic. You understand that customers who subscribe to the long-distance service will not be able to access alternative long-distance providers by dialing "1+".

1.3   **Entertainment Service.** We will arrange for entertainment service to be offered to you and your residents by an entertainment-service provider. You acknowledge that the package of channels offered is subject to change depending on various factors, including changes in programming available to the entertainment-service provider, legal requirements to carry certain channels, and channel capacity.

1.4   **Alarm Service.** We will arrange for alarm service to be offered to you and your residents by an alarm-service provider. The alarm-service provider will install an alarm system in a unit when a resident orders monitoring service. The resident will enter into an agreement with the alarm-service provider.

1.5   **Additional Service.** We may decide to offer you and your residents additional services that can be delivered to your residents over our communications system. We will give you prior written notice of any additional service to be offered. The royalty fee for any additional services will be the same as the royalty fee for entertainment services unless we notify you that we wish to negotiate a different royalty fee. If we do, you and we must agree to a royalty fee (see § 3) before we will begin the additional service for residents.

> Here, the ubiquitous but much-litigated contract verb *shall* has been replaced by *will* (mandatory) and *may* (permissive). The result is a much clearer provision.

2   **Rates**

The initial rates to be charged the customers for the services will be our standard rates for the metropolitan area in which the property is located. Upon giving notice to customers, we or our affiliates may change rates for any service as legally allowable. Customers will be billed and are responsible for paying taxes, franchise fees, and other fees assessed in conjunction with the services.

3   **Royalty Fee**

We will pay you a royalty fee equal to a percentage of the gross collected revenues, as defined in *Exhibit B*. The royalty fee will be calculated for each preceding quarter within 30 days after the end of the calendar quarter during the initial term and during any renewal term. We will provide you with a quarterly statement of gross collected revenues detailing the sources of revenue. Once a year, you will be allowed to review and audit—during business hours at our offices—our records relating to the statement of gross collected revenues. Either you or we will correct any error by paying the deficient amount to the other by the 20th day of the month after the review or audit. We may deduct from a royalty fee any overdue amount payable by you for services we provided to you.

4   **Communications System**

4.1   **Construction, Installation, and Maintenance.** At no charge to you, we will have the communications system designed, constructed, installed (to the extent that existing wiring and facilities are not available), and maintained as necessary to provide the services to the property in accordance with industry standards and applicable laws. We will arrange to release any liens affecting how the communications system is designed, built, installed, or maintained; and we will do that within 30 days of receiving notice of any such lien. You will cooperate with us and the service providers in obtaining permits, licenses, consents, and other requirements that may be necessary for us to install and operate the communications system and provide services, and we will pay your reasonable costs of cooperating in this manner.

4.2   **Schedule.** We will begin establishing the communications system for each stage of the property according to the construction schedule described in *Exhibit C*. You will ensure that the control room described in § 5.6 is completed at your expense—with electric power and suitable for installation of our equipment—no later than 30 days before the date scheduled in *Exhibit C* for the first resident's occupancy. If the control room is not completed on time, you will be responsible for our extra costs resulting from the delay.

4.3   **Exclusive Control.** We or our service providers will retain full ownership of the respective components of the communications system—including all inside wiring installed on the property—as well as the exclusive right to control and operate the communications system and all other wiring, equipment, and facilities that we can use under § 5.4. You and we may not permit the communications system or any other wiring, equipment, or facilities to be used by any service provider other than those expressly permitted under this Agreement. The communications system will not be considered a fixture of the property. You must not access, operate, or move the communications system. You acknowledge that if a resident does not subscribe to the alarm service, the alarm-service provider may remove the alarm equipment from the resident's unit and install it in another unit. But if this occurs, the alarm-service provider must install a faceplate over the opening for that equipment.

5   **Your Basic Obligations; Grant of Easement and Incidental Rights**

5.1   **Easement.** You grant us a nonexclusive easement on the property for purposes of constructing, installing, operating, maintaining, and removing the communications system. You reserve the right to cross this easement and to grant other easements on the property, but other easements must not interfere with this easement granted to us. This easement covers only us, the entertainment-service provider, the alarm-service provider, and any subcontractor carrying out one of the easement's purposes on our behalf. We do not otherwise have the right to apportion the easement or permit access to the property by third parties. The easement's term ends when the initial term expires, but if we choose to extend the Agreement for the renewal term, the easement's term will end when the renewal term expires. At the time of signing this Agreement, you and we will also execute (1) an

Easement and Memorandum of Agreement (in the form of *Exhibit D*), and (2) a UCC-1 financing statement in favor of us and the service providers to demonstrate our ownership interests in the communications system. We may record these instruments at any time.

5.2   **Grant of Rights.** You acknowledge that we will spend substantial time, resources, and money in meeting our obligations under this Agreement, and that we are relying on your promises in this Agreement in order to recoup our investment by providing the services to the property and by collecting revenues from customers. You therefore grant us the following rights:

(A) the exclusive right to plan, construct, operate, maintain, and remove the communications system on the property;

(B) the exclusive right to offer local and long-distance telephone service— as well as custom communications features and other enhanced services—to residents, subject to applicable laws;

(C) the exclusive right to offer entertainment service and alarm service to residents, subject to applicable laws;

(D) the exclusive right to offer additional services to residents under § 1.5, subject to applicable laws; and

(E) the exclusive right for us—or for the entertainment-service provider or the alarm-service provider—to enter the property to market services to residents. This right will not prohibit others from entering the property for other purposes. All on-site solicitation under this paragraph will occur at reasonable times, will be conducted professionally, and will not impose unduly on the residents.

> List items are syntactic parallels: all are direct objects of the verb *grant*.

5.3   **Our Exclusive Rights.** You have not retained any interest in the property obligating or allowing you to grant any rights similar to or competitive with those granted in § 5.2. If any other provider of services obtains the right to offer services to the property by applicable laws, you may permit that provider to offer or provide any services required by those laws to the extent required. But during the Agreement's term you will not do any of the following:

(A) agree to promote, market, or sell services that compete with the services we provide;

(B) offer competing services within the property;

(C) grant a third party the right to offer competing services within the property; or

(D) allow residents to install or operate any system or device—including antennas and satellite dishes—capable of providing substitute services for the services we offer.

5.4   **Wiring Responsibility; Electricity.** You will appoint us as your agent to make the necessary arrangements with the local-exchange carrier to ensure your right to use, remove, and rearrange all existing carrier-owned wiring and cabling from the demarcation point to all locations on the property. (To this end, you will execute the letter of agency attached as *Exhibit G*.) You will allow us, at no charge, to use any wiring, poles, conduits, and other facilities or equipment that you own or have the right to use. We will provide, at the resident's request and expense, additional wiring or outlets within the units to add or change services or equipment locations. You will arrange for the local electric company to meter all equipment that we use, and we will pay the utility provider directly for electricity used.

5.5   **Marketing and Sales.**

(A) You will use your best efforts to market and sell the services to residents and prospective residents. Specifically, you or your rental agents will do the following:

List items are syntactic parallels: all are verb phrases specifying what the party agrees to do.

(1) describe the components of each of the services—including the available features, pricing, ordering procedures, and benefits—both during your initial meeting with a resident or prospective resident and when the resident signs a lease;

(2) provide residents and prospective residents with our current publications describing the services;

(3) take orders for the services from any resident or prospective resident who wishes to subscribe;

(4) provide us with notice—within three business days of your getting it—of a resident who has entered into or terminated a lease, or vacated a unit previously occupied or leased;

(5) report to us residents' requests or comments about the services;

(6) make rental agents available for training by us on the marketing of the services and comply with our marketing policies and procedures; and

(7) display marketing and sales materials in leasing offices and common areas.

(B) You acknowledge that we or any service provider may require residents to provide a deposit for receiving a service. You also acknowledge that we may reasonably try to remarket services to residents who order less than all the available services. If a new resident does not order all the services, you will give us that resident's name and address within three business days of when the resident signs a lease. You will forward to us a resident's service order by the end of the next business day after the order has been placed. If you do not timely forward a service order, you will forfeit the first month's royalty fee for that resident. You will allow us and the service providers to periodically host an event on the property, at our expense, to introduce services to residents and prospective residents.

5.6   **Control Room.** The control room—for use by us and our service providers—is a secure, enclosed, climate-controlled room located on the property. You lease to us exclusively the control room (as described in

Exhibit E), where our equipment may be installed, operated, maintained, or removed. The control room will be at least 10 x 10 feet in size. We—as well as our service providers—will have access to the control room 24 hours a day, every day of the year.

5.7   Contracts with Residents. You have no responsibility—express or implied—for any contractual liabilities or obligations under a separate agreement between us and a resident or between a service provider and a resident. All solicitations and contracts with residents and prospective residents will clearly state that you are not affiliated with us or with the service providers—and that you have no responsibility for the services.

5.8   Insurance.

(A) You will purchase and maintain during the Agreement's term the following types of insurance:

(1) Fire and extended-coverage policies that insure the buildings on the property for at least the full replacement cost of those buildings.

(2) A commercial general-liability policy that covers premises operations, broad-form property damage, personal-injury hazards, and contractual liability.

(B) The liability limits under these policies will be $2 million per occurrence, with a combined single limit for bodily-injury and property-damage liability. You will give us a certificate of insurance attesting to the existence of the coverage and providing that the policies cannot be canceled without 30 days' notice to us. The policies must name us as an additional insured and must be issued by a carrier with an A.M. Best rating of A- or better. You may obtain the coverage under a blanket insurance policy.

5.9   Casualty.

(A) If a casualty to the property occurs—whether by fire or other means—and renders one or more units uninhabitable, you must, within 30 days of the casualty, notify us in writing of either:

(1) your agreement to restore the property and to begin and diligently pursue restoration; or

(2) your choice to terminate this Agreement, either in whole if no units are restored or in part if only some units are restored.

(B) If you agree to restore the property, we will repair or replace any parts of the communications system damaged as a result of the casualty. If you terminate this Agreement in part, we may choose to terminate the Agreement in whole if continuing to provide services would require the replacement of centralized equipment and if, in our opinion, this replacement would not be economically justified in light of the reduced number of units to be served after the casualty.

-6-

5.10 Your Representations and Warranties; Lienholder Consent.

    (A) You represent and warrant that the following statements are true:

        (1) you are the sole legal and beneficial owner in fee simple of the property, which is subject to no encumbrances other than any listed in *Exhibit A*;

        (2) you have full power and authority to enter into this Agreement and to grant the easements and licenses provided for in the Agreement, and the signatory below has been authorized to so act;

        (3) no person or entity holds any interest in the property that conflicts with any interest granted to us under this Agreement;

        (4) the property is not part of a bankruptcy proceeding, foreclosure action, or deed-in-lieu-of-foreclosure transaction;

        (5) you are not in default on any mortgages or encumbrances on the property;

        (6) no purchase contracts exist with respect to the property;

        (7) the property is not governed by any rent-control laws, nor is it being subsidized under any law, regulation, or ordinance (except as disclosed in *Exhibit A*); and

        (8) the property—as well as your operation of it—complies in all material respects with all applicable laws, including laws relating to the security of residents, the property, and each unit.

    (B) If any part of the property is or becomes encumbered by a lien or security interest, you will obtain from the lienholder a consent form (as set forth in *Exhibit F*) and will agree to the terms of this consent. You will deliver this consent to us either within 30 days of the date of this Agreement or by the date when the lien or security interest attaches, whichever is later.

5.11 Access to Units. If necessary for installation or repair of a service or the communications system, you will provide access to a resident's unit. If the resident is not home when our personnel need access, your representative will accompany our personnel into the unit.

5.12 Duty to Report. You will use reasonable efforts to maintain the property in a manner that preserves the integrity of the communications system and the property. You will promptly notify us of any condition or occurrence that might affect the security of the property, residents, units, communications system, or provision of services.

6 Our Basic Obligations

6.1 Maintenance and Repair. We—or the service providers, as appropriate—will maintain and repair the communications system in accordance with industry standards.

6.2 Billing and Collections. We are responsible for all billing and collection activities associated with the services. You will not be responsible for a delinquent account of any customer (other than you). We may establish our own bad-debt policy, including disconnection of a customer's service. You are responsible for paying us only for services provided to you.

6.3   **Marketing and Sales.** We will provide you with marketing materials, service-order forms, sales support, and sales training so that you and your employees can market and sell the services as provided in § 5.5.

7   **Term**

7.1   **Initial Term.** The initial term of this Agreement is ten years. It begins on the date of this Agreement. If a lienholder's consent is required under § 5.10(B), this Agreement will become effective when you deliver that consent.

7.2   **Renewal Term.** In exchange for our payment of $100, you grant us the option to renew the initial term for a renewal term of five years. To exercise this option, we will notify you in writing at least 180 days before the initial term expires. The royalty fee for the renewal term will be the same as the royalty fee for the initial term unless we notify you that we wish to negotiate a different royalty fee. This Agreement—along with all its easements, interests, and obligations—will then be renewed for the renewal term.

7.3   **Early Termination.** In addition to our right of termination under § 5.9, we may terminate this Agreement—in whole or in part—without liability to you if we reasonably determine that offering or providing services to the property has become infeasible due to changes in applicable laws or regulations and if we give 90 days' written notice.

8   **Default and Remedies**

8.1   **Default.** A default under this Agreement occurs upon any of the following events:

(A) if you or we fail to meet or perform any material term, provision, or obligation contained in this Agreement and then do not cure this failure within 30 days after receiving notice from the other party;

(B) if you or we become a debtor in a bankruptcy proceeding or similar action that is not permanently dismissed or discharged within 60 days; or

(C) if you or we become insolvent.

8.2   **Remedies.**

(A) If either party defaults, the nondefaulting party may do all of the following:

(1) terminate this Agreement by giving 30 days' written notice to the defaulting party;

(2) sue the defaulting party for damages; and

(3) seek any other available legal or equitable remedy.

(B) The parties agree that a default may result in irreparable damage for which no adequate remedy may be available. The parties therefore agree that injunctive or other equitable relief—including specific performance—will be available in addition to all other available remedies.

9 No Warranties; Limitation of Liability

Except as expressly stated in this Agreement, we make no representations or warranties—express or implied—regarding the communications system or the provision of services, including an implied warranty of merchantability or fitness for a particular purpose. Neither party to this Agreement will be liable to the other party, to customers of a party, or to a third party for any indirect, special, punitive, or consequential damages, including damages based on loss of service, revenues, profits, or business opportunities.

10 Indemnity

10.1 Yours. Except for claims caused by the conduct or negligence of you, your employees, your agents, residents, or any third party that has entered the property with your permission, we will indemnify and defend you and your directors, officers, employees, agents, representatives, and affiliates from all claims resulting from:

(A) the design, construction, installation, operation, or maintenance of the communications system; and

(B) a default by us that has not been cured.

10.2 Ours. You will indemnify us and our directors, officers, employees, agents, representatives, and affiliates from all loss or damage to any part of the communications system caused by you, your employees, your agents, residents, or any third party that has entered the property with your permission. You will also indemnify and defend us and our directors, officers, employees, agents, representatives, and affiliates from all claims resulting from:

(A) any matter or event outside the scope of our express obligations under this Agreement; and

(B) a default by you that has not been cured.

11 Removal of Communications System

After this Agreement has expired or been terminated, we may remove the communications system in whole or in part, including all transformers, switches, electrical equipment, wiring, and cable installed by us or the service providers. We will pay for this removal unless the Agreement was terminated because of your default, in which case you will bear the cost. After removing the communications system, we will, if necessary, fully repair and restore all portions of the property from which the system has been removed. Instead of removing the communications system, we may choose to disable it. Once the system is disabled, title to the system will vest in you, and we will have no further interest in the disabled system. You may then sell or use the system as you wish.

12 Assignment

12.1 **Assignment by Us.** We may assign our interests or duties under this Agreement to any parent, affiliate, successor, or subsidiary that we may have. We may also assign this Agreement to any entity that purchases the cable-television system of the entertainment-service provider. We must notify you in writing of any assignment within 30 days.

12.2 **Assignment by You.** If you transfer or assign the property, the new owner must assume your obligations and affirm the easement and other rights granted to us under this Agreement.

12.3 **Real Right and Covenant.** The easement and other rights granted to us run with the title to the property and are binding on you and on all subsequent owners, as well as on others who may claim an interest in the property. You agree that the easement and other interests granted to us are a real-property interest in the property and that the other rights and benefits granted to us are coupled with and incidental to this real-property interest.

13 Confidential Information

13.1 **Confidentiality Agreement.** The parties will keep this Agreement and its terms confidential. The parties will also keep confidential any information that is provided by one party to the other and that is marked confidential. The parties may not use confidential information for any purpose other than performance of this Agreement.

13.2 **Survival.** The covenants in § 13.1 will survive the expiration or termination of this Agreement.

14 Use and Protection of Proprietary Names

Neither party may use any proprietary name of the other except as specifically provided in writing by the owner of the name.

15 Miscellaneous Provisions

15.1 **Entire Agreement.** This Agreement constitutes the sole agreement of the Parties with respect to its subject matter. It supersedes any prior written or oral agreements or communications between the Parties. It may not be modified except in a writing signed by the Parties.

15.2 **No Assignment.** Neither party may assign this Agreement without the other party's prior written consent, which must not be unreasonably withheld. A party's entering into contracts with subcontractors is not considered an assignment.

15.3 **Successors and Representatives.** This Agreement binds and inures to the benefit of the Parties and their respective heirs, personal representatives, successors, and (where permitted) assignees.

15.4 **Notices.** All notices and other communications required or permitted under this Agreement must be in writing and must be sent to the party at that party's address set forth below or at whatever other address the party specifies in writing.

15.5 **Severability.** If any part of this Agreement is for any reason held to be unenforceable, the rest of it remains fully enforceable.

15.6 **"Including."** Unless the context requires otherwise, the term "including" means "including but not limited to."

15.7 **Headings.** Headings are for convenience only and do not affect the interpretation of this Agreement.

15.8 **Applicable Law.** Minnesota law applies to this Agreement without regard for any choice-of-law rules that might direct the application of the laws of any other jurisdiction.

15.9 **Counterparts.** This Agreement may be signed in counterparts, each one of which is considered an original, but all of which constitute one and the same instrument.

16 Definitions.

- "Affiliate" means any corporation, partnership, limited-liability company, or similar entity in which Time Warner Inc. or Time Warner Entertainment Company, L.P. has a direct or indirect ownership interest of 25% or more.

- "Alarm service" means the provision of monitored intrusion alarm services.

- "Communications system" means all facilities and equipment necessary or desirable in our opinion to provide the initial and continued delivery of services under this Agreement. This includes wires, poles, conduits, pipes, antennas, switch and alarm equipment, software, central processing units, and associated facilities and equipment located on the property (some of which may be allocated to particular services).

- "Custom communications features" means custom telephone-related communications services such as call waiting, call forwarding, speed dialing, and voice mail.

- "Entertainment service" means the provision of cable-television and other video-and-sound services, including the same package of basic, premium, pay-per-view, and interactive-game services generally offered to residential customers by the entertainment-service provider.

- "Local telephone service" means the provision of shared access to the local telephone network of the local-exchange carrier, access to 911, operator- and directory-assistance services, and local telecommunications services by our affiliate to the extent permitted by applicable laws.

> Definitions appear at the end of the contract, where they are unobtrusive yet easy to find.

-11-

- "Long-distance telephone service" means the provision of telecommunications services beyond the toll-free local calling area, including access to long-distance operator- and directory-assistance services.
- "Service" means any telephone service, entertainment service, alarm service, or additional service offered to you or to the residents during the term of this Agreement.

Dated: _____

TIME WARNER *Connect* **(referred to as "we" throughout)**
a New York General Partnership

By: _____

Its: _____

OWNER (referred to as "you" throughout)

_____

a _____

Address: _____

_____

_____

Phone: _____

Fax: _____

By: _____

Its: _____

-12-

KEY TO BASIC EXERCISES

What follows are model answers for 32 of the basic exercises — the ones for which a model is possible. Some exercises — namely, those for §§ 4, 19, 21, 22, 26–28, 30, 33, 41–47, 49, and 50 — don't lend themselves to "model" answers, so they don't appear here.

§ 1 Case: *People v. Nelson*, 132 Cal. Rptr. 3d 856 (Ct. App. 2011)

Facts: Carl Nelson stopped his car on the roadway at a red light, got out his cellphone, dialed, and held it up to his ear. When he noticed a motorcycle police officer watching him, he put the phone away. Then the light turned green, and he drove into the intersection. The officer stopped him and cited him for using the phone while driving. On appeal, Nelson asserted that as the California Supreme Court defined *driving*, sitting in a stopped vehicle did not qualify. The People responded that the statute forbids operating a vehicle on a public roadway, so it didn't matter that Nelson had briefly stopped.

Question: California law forbids using a hand-held wireless telephone while driving. Does *while driving* mean that the car must actually be in motion when the phone is in use?

Holding: No. Mr. Nelson was driving even though his car wasn't moving. The court of appeals affirmed his conviction.

Reasoning: The court of appeals analyzed three factors in its decision: (1) the language of the statute at issue and other similar statutes suggests that the terms *drive* and *while driving* encompass a driver's fleeting pauses at traffic signals while on public roads; (2) the legislature used *drive* and *operate* interchangeably, and the statute was enacted to address the unsafe practice of using hand-held wireless telephones while operating motor vehicles, without restriction to only moving vehicles; and (3) applying the statute to only moving vehicles would result in significant safety hazards on public roads, such as drivers using their phones in stop-and-go traffic, at stop signs, and during other momentary pauses, thereby creating a sea of distracted drivers who are likely to begin a phone call while stopped but then find it difficult to end those calls when traffic resumes moving.

§2 Nonlinear Outline

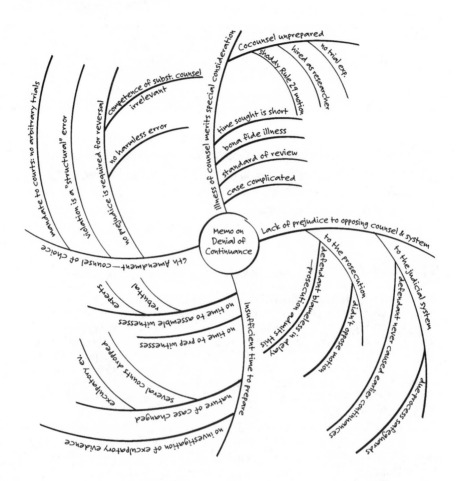

Linear Outline

1. Executive Summary
   - Issue: Charged with drug trafficking, Oscar Winchell retained Millard Gilmer, a veteran criminal-defense lawyer (assisted by Norman Newman, a first-year lawyer). Six weeks before trial, Gilmer had emergency heart surgery; he required eight weeks to recuperate. Winchell moved for a one-month continuance (unopposed), and the court denied the motion. With Newman as his only attorney, Winchell was tried and convicted. Was denying the continuance reversible error?

- Answer: An appellate court would likely hold that if lead counsel suddenly fell ill and cocounsel was too inexperienced to handle the case, the trial court erred in not granting a continuance for three reasons:

  (1) The refusal to postpone the trial resulted in a fundamentally unfair trial.

  (2) Newman had insufficient time and experience to prepare adequately for a trial of this magnitude and a case of this complexity.

  (3) Winchell has a constitutionally guaranteed right to counsel of choice, and this right cannot be arbitrarily denied. Winchell had not retained Newman as trial counsel. Rather, Newman had been associated in a research capacity only.

2. When illness of counsel is the ground for a continuance, reversal need not be predicated on a finding of abuse of discretion but may be based simply on the resulting unfairness of the trial. *Arabian Am. Oil v. Scarfone*, 939 F.2d 1472, 1479 n.17 (11th Cir. 1991).

   - Although the general standard of review for the denial of such a request is abuse of discretion, the caselaw establishes an attorney-illness exception.

   - The facts of this case satisfy the requirements for applying the exception and reversal: counsel was ill, cocounsel was relatively unprepared and inexperienced, the time sought for continuance was short, and the case was complicated. *Smith-Weik Mach. Corp. v. Murdock Mach. Corp.*, 423 F.2d 842 (5th Cir. 1970).

3. In the alternative, the court's denial of the continuance was an abuse of discretion because it left inexperienced cocounsel unguided — and with only five weeks to prepare for his first trial.

   - A showing of abuse of discretion, resulting in specific substantial prejudice, mandates reversal of a conviction.

   - The facts of this case are essentially indistinguishable from the facts of *United States v. Verderame*, 51 F.3d 249 (11th Cir. 1995), a case in which the Eleventh Circuit reversed a conviction on the ground that without the continuance, there was insufficient time to prepare.

   - Neither the prosecution nor the judicial system would have been prejudiced by the delay.

- The prosecutor did not oppose a continuance.
- As to two earlier continuances, both the court and the prosecutor stated on the record that Winchell was blameless.
- The record demonstrates how the denial of a continuance substantially prejudiced the defense. This prejudice resulted mostly from Newman's inexperience.
- Even an experienced advocate would have found the time insufficient to (a) digest copious discovery, (b) investigate new exculpatory evidence, and (c) prepare or assemble witnesses.
- No motion was made for an order directing the prosecutor to define the charged narcotics conspiracy or to list the participants.

4. In the second alternative, the denial was structural error. The right to counsel of choice is a component of due process, requiring courts to balance a defendant's choice of counsel against the general interest in a fast and efficient trial. *Gandy v. Alabama*, 569 F.2d 1318, 1326 (5th Cir. 1979).

- Arbitrary action prohibiting the use of counsel of choice violates due process. *Gandy*, 569 F.2d at 1326.
- Violation of the right to counsel of choice is a structural error, requiring automatic reversal. *United States v. Rankin*, 779 F.2d 956 (3d Cir. 1986).
- This ground requires no proof of prejudice: the right is either respected or denied.
- Competence of substitute counsel is irrelevant.
- No harmless-error analysis applies. *Rankin*, 779 F.2d at 958.

5. Conclusion
- the likelihood of success on appeal
- briefing schedule
- likely time allotment for oral argument — what the clerk says
- additional avenues of reversible error to explore

§ 3

- In March 2010, Gilbert Spaulding applied to the Workforce Commission for extended unemployment benefits. The commission denied the request because Spaulding was ineligible for the benefits during the period for which he sought them. The trial court affirmed.
- Plaintiff, Pilsen Corporation, moved for a partial summary judgment on the discrete issue of fraud. The trial court granted the motion,

and the court of appeals affirmed. On further appeal, however, the state supreme court reversed.

- Davis Energy owns a fuel-storage yard that can be reached only by a private road. For seven years, owners of adjacent lots have used the road to reach their property. For the past three years, Davis has had a guard at the road's entrance but has posted no other notice about private property or permission to enter. Has Davis, through its actions or silence, granted its neighbors an easement to use the road?

- Plaintiff Los Angeles Dodgers, a corporation owning a professional baseball team, began in New York as the Brooklyn Dodgers. In 1958, the team moved the site of its home games from New York to California and changed its name. The organization's principal corporate offices are now in Los Angeles.

§ 5
- The Business Corporation Law does not address whether a New York corporation can indemnify nonemployees.

- Even assuming that the fog caused Cetera's accident, Pardone had no duty to prevent such a freakish and unforeseeable injury.

- Before the initial public offering, no one knew or had reason to know that Palm Harbor could not be properly completed on time.

- Beale has not alleged facts that, if true, would establish either public injury or reduced competition among the nation's law schools. So her restraint-of-trade claim must be dismissed.

- The court examined many cases but found few that imposed a duty to disclose the illegal conduct of candidates for elected office.

§ 6
- Oral argument would be of little benefit for two reasons. First, the dispositive issue has recently been decided by the Texas Supreme Court [footnote citation] and by this Court [footnote citation]. Second, the facts and legal arguments are adequately presented in the briefs and the record. [70 words]

- No cases explicitly hold that Kansas requires a corporation to have a valid business purpose to engage in certain specified corporate transactions. But in 2013 the Supreme Court of Kansas decided a case that bears on the question. The case involved a cash-out merger in which the dissenters claimed that the defendant's board of directors had breached its fiduciary duties to them. The court found that a corporation need not show a valid corporate purpose for eliminating stockholders. [80 words]

- The court of appeals cited two salient points. First, the Environmental Protection Agency (EPA) had already issued the applicant a National Pollution Elimination System permit for the actual discharge of wastewater from the outfall pipe. Second, under the Clean Water Act, the issuance and conditions of such permits are generally exempt from compliance with the Environmental Impact Statement (EIS) requirement. So the court concluded that the Corps had properly excluded the environmental implications of the outfall-pipe discharges from its analysis. The court considered only the construction and maintenance of the pipeline itself in determining that issuing the permit did not constitute a major federal action. [107 words]

§ 7
- While struggling as a single parent to provide for her children, Ms. Lenderfield accrued considerable debt to her family and others.
- Chesapeake incorrectly asserts that it is not a proper defendant in this case and that therefore relief cannot be granted.
- Finding that Officer McGee was acting more as a school employee than as a police officer in searching Robinson, the court ruled that an official's primary role is not law enforcement.

§ 8
- The court relied heavily on the district court's statement that (1) the would-be intervenors retained the right to appear through counsel, to participate in the fairness hearing, and to conduct discovery, and (2) they had standing to appeal the court's approval or disapproval of the class-action settlement.
- Tenant will probably not be able to have the lease declared void and unenforceable for vagueness. It contains all the essential elements of a lease: a description of the premises, the amount of rent to be paid, the term of the lease, and the identity of the parties.
- The *Younger* doctrine also applies to a state civil proceeding that (1) is ongoing, (2) implicates important state interests, and (3) affords an adequate opportunity to raise federal claims.

§ 9
- After the plaintiff testified, three witnesses testified for the corporation.
- The court decides this purely legal question.
- The court should deny McCormick's motion for partial summary judgment on the duty to defend.

- The court should disregard Thompson's opposition because it violates California Rule of Court 313.

§ 10   • Notice will be effective only if it is delivered in person or by certified mail, return receipt requested.

- Without contrary proof, the court should presume that the administrator's functions continue.

- Termination will be approved only after the administrator reviews the application and finds it complete.

- The jurors may have believed that Payton's mitigation evidence was within their reach. They certainly had judicial direction.

§ 11   • On August 27, in response to the Governor's Plea to the Jurisdiction, this Court dismissed the whistleblower claims against the Governor.

- The single most important factor in determining whether, within the meaning of the Act, a party is in charge of the work is the right to stop the work.

- The Commission is not now in a position to provide additional affidavits and other evidence to support its contention that Bulworth and Islington are an integrated enterprise.

- For good cause, the court may authorize a preappearance interview between the interpreter and the party or witness.

- Arguing that it had no control over the release of the hazardous substance that created the emergency, Silver Sidings contests whether, under the Spill Bill, the Department of Natural Resources has jurisdiction. But Silver Sidings is, under the Spill Bill's definition, "a person having control over a hazardous substance involved in a hazardous-substance emergency." Four statutory factors demonstrate this: (1) Silver Sidings owned the property where the release occurred, (2) it owned the underground storage tanks from which the hazardous substance was released, (3) it permitted the hazardous substance to be stored in its tanks on its property, and (4) it had every right as a landowner to control the use of its land and tanks.

§ 12   • On July 15, 2010, in a prehearing conference, the court extended Rawson's time to respond to Vicker's motion until August 6. But Rawson failed to file a response.

- An employee who is subpoenaed to testify in a judicial or administrative proceeding must give the company prompt notice of the subpoena so that it can decide whether to seek a protective order.
- The court asks whether the plaintiff is guilty of unreasonable delay in asserting its rights. This determination is within the court's discretion. The emphasis is on the delay's reasonableness, not its length.
- After the Bank dishonored and returned the forged check, the US Attorney subpoenaed the Bank, directing it to deliver to his office, upon receipt, all bank checks, cashier's checks, and similar items stolen in the July 2, 2010 robbery.

§ 13
- Jones agrees with Smith.
- The professional fees in this project depend entirely on what planning techniques the client favors.
- The judge believes she has discretion to determine whether the crime-fraud exception applies.
- With or without an express agreement, most courts hold that the authority continues for a reasonable time in light of all the circumstances.

§ 14
- Jenkins knew about the computer's access port.
- This Court correctly dismissed the plaintiff's claims.
- Courts have identified several factors in determining whether a defendant's use of another's registered trademark is likely to cause confusion, mistake, or deception.
- A party can preemptively protect the enforceability of the contract's provisions by inserting a severability clause.
- A party may waive a provision of this agreement only by signing a written waiver.

§ 15
- An interested party may apply to modify or revoke an antidumping order (or to terminate a suspension agreement) during an annual administrative review. The board normally won't consider revoking an order unless there have been no sales at less than fair value for at least three consecutive years. (*Suspension* can't be changed in the phrase *suspension agreement*.)
- In analyzing the ADA claim, the court noted that the company terminated the decedent and reduced his AIDS benefits before the ADA became effective. Plaintiff nonetheless alleged that limiting AIDS

benefits beyond the ADA's effective date—in effect discriminating between plan members with AIDS and members without AIDS—violated the general rule of Title I.

- A finding that reasonable grounds exist to revoke parole should first be made by someone directly involved in the case. But the preliminary evaluation and resulting recommendations should be in the hands of someone not directly involved. (The words *evaluation* and *recommendations* probably need to be retained.)

§ 16
- Licensee will perform the work in compliance with all applicable laws.
- While the witness's truthfulness may be challenged on cross-examination, it cannot be further challenged through extrinsic evidence of matters not already in the record.
- If you fail to perform an obligation under this agreement, we may choose to perform the obligation and then recover from you the cost of our performance. (For purposes of this revision, *the bailor* becomes *we*; *the bailee* becomes *you*.)
- Seller must assist Buyer in this process but will not bear the associated costs.

§ 17   Foster does not dispute that his complaint against Pine National wasn't filed until after the applicable limitations period had expired. Rather, Foster seeks to avoid time-bar by arguing that (1) the statute is tolled because this is a case of misnomer and (2) the equitable exception described by the Texas Supreme Court in *Enserch Corp. v. Parker* [footnote citation] applies. Foster argues that the question whether Pine National was prejudiced by the late filing creates, under the exception, a material issue of fact precluding summary judgment.

Yet neither argument states a valid ground for tolling the statute. First, the undisputed facts show, as a matter of law, that this is not a case of misnomer but of misidentification. And cases of misidentification do not toll limitations. Second, the equitable exception is unavailable on these facts. Although Foster argues that the late filing creates a material fact issue, prejudice to Pine National is irrelevant under the *Enserch* exception. So Foster has failed to show any basis for applying the exception. His claims are time-barred as a matter of law.

§ 18   Appellant provides a substantially correct statement of the procedural history. On July 27, 2010, Keith W. Hillman filed for benefits with the

Criminal Injuries Compensation Fund. Exactly a month later, the Director of the Division of Crime Victims' Compensation denied the claim because Hillman's conduct had contributed to his injury and because Hillman had not cooperated with law enforcement. In December 2010, Hillman requested a review of the denial. The deputy commissioner held a hearing in April 2011.

§ 20
- Enclosed are the following documents: [list]. (*Or*: Here are the four documents you requested. You'll find that . . .)
- As you requested, I met with Roger Smith today. (The case is referred to in the subject line. Omit any reference to it in this sentence.)
- The discovery cutoff in this case is Monday, March 20, 2014.
- After talking with Alex in your office this morning, I called the trustee.
- We would like to retain you as a consultant in this case.
- Thank you. If you have any questions, please call.

§ 23
In a Texas federal district court, R&B Music sought injunctive relief against the McCoys to prevent them from any further use or disclosure of R&B's trade secrets. A day later, the Texas court issued an order restraining the McCoys from using or disclosing certain R&B property and proprietary information. At the same time, the court set an evidentiary hearing on R&B's preliminary-injunction motion, giving the parties ten days' notice.

A day before the scheduled hearing, the McCoys moved to dismiss for an alleged lack of venue and personal jurisdiction. Alternatively, they asked the court to transfer the case to an Illinois federal court under 28 U.S.C. § 1404 or § 1406.

When the parties arrived for the injunction hearing, the Texas court indicated its intent to hear testimony and rule on the McCoys' dismissal or transfer motion, to which R&B had been given no chance to respond. The testimony established that the McCoys had had significant contacts in Texas for the past eight years—including daily phone calls and faxes to and from R&B; their three visits to R&B's Texas headquarters; and their work in negotiating R&B contracts with Texas musicians.

The next day, the Texas court transferred the case to this Court, noting that the transfer was for the reasons stated on the record. As the transcript reveals, the Texas court decided that while it had personal jurisdiction over John McCoy, it lacked personal jurisdiction over Kate McCoy. According to the court, the case should be transferred because "to accord relief to R&B down here while leaving the Illinois court to deal with Kate McCoy simply would not provide an effective situation" for any of the parties. The judge did not indicate which statutory section governed the transfer.

In the same order, the Texas court further ruled that its earlier order restricting both John and Kate McCoy from using or disclosing R&B's trade secrets would remain in effect pending further orders of the Illinois court. After the case arrived in Illinois, R&B filed a supplemental motion for preliminary injunction, asking this Court to extend and expand the injunctive relief that the Texas court had already granted.

§ 24   The modern legal researcher must work in two realms: paper and electronic.

§ 25   1. The automobile made its first appearance on the streets, for all practical purposes, in the first decade of this century.
2. **By 1940,** the United States had become an **automobile society.** (*By 1940*: temporal progression; *automobile society*: echo link.)
3. **The numbers** have **continued** to rise, as automobiles choke the roads and highways and millions of people, living in the land of suburban sprawl, use the automobile as their lifeline — connecting them to work, shopping, and the outside world in general. (*The numbers*: pointing word plus echo link; *continued*: echo link.)
4. **Thus,** a person who parks overtime and gets a "ticket" will get an order to appear in court and face the music. (Explicit connective.)
5. In many localities, **traffic matters** got handled by municipal courts, police courts, justices of the peace, and sometimes specialized departments of a municipal court. (Echo link.)
6. The **traffic court judge,** as one would expect, did not have the prestige and dignity of a higher-grade judge. (Echo link.)
7. The root of **this evil** was, perhaps, the fact that defendants did not — and do not — see themselves as criminals, but rather as unlucky people who got caught breaking a rule that everybody breaks once in a while. (Pointing word plus echo link.)
8. **This attitude** came to the surface in a 1958 American Bar Association report on traffic matters in Oklahoma. (Pointing word plus echo link.)

§ 29 This Court held that Julia was entitled to damages for loss of consortium and affirmed that portion of the judgment. But the Court reversed on mental anguish because Julia did not witness the accident:

> [A] claim for negligent infliction of mental anguish that is not based on the wrongful-death statute requires that the plaintiff prove that he or she was, among other things, located at or near the scene of the accident, and that the mental anguish resulted from a direct emotional impact upon the plaintiff from the sensory and contemporaneous observation of the incident, as contrasted with learning of the accident from others after the occurrence. Julia has not met either of these requirements and therefore may not recover for mental anguish.

Thus, . . .

§ 31
- Nothing in this Agreement gives anyone, other than the parties and the Buyer's permitted assignees, any rights or remedies under the Agreement.
- The Corporation and the Executive agree that they have negotiated this Agreement at arm's length and that legal counsel for both parties have had an adequate opportunity to review this Agreement so that any court will fully enforce it as written.
- The employee agrees not to compete and further agrees that the limitations relating to time, geographical area, and scope of activity to be restrained are reasonable. This agreement is supported by independent, valuable consideration as required by Texas Business and Commerce Code § 15.50.

§ 32 (1) **Commitment.** This letter defines the commitment made on behalf of Lucky Development Company (Seller) to sell to ABC Company (Buyer) 111.3 acres of land out of the Benbow House Survey, Abstract 247.

(2) **Buyer Obligations.** Buyer must pay, in cash, a sum equal to the product of $5.50 multiplied by the total number of square feet within the land's boundaries. Payment must be made under the terms of a Sale-and-Purchase Agreement acceptable to and executed by both Buyer and Seller. Buyer must exercise its best efforts to

(a) enter into the Sale-and-Purchase Agreement within the stated time; and

(b) secure any essential commitments from high-quality department and specialty stores to establish, construct, and operate a regional mall.

(3) Limitation of Commitment. No sale or purchase agreement or contract of sale is intended until Buyer and Seller agree to the Sale-and-Purchase Agreement. If Buyer and Seller do not agree within 60 days from the date of this letter, neither party will have *any* liabilities or obligations to the other.

§ 34   7.7 Insurance

(A) Policies. Borrower must provide the insurance policies described in Exhibit I, together with all other insurance policies that Lender may reasonably require from time to time. All insurance policies must:

(1) be continuously maintained at Borrower's sole expense;

(2) be issued by reputable, responsible insurers that are satisfactory to Lender;

(3) be in form, substance, and amount satisfactory to Lender;

(4) with respect to liability insurance, name Lender as an additional insured;

(5) provide that the policies cannot be canceled or modified without 60 days' prior written notice to Lender; and

(6) with respect to insurance covering damage to the Mortgaged Property, name Lender as a mortgagee, contain a "lender's loss payable" endorsement in form and substance satisfactory to Lender, and contain an agreed-value clause sufficient to eliminate any risk of coinsurance.

(B) Proof of Coverage. Upon request, Borrower must deliver to Lender the original policies, copies of them, or certificates evidencing the policies.

§ 35 • Escrow Agent is entitled to receive an annual fee in accordance with standard charges for services to be rendered under this Agreement.

• Each member may transfer all or any part of his membership interest to any other member without restriction of any kind.

• The occurrence of any one or more of the following constitutes an event of default: (a) if Borrower fails to pay any installment of principal or interest on an advance. . . .

• After completing its work, Licensee must restore the License Area to the condition in which Licensee found it upon first entering.

- The sender fully complies with the requirement to send notice when the sender obtains electronic confirmation. (This one expresses a status, not a duty. An alternative wording: *The sender has fully complied with the requirement to send notice when . . .*)

§ 36
- The Buyer must pay in full for product previously delivered. But the quantity of product whose delivery or acceptance is excused by force majeure will be deducted without liability from the quantity otherwise subject to delivery or acceptance.
- For travel and subsistence expenses actually and necessarily incurred by Contractor in performing this Contract, Contractor will be reimbursed in the same manner as in the current Commissioner's Plan, but not in an amount that exceeds $2,000 or the amounts provided for under the Plan.
- The Borrower may, at any time and from time to time, prepay the Loans in whole or in part, without premium or penalty, upon at least one business day's notice to the Lender, specifying the date and the amount of the prepayment. Each prepayment must be accompanied by the payment of all accrued but unpaid interest on the amount prepaid to the date of the prepayment.

§ 37
- AmCorp and Havasu have the sole right to use inventions covered by this Agreement and to obtain patent, copyright, trade-secret, and any other form of legal protection for the inventions.
- Immediately upon notice from Pantheon, Licensee must discontinue producing licensed items at every print shop.
- No change, waiver, or discharge of this Agreement is valid unless in a writing that is signed by an authorized representative of the party against whom the change, waiver, or discharge is sought to be enforced.
- The settlement is binding on all classes of creditors and stockholders of this Corporation.

§ 38
- An employee who has earned more than 25 credits is eligible for positions under § 7.
- The fire marshal is responsible for issuing any permit listed in this section.
- Each shareholder of the corporation has only one vote.
- If an appealing party has not satisfied the requisites for an interlocutory appeal, that party's appeal will be dismissed.

- When an issue not raised by the pleadings is tried with the parties' express or implied consent, it must be treated in all respects as if it had been raised by the pleadings.

§ 39   Before the entry of the final decree on June 5, 2010, the parties participated in four hearings before three Commissioners in Chancery, took three additional sets of depositions of healthcare providers, and had at least 12 live hearings. The court granted a divorce on the ground of separation in excess of one year, granted spousal support and $5,000 in costs and attorney's fees to the wife, and equitably distributed the property.

§ 40   Two of the three passages seem to have real meaning, but they are all poorly expressed.

- I'm not sure I understand this sentence. It might mean this: "It is illegal for a savings and loan holding company to obtain control of an uninsured institution or to retain control (for longer than 12 months) of any institution that has become uninsured."
- This is an odd, even surprising provision because it seems to give the nonspouse in a bigamous relationship more rights than the bigamist's innocent spouse. It seems to mean this: " 'Spouse' means the person (1) to whom the Cardholder is legally married, or (2) with whom the Cardholder has been cohabiting as husband and wife for at least two years. If the Cardholder is legally married but has been cohabiting with someone outside the marriage for at least two years as husband and wife, then that someone is considered the spouse."
- This is a weird contractual provision. If you sign the agreement, you seem to be violating it no matter what you do. So it seems to have no genuine meaning at all. But it might be trying to say something like this: "In imposing requirements, standards, and rates, the 911 provider must treat the Company just as it treats an incumbent local-exchange company."

§ 48   The following abbreviations appear in these answers:

GMAU   Bryan A. Garner, *Garner's Modern American Usage* (3d ed. 2009).
MAU   Wilson Follett, *Modern American Usage: A Guide* (Erik Wensberg ed., 2d ed. 2011).
AHBEU   *American Heritage Book of English Usage* (1996).
U&A   Eric Partridge, *Usage and Abusage* (Janet Whitcut ed., new ed. 1995).
GDLU   Bryan A. Garner, *Garner's Dictionary of Legal Usage* (3d ed. 2011).
AU&S   Roy Copperud, *American Usage and Style: The Consensus* (1980).
S&W   William Strunk Jr. & E. B. White, *The Elements of Style* (4th ed. 2000).

> *MEU2*   H. W. Fowler, *A Dictionary of Modern English Usage* (Ernest Gowers ed., 2d ed. 1965).
> *TCW*   Theodore M. Bernstein, *The Careful Writer* (1965).

- When Margot arrived, Rodney told her that David had laid down because of his pain. (*Laid* should be *lain*.)
    GMAU at 501–02.
    MAU at 175.
    AHBEU at 113.
    U&A at 170.
    GDLU at 528.
    S&W at 51.
    MEU2 at 327.
    TCW at 254–55.

- Mrs. Clements testified that Kenneth was waiving the gun wildly and pointing it at Bill. (*Waiving* should be *waving*.)
    GMAU at 850.
    U&A at 372.
    GDLU at 934.
    AU&S at 411.
    MEU2 at 685.

- Counsel testified that because the testimony would have harmed her case, she opted to forego it for reasons of trial strategy. (*Forego* should be *forgo*.)
    GMAU at 368.
    AHBEU at 97.
    U&A at 120.
    GDLU at 371–72.
    MEU2 at 205.

- Since the *Oneida* line of cases are now binding federal law in California, this Court is bound to follow them. (*Are* should be *is*; the subject is *line*.)
    GMAU at 801–03.
    AHBEU at 36.
    U&A at 211.
    GDLU at 881–82.
    AU&S at 366.
    MEU2 at 402.
    TCW at 301–02.

- The cost of any arbitration proceedings will be born by the party designated by the arbitrators. (*Born* should be *borne*.)
     GMAU at 111.
     AHBEU at 78.
     U&A at 49.
     AU&S at 52.
     MEU2 at 62.

- The gas would likely be inventory under the Idaho statutes defining the term, but these provisions might not apply since they do not effect Idaho taxable income. (*Effect* should be *affect*.)
     GMAU at 26.
     AHBEU at 69.
     U&A at 8.
     GDLU at 34–35.
     AU&S at 52.
     S&W at 45.
     MEU2 at 13.
     TCW at 29.

- Texas law prohibits the unjustified interference with a parties' existing or prospective contractual relations. (*Parties'* should be *party's*.)
     GMAU at 635–38.
     AHBEU at 241.
     GDLU at 684–85.
     S&W at 1.

- For the reasons stated in Jones's initial motion, Jones maintains that the Court's August 27 order precludes Fillmore from preceding on count six in this action. (*Preceding* should be *proceeding*.)
     GMAU at 649.
     GDLU at 696.
     AU&S at 300.
     TCW at 347.

- The laws of the State of Massachusetts (irrespective of its choice-of-law principals) govern the validity of this Agreement, the construction of its terms, and the interpretation and enforcement of the parties' rights and duties. (*Principals* should be *principles*.)
     GMAU at 659.
     AHBEU at 128.
     U&A at 256.
     GDLU at 708.

AU&S at 304.
TCW at 347.

- Neither Mr. Robinson's affidavit nor Plaintiffs' deposition testimony carry the force of law. (*Carry* should be *carries*.)
    GMAU at 637.
    MAU at 116.
    U&A at 204.
    GDLU at 684–85.
    MEU2 at 386–87.
    TCW at 121–22.

BIBLIOGRAPHY

General Writing Guides

Baker, Sheridan. *The Practical Stylist.* 8th ed. N.Y.: Longman, 1998.

Graves, Robert; and Alan Hodge. *The Reader over Your Shoulder: A Handbook for Writers of English Prose.* 2d ed. N.Y.: Random House, 1979.

Payne, Lucile Vaughan. *The Lively Art of Writing: Understanding Forms.* Reprint, Chicago: Follett, 1982.

Strunk, William, Jr.; and E. B. White. *The Elements of Style.* 4th ed. N.Y.: Macmillan, 2000.

Trimble, John R. *Writing with Style.* 3d ed. Upper Saddle River, N.J.: Pearson, 2011.

Zinsser, William. *On Writing Well: The Classic Guide to Writing Nonfiction.* 30th anniversary ed. N.Y.: HarperCollins, 2006.

Usage Guides

Bernstein, Theodore M. *The Careful Writer: A Modern Guide to English Usage.* N.Y.: Athenaeum, 1965.

Burchfield, R. W. *The New Fowler's Modern English Usage.* 3d rev. ed. Oxford: Oxford Univ. Press, 2004.

Evans, Bergen; and Cornelia Evans. *A Dictionary of Contemporary American Usage.* N.Y.: Random House, 1957.

Follett, Wilson. *Modern American Usage: A Guide.* 1st rev. ed. Revised by Erik Wensberg. N.Y.: Hill & Wang, 1998.

Fowler, H. W. *A Dictionary of Modern English Usage.* 2d ed. Revised by Ernest Gowers. N.Y.: Oxford Univ. Press, 1965.

Garner, Bryan A. *Garner's Dictionary of Legal Usage.* 3d ed. Oxford: Oxford Univ. Press, 2011.

Garner, Bryan A. *Garner's Modern American Usage.* 3d ed. Oxford: Oxford Univ. Press, 2009.

Garner, Bryan A. "Grammar and Usage." In *The Chicago Manual of Style,* 201–304. 16th ed. Chicago: Univ. of Chicago Press, 2010.

Partridge, Eric. *Usage and Abusage: A Guide to Good English.* New ed. Revised by Janet Whitcut. N.Y.: Norton, 1994.

Plain English

Adler, Mark. *Clarity for Lawyers: The Use of Plain English in Legal Writing.* 2d ed. London: Law Society, 2007.

Eagleson, Robert D.; Gloria Jones; and Sue Hassall. *Writing in Plain English.* Canberra: AGPS, 1990.

Flesch, Rudolf. *The Art of Plain Talk*. N.Y.: Harper & Bros., 1946.

Gowers, Ernest. *The Complete Plain Words*. 1st Am. ed. Revised by Sidney Greenbaum and Janet Whitcut. Boston: D. R. Godine, 2002.

Gunning, Robert. *The Technique of Clear Writing*. Rev. ed. N.Y.: McGraw-Hill, 1968.

Lauchman, Richard. *Plain Style: Techniques for Simple, Concise, Emphatic Business Writing*. N.Y.: AMACOM, 1993.

Steinberg, Erwin R., ed. *Plain Language: Principles and Practice*. Detroit: Wayne State Univ. Press, 1991.

Style Manuals

The Associated Press Stylebook and Briefing on Media Law. Darrell Christian, Sally Jacobsen & David Minthorn, eds. 2013 ed. N.Y.: Basic Books, 2013.

The Chicago Manual of Style. 16th ed. Chicago: Univ. of Chicago Press, 2010.

Sabin, William A. *The Gregg Reference Manual: A Manual of Style, Grammar, Usage, and Formatting*. Tribute ed. N.Y.: McGraw-Hill, 2011.

Law Dictionaries

Garner, Bryan A., ed. *Black's Law Dictionary*. 9th ed. St. Paul: West, 2009.

Greenberg, Daniel, ed. *Jowitt's Dictionary of English Law*. 3d ed. London: Sweet & Maxwell, 2010.

Words and Phrases. 90 vols. & supps. St. Paul: West, 1940–.

Legal Language Generally

Freedman, Adam. *The Party of the First Part: The Curious World of Legalese*. N.Y.: Henry Holt, 2007.

Garner, Bryan A. *Garner on Language and Writing*. Chicago: ABA, 2009.

Mellinkoff, David. *The Language of the Law*. Boston: Little, Brown, 1963.

Mertz, Elizabeth. *The Language of Law School: Learning to Think Like a Lawyer*. Oxford: Oxford Univ. Press, 2007.

Robinson, Marlyn, ed. *Language and the Law: Proceedings of a Conference*. Buffalo, N.Y.: William S. Hein, 2003.

Schauer, Frederick, ed. *Law and Language*. N.Y.: N.Y. Univ. Press, 1993.

Tiersma, Peter M. *Legal Language*. Chicago: Univ. of Chicago Press, 1999.

Tiersma, Peter M. *Parchment, Paper, Pixels: Law and the Technologies of Communication*. Chicago: Univ. of Chicago Press, 2010.

Tiersma, Peter M.; and Lawrence Solan, eds. *The Oxford Handbook of Language and Law*. N.Y.: Oxford Univ. Press, 2012.

Legal-Writing Style

Asprey, Michèle M. *Plain Language for Lawyers*. 4th ed. Sydney: Federation, 2010.

Charrow, Veda R.; Myra K. Erhardt; and Robert P. Charrow. *Clear and Effective Legal Writing*. 4th ed., N.Y.: Aspen, 2007.

Garner, Bryan A. *The Elements of Legal Style*. 2d ed. N.Y.: Oxford Univ. Press, 2002.

Garner, Bryan A. *The Redbook: A Manual on Legal Style*. 3d ed. St. Paul: West, 2013.

Good, C. Edward. *Mightier than the Sword*. Charlottesville, Va.: Blue Jeans, 1989.

Kimble, Joseph. *Lifting the Fog of Legalese: Essays on Plain Language*. Durham, N.C.: Carolina Academic, 2006.

Painter, Mark. *The Legal Writer.* 3d ed. Cincinnati: Jarndyce & Jarndyce, 2005.

Schiess, Wayne. *Better Legal Writing: 15 Topics for Advanced Legal Writers.* Buffalo, N.Y.: William S. Hein, 2005.

Schiess, Wayne. *Writing for the Legal Audience.* Durham, N.C.: Carolina Academic, 2003.

Volokh, Eugene. *Academic Legal Writing: Law Review Articles, Student Notes, Seminar Papers, and Getting on Law Review.* 4th ed. N.Y.: Foundation, 2010.

Wydick, Richard C. *Plain English for Lawyers.* 5th ed. Durham, N.C.: Carolina Academic, 2005.

Brief-Writing

Garner, Bryan A. *The Winning Brief: 100 Tips on Persuasive Briefing in Trial and Appellate Courts.* 2d ed. N.Y.: Oxford Univ. Press, 2004.

Peck, Girvan. *Writing Persuasive Briefs.* Boston: Little, Brown, 1984.

Rossman, George, ed. *Classic Essays on Legal Advocacy.* 1960. Reprint, Clark, N.J.: Lawbook Exchange, 2010.

Scalia, Antonin; and Bryan A. Garner. *Making Your Case: The Art of Persuading Judges.* St. Paul: West, 2008.

Commercial Drafting

Burnham, Scott J. *The Contract Drafting Guidebook.* Charlottesville, Va.: Michie, 1992.

Burnham, Scott J. *Drafting and Analyzing Contracts.* Newark: LexisNexis, 2003.

Butt, Peter; and Richard Castle. *Modern Legal Drafting: A Guide to Using Clearer Language.* 2d ed. N.Y.: Cambridge Univ. Press, 2006.

Child, Barbara. *Drafting Legal Documents.* 2d ed. St. Paul: West, 1992.

Dickerson, Reed. *The Fundamentals of Legal Drafting.* 2d ed. Boston: Little, Brown, 1986.

Felsenfeld, Carl; and Alan Siegel. *Writing Contracts in Plain English.* St. Paul: West, 1981.

Flesch, Rudolf. *How to Write Plain English: A Book for Lawyers and Consumers.* N.Y.: Harper & Row, 1979.

Garner, Bryan A. *Securities Disclosure in Plain English.* Chicago: CCH, 1999.

Kuney, George W. *The Elements of Contract Drafting.* 3d ed. St. Paul: Thomson/West, 2011.

Piesse, E. L. *The Elements of Drafting.* 10th ed. Revised by J. K. Aitken and Peter J. Butt. Sydney: Lawbook, 2004.

Schiess, Wayne. *Preparing Legal Documents Nonlawyers Can Read and Understand.* Chicago: ABA, 2008.

Wincor, Richard. *Contracts in Plain English.* N.Y.: McGraw-Hill, 1976.

Legislative Drafting

Cutts, Martin. *Lucid Law.* 2d rev. ed. High Peak, U.K.: Plain Language Commission, 2000.

Haggard, Thomas R.; and George W. Kuney. *Legal Drafting in a Nutshell.* 3d ed. St. Paul: West, 2007.

Legal Interpretation

Scalia, Antonin; and Bryan A. Garner. *Reading Law: The Interpretation of Legal Texts*. St. Paul: Thomson/West, 2012.

Jury Instructions

Tiersma, Peter M. *Communicating with Juries*. Williamsburg, Va.: National Center for State Courts, 2006.

Legal Citations

The Bluebook: A Uniform System of Citation. 19th ed. Cambridge, Mass.: Harvard Law Review, 2010.

Dickerson, Darby. *ALWD Citation Manual: A Professional System of Citation*. 4th ed. Frederick, Md.: Aspen, 2010.

INDEX